MYSTICAL DRAGON MAGICK

Many of Llewellyn's authors have websites with additional information and resources.
For more information, please visit our website at www.llewellyn.com.

MYSTICAL DRAGON MAGICK

TEACHINGS OF THE FIVE INNER RINGS

D. J. CONWAY

Llewellyn Publications
Woodbury, Minnesota

First Edition
First Printing, 2007

Book design by Steffani Sawyer
Editing by Brett Fechheimer
Cover illustration ©2007 John Blumen
Cover design by Kevin R. Brown
Interior art by Vicki Visconti pp. 17, 67, 151, 189, 217
 Kevin R. Brown pp. 133-140, 161-165, 176, 178, 203-205
 © 2007 Dover pp. 1, 9, 29, 48, 55, 232, 239
Llewellyn is a registered trademark of Llewellyn Worldwide, Ltd.

Library of Congress Cataloging-in-Publication Data

Conway, D. J. (Deanna J.)
 Mystical dragon magick : teachings of the five inner rings / by D. J. Conway. — 1st ed.
  p. cm.

 ISBN 978-0-7387-1099-0

 1. Dragons. I. Title.
 GR830.D7C664 2007
 299'.93—dc22
                              2007024773

Llewellyn Publications
A Division of Llewellyn Worldwide, Ltd.
2143 Wooddale Drive, Dept. 978-0-7387-1099-0
Woodbury, Minnesota 55125-2989, U.S.A.
www.llewellyn.com

Printed in the United States of America

Other Books by D. J. Conway

Animal Magick

By Oak, Ash, & Thorn

The Celtic Dragon Tarot

Celtic Magic

Dancing with Dragons

Magickal Mystical Creatures

Maiden, Mother, Crone

Moon Magick

Norse Magic

Shapeshifter Tarot

Forthcoming Books by D. J. Conway

Guides, Guardians, & Angels

To Ken, who appeared unexpectedly in my life at the right time,
under very unusual circumstances.
Welcome to the uncertain world of writers and psychics, with accompanying
dragons, faeries, elves, mystic teachers, and Otherworld spirits.

My thanks, also, to all of the fantastic dragon help.

CONTENTS

FOUR 189

The Way of the Dragon Warrior
Fourth of the Inner Rings

FIVE 217

The Way of the Dragon Mystic
Fifth of the Inner Rings

SIX 239

Continuing the Great Journey

INTRODUCTION

Still Dancing with Dragons

HERE BE DRAGONS!

After *Dancing with Dragons* was published in 1994, I discovered that a huge section of the population around the world was fascinated by dragons and believed in them as I do. One of the most interesting e-mails came from an older woman who asked me if I had been trained in the dragon magick of Lebanon. It seems that the rituals in *Dancing with Dragons* use nearly the exact wording of the rituals in that magickal path. It is nice to have the dragon information substantiated by the surviving rituals of an ancient group.

The Otherworld and all its beings, especially dragons, have always been part of my life. I was born with my psychic senses alert and with the ability to tap previously learned esoteric knowledge. Although my large extended family was full of closet psychics, few of them talked about their experiences. I soon learned that talking with my deceased grandmother brought trouble. Only the discretion of public silence was safe. Communicating with the deceased and dragons was best done when I was alone.

Dragons among the trees beyond the fields of dairy cows seemed normal to a child barely a year old. When I was old enough to wander those fields alone, I spent every possible moment with those dragons, as well as a host of nature spirits. When dragon teachers appeared, it was a pleasant surprise, not a shock. The shock came when I entered school and discovered there were no books on dragons in the library.

Many years later, when the dragons asked me to write *Dancing with Dragons*, I became their "interpreter" for the knowledge they wanted to share. However, the dragons refused to let me write all I knew about them at that time. "Not yet," was their response.

In that first dragon book, I wrote at length about whether dragons are real or imaginary. They are quite real. They simply have chosen to live in the Otherworld, a plane of existence with different vibrations. The Otherworld's vibrations allow these entities to exist in the same "place" as our physical plane without our seeing them. That is, unless the beings of that world want to be seen. Humans have the unfortunate habit of tearing things apart to prove they exist.

Many writers use the words *astral* and *Otherworld* interchangeably. I'm not sure I agree. The huge *Oxford English Dictionary* notes that *astral* comes from the Latin word *astralis* (meaning "star") and defines it as "consisting of a super-sensible substance beyond the tangible world in refinement." The *OED* also states that "the 'Otherworld' is a world beyond present reality." Sounds like the same place, doesn't it? Yet during sleep and deliberate astral travel, not everyone journeys into the Otherworld. In my experience, there is a thin layer of slightly more refined vibrations between the dense vibrations of the physical plane and the ones higher yet of the Otherworld. I base this idea on the shamanic tradition of thousands of years, a tradition in which one must be concentrating on the Otherworld in order to reach it. Therefore, it seems sensible that another layer of "stuff" lies between the two planes. Otherwise, one could idly—and unintentionally—walk between the worlds all the time, just by letting one's thoughts drift off reality. A frightening thought to most people. And probably to the beings in the Otherworld.

In *Dancing with Dragons*, I presented several areas of meditation and magick through which certain dragons could interact with human magicians. Or non-magicians, for that matter. I wanted people to be comfortable that dragons are basically friendly to curious humans and quite willing to work with—and create lasting relationships with—those of us who desire it. By explaining as clearly as I could the various methods of contacting dragons, many readers discovered the delight of "dancing" with dragons any time they wished to.

A good many of those readers were excited to learn that anyone could have the company of a guardian dragon, maybe even two, as I had with Nip and Tuck. Dragons rarely give you their real names, so I doubt Nip and Tuck are their true names. That pair is just too full of mischief to be serious, except about their duties.

Thinking the first dragon book would be the only one I was to write, I went on to other writing projects. I felt I had done a pretty good job of opening the door to other realities for people.

In 2005, the elder dragons informed me that it was time to write a second dragon book for serious students of dragon magick, this one containing secret information about the Five Inner Rings. They gave me a detailed outline and, over the next nine months or so, worked with me on expanding the outline with details not revealed before. Even I had been unaware of the depths of a few lessons.

About the time I started this book, Nip and Tuck graduated from being guardians, leaving me a little lost without them. I was widowed in 2002 and suffered dangerous health problems early in 2003. Three years later, however, my present husband and I were led to find each other under unusual circumstances. I'm sure Ken and I had more help than we realized when that meeting was arranged. At the same time, the beautiful white and gold Nesta took over guardian position. The mischievous Nip and Tuck still check in occasionally. Nesta is quick to tell them she has everything under control. Tinsel and Rudy, the two babies I mentioned in the first book, are still with me.

If you haven't made the acquaintance of a guardian dragon, perhaps you are wondering what they are. A guardian dragon is an adolescent who is learning to work with humans. Although they lack the size, strength, and knowledge of the older, larger dragons, guardians help humans, particularly magicians, by protecting, aiding in spells and rituals, and in the development of meditation and the psychic arts, especially divination. It seems to be customary to get acquainted with a guardian dragon before you meet the larger dragons. Perhaps this happens because the guardians are small enough not to frighten the humans to whom they appear.

"Appearing" doesn't mean actually having a dragon manifest in front of you, although that can happen. Appearing is more like sensing a presence close to or behind you. Often you will see them with your inner eyes, as a fleeting movement in the corner of your eye, or in pictures in your mind. Their conversations are by telepathy. You will know the thoughts aren't yours, because the words, tones, and information aren't in your style of thinking.

These smaller dragons can range in size from knee-high to your own height. They become a type of astral watchdog for you, your family, and your property. That includes any pets you might have. The cats have always known Nip and Tuck, so they were leery for a time with Nesta. Now they accept her presence. They are probably happy that she doesn't tease them as the other two did.

You "feed" your guardian companions on love and respect and allow them to consume any leftover magickal energy drifting around. Guardians are always watched over by an older dragon, very likely because they can be very exuberant and active. So don't be shocked if you glimpse a shadowy large form unobtrusively standing around.

There are often much smaller, younger dragons with the guardian. These are usually siblings who need a dragon-sitter. The babies are about the length of your hand. Colors vary in all the younger dragons, revealing that the babies and guardians come from different dragon clans. The smaller dragons are lighter in color and their scales soft to the touch, again a clue to their young age. Older dragons have hard, defined scales and sharper, darker coloring.

Dragons age very slowly. Therefore, the juvenile and adolescent stages can last well over five hundred years. This is a relatively short period of time for long-lived dragons, who count centuries as we do months.

The dragon elders dictated the way in which I present the information in this book. So if you are eager to find out everything about them, be patient. What you learn in each Ring as a student will be some new, often slightly different, information, while you are building up to the next Ring.

The Five Inner Rings themselves lie in the Otherworld, while much of what you learn will be practiced in this world. There is little written clearly about the Rings, just hints and a fine thread, primarily through Eastern myths and legends. The Dragon Warrior section has been kept alive in martial arts, but only as it applies to being a warrior. And little of the martial arts teachings are similar to the Dragon Warrior any longer.

The Rings might be compared to a college of Otherworld training. The area of the Five Inner Rings lies in the Otherworld realm, with connections to more than one level of that place. The only way I've seen the Rings is as concentric circles around an open center. There is only one Gate to each Ring, plus the one through which you enter from outside, and you can't go through any door to the next Ring unless the dragon at the Gate allows you to do so. This permission is given only after the appropriate initiation for that section. This is one field of learning in which you can't get "passed along," nor can you buy your way to a degree. You earn your way, or you don't go through.

Don't be concerned about how to reach the Rings. You can reach the Otherworld most easily through meditation. When you relax deeply while concentrating on your goal, you slide automatically into astral travel. Your concentration on the goal sees that you reach the correct place. Don't worry that what you see and experience in your mind might be illusion, because it isn't. All your inner senses, which duplicate the senses you use every day, will come alive in the Otherworld. All of it is truly happening, simply on another level of vibration.

If you prefer to "experience," and not have to remember the order of happenings in meditations given in this book, record them on an audiotape you can play while meditating. Then you can open yourself to everything you see, hear, and experience without worry. Meditation is simple, once you grasp the relaxing part. Remember, if you think too much about relaxing, it will only be harder. Practice and regular meditation soon solve the relaxing technique. You will become so engrossed with what happens in the Otherworld that you won't have time to worry.

To get comfortable with meditation, use the following short meditation to start on your way. It will introduce you to the Inner Ring of Apprentice, the first step along your dragon journey. And perhaps it will make you stretch into an entirely new way of looking at, and thinking about, the layers of "reality" in which we live. May your journey through the Five Inner Rings open your life to all the potentials around you.

Entering the Five Inner Rings

The beginning and the ending of a guided meditation are done in the same manner each time. Therefore, the beginning and the ending will not be included in other meditations in this book. If you prerecord the meditations, which makes meditation so much easier, simply speak the beginning and the ending in the proper places.

In preparation for meditation, silence your phone and doorbell. Make certain that pets do not have access to you during this time. Request also that any humans stay away and not talk to you. If necessary, hang a "do not disturb" sign on the door. Use soft, instrumental music as a background to blot out small irritating noises.

Using candles and incense are not required. If you do use them, make certain they are not near anything flammable and that they won't topple over. You also don't want your room to become choked with fumes.

I don't recommend meditating while lying down, since this is one of the easiest ways to fall sleep. Instead, select a comfortable chair in which you sit upright with your feet on the floor. When deep in your meditation, you will be in an astral travel or a shamanic trance journey.

You will not be aware of time, because time is a man-made theory. Nor are you likely to be fully aware of what is happening around you, unless the mind senses danger. In this case, you will be able to return to your body at once. The same applies if you are fearful of anything you see during this time. You are never trapped, caught, in danger of losing your soul, or whatever else people fear; you can open your eyes anytime and be back in normal time and place.

(Beginning of meditation)

Sit in the chair, back straight, feet flat on the floor, with your hands in your lap. Take three slow, deep breaths, relaxing more of your body's muscles each time. Visualize yourself surrounded by brilliant white light, with your guardian spirits at your side. Your body relaxes more and more until you feel light and very comfortable. See yourself standing beside a well. If anything or anyone in your life is upsetting you, drop it or them into the well. They fall down into the darkness away from you. Walk away from the well, leaving every annoying person and thing behind.

(End of beginning)

You feel yourself moving so fast, it seems as if you are not moving at all. A huge wooden door bound with iron scrollwork and hinges appears before you at the same time the velvety darkness around you fades to bright sunlight. As you stand looking at the massive door, you reach up to pull the heavy chain attached to a bell. The deep sound reverberates over and over until the door slowly opens.

"Why have you come here?" asks the brightly colored dragon just inside the door.

When you answer that you wish to study within the Five Inner Rings, the dragon beckons you inside. As the door closes behind you, you become aware that, although you sense the circular shape of the First Ring, what you see is a spacious, narrow room with slightly curved walls. Sunlight seems to stream through skylights, but you can't see the ceiling.

As you look to the right, then the left, you see endless lines of tables holding a selection of objects, shelves against the walls full of scrolls and books, and diagrams and maps hung on the walls in between open cabinets containing jars of dried herbs and tall bottles of oils.

"Do you desire to study with the dragons?" the Gate dragon asks. "If you are certain, I ask you to sign the registry." The large clawed foot points to a table beside the closed door. On the table is a quill pen in an ink bottle and an open book.

If you truthfully intend to pursue the study of dragon magick, you step forward and sign your name beneath the other names you see in the book.

When you are finished, the Gate guardian fastens a tiny silver dragon figure to your clothing. You are then allowed to ask the guardian one question.

The guardian leads you down the room to a bright cone of light that reaches from the stone floor upward endlessly.

"When you come again, say you are a student of the Five Inner Rings," the dragon tells you. "We hope to see you soon."

The clawed hand points toward the brilliant cone.

(Ending) *As you walk into the light, you find yourself back inside your physical body. Move your fingers and feet slowly until you feel comfortable once more on the physical plane. The meditation is ended.*

(End of meditation)

European and Eastern Dragons

This world's ancient mythologies from nearly every culture tell tales about dragons. The descriptions of these creatures differ according to the culture studied. Basically, however, dragons can be divided into two large groups: Western and Eastern. The few strange descriptions of dragons that fall between these two categories are rare.

The dragons of the Western world, primarily Europe, are quite large with heavy, muscular bodies covered with thick, tough scales. They have a long sinuous neck with a triangular-shaped head, two leather-like wings, and a long narrow tail. The hind legs are large and powerful, while the forelegs are much shorter. However, the West also has *wyverns* (dragons with only two back legs), and a winged but legless version called the Worm. They are known to breathe fire and smoke when agitated. Their scale colors run the gamut of hues. However, no particular colors seem to be associated with special dragon families, the areas where the dragons are found, or their ages.

The blood (life force) of Western dragons is very corrosive and poisonous yet highly valued for its magickal qualities. Most Western dragons are not friendly or beneficial toward humans, probably because they were so widely harassed and hunted.

Eastern dragons act quite differently and are held in high regard by the peoples of the Far East. Most dragons of this class have four legs of equal size, a long serpentine body, and a varying number of claws. The five-clawed dragons, five claws on each foot, are so rare that Chinese emperors adopted them as a sacred ancestor, enacting laws that ensured that only top royalty could use their pictures. All other dragons have either three or four claws on each foot.

Although hot-tempered when provoked, they do not breathe fire often or go on destructive rampages. Portraits of Eastern dragons, embroidered on surviving clothing and wall hangings, picture them as primarily wingless. However, they can propel themselves through the air by balancing between the winds and the Earth's magnetic field. The Chinese divide the dragon population into four groups with different characteristics. Primarily, these classes rule over seas and rivers, the skies, precious metals and gems, and releasing the rain.

Dragons are so popular in the Orient that experts have studied them for years. The experts discovered that colors were indicative of a dragon's age, that dragons laid eggs that took at least a thousand years to hatch, and that they could change forms through concentration or extreme anger. Eastern dragons had the very special ability to shapeshift into a human. This trait isn't mentioned in European tales.

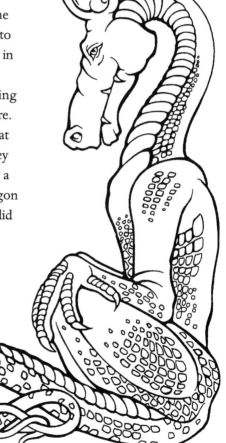

Chinese doctors were as interested in using dragon parts in medicine as European doctors were. However, the Chinese knew from their studies that dragons shed their skin and bones periodically. They also gathered dragon foam from the ocean after a fight or storm. The red, sometimes black, dragon blood was poisonous and unusable. However, it did turn into amber when it fell onto the ground.

Some characteristics are common to both the Western and Eastern species. Western dragons are less cooperative with humans than Eastern dragons, probably because they are treated with less respect. Neither is less powerful in magick than the other; they merely have different ways of doing things. They use guile and riddles until they are certain of a human's intentions toward them.

After they reach a certain level of maturity, the younger ones of the dragon species begin their work with humans by becoming personal or guardian dragons. Many of them decide to stay with one human for the human's lifetime, especially if the two forge a strong bond. If the atmosphere is safe, and the Apprentice trustworthy, often the very small dragons are allowed to do this. These young ones may be the length of your hand or smaller; they have not taken on permanent coloring yet. They are supposed to just observe, but frequently they end up befriending the Apprentice and any animals in the vicinity. Since dragons take much more time than humans to mature, it isn't likely you will see any change in size and/or appearance of the tiny dragons.

Soon after the arrival of the guardian dragon, usually in timing with a certain point in a human magician's training, larger and older dragons make an appearance to regularly teach and work with the Apprentice. These teachers do not accept excuses for slacking on practice. If you make too many excuses, or don't put in the learning time you should, these older dragons can and will discontinue teaching you. Your name also goes on a kind of dragon "blacklist." You only can remove yourself from this "list" by practicing diligently on your own and hoping for a reprieve.

Dragons have always held a high position in Eastern cultures. They still are honored each year at the Chinese New Year festivals. There are no Western festivals for honoring dragons. However, dragons have come into favor in the West in the last ten years or so. Even a few positive movies have been made about them. You can now see a small hole in the wall of prejudice. Perhaps you, as an example of a dragon magician quietly living life, will be one to help breach the wall. You never know.

Understanding Dragon Magick

Magick! The very word conjures up a variety of different mental images to humans. To the majority, their idea of magick is of instant gratification, of obtaining whatever they desire. A snap of the fingers, a wiggle of the nose, and *voilà*! What they wanted has appeared without any effort on their part.

However, practitioners of genuine, non-theatrical magick know that magick isn't instantaneous and that it requires much time and energy to prepare for and then perform. After that, one must be patient until the manifestation appears. The magician gathers the herbs, stones, candles, and other objects that signal to the linear, or left, brain that it has a schedule of ritualized duties to follow. This leaves the creative, or right, brain free to leap beyond the linear-imposed boundaries of "reality" and to mold universal energy into a desired result. The results rarely happen soon, especially if you are an unskilled magician, so take time to develop in the Otherworld realm before making your desire manifest in the physical world.

In order to do this, you have to trick part of your brain into cooperating. The right brain ignores all linear rules because this half of the brain sees "reality" and "possibility" in terms of the infinite, a concept the left brain cannot conceive of as real. There is no such thing as time to the right brain. To the left brain, everything runs on time. Whatever can't be seen by the human eyes, touched, tasted, or trapped in a laboratory vial cannot possibly be real, the left brain tells us. Yet it can't explain certain things that happen, no matter how hard it tries.

The art of magick in all its forms has been practiced and studied for thousands of years, a minimum of 4,500 years to be exact. If magick didn't work, if tangible results weren't seen, humans would have given up on it centuries ago. But we are still learning about magick and new (to us) methods of making it more efficient and productive.

Dragon is another word that creates a sense of anticipation in humans. Many cultures around the world not only practice magick, but they believe in dragons. Somehow, magick and dragons just seem to go together. The dragons themselves are magickal creatures, but the connection goes beyond that. Dragons are masters in using magick.

It is rare to find a culture that doesn't have tales of dragons in its history and folklore. These dragons may be described as having different forms from those in Europe and the Far East with which we are familiar, but they are still dragons.

Magicians worldwide know the value of befriending a dragon and getting it to add energy to the spells. In fact, a willing dragon as a co-magician in magick can triple the human magician's creative power before the spellwork even starts. If the magician cements the bond between with a co-magician dragon in a positive way—as equal partners, each able to contribute a different ingredient to the potion—spells begin to manifest faster. The human gains not only the physical result wanted, but learns new magickal methods and ways to communicate with beings of the Otherworld.

In *Dancing with Dragons*, I introduced several categories of dragons and ways to interact with them as co-magicians. I plan to expand the methods of magick in this book, along with introducing many more dragon secrets and ways of doing dragon magick. I assume you are familiar with the dragons and at least some of the information in *Dancing with Dragons*. If you are, these lessons will not give you much difficulty. Just a stretch in your magickal muscles. If you are not familiar with the first book, you will have to work a little harder, but learning will not be impossible.

This book can be used entirely on a mundane level. Doing the spells and meditations can benefit any magician. Self-discipline, visualization, patience, and perseverance are valuable traits to cultivate so you can be the director, and not the victim, of your life events.

However, if a person is searching for a dragon guide to higher spiritual paths and more effective magick, and is willing to invest the necessary time and effort, then this book will unfold its information in a different way. According to the true desire in the seeker and the readiness of the pupil, the hidden Dragon Gates in the Otherworld will be revealed. The secret doors to the Five Inner Rings will give up their mysteries.

The door to each Inner Ring opens into a different, but higher, state of spiritual consciousness and a broader, deeper range of Otherworld magickal information. Each state of consciousness is related to a dragon level of teaching. That is why this book is divided into five stages of initiation, each stage matching one of the traditional Five Inner Rings of dragon magick.

The Five Inner Rings were originated by the dragons as a safe method of dispersing ancient knowledge to humans. The magick and other information written here is known by very few humans now alive. I was contacted by an ancient dragon group still practicing in Lebanon who wondered how I had come to know the dragon secrets. I was as surprised as they were that other people were working with dragons and had done so for several centuries. They assured me that my rites and magick matched theirs almost word

for word—even the dragon names. All I could answer was, "The dragons told me." There was one more communiqué to encourage me to keep working, then no other answers. I suspect they dare not be exposed as magicians in a predominantly Muslim country.

The dragons also control who can pass through a Ring Gate, and when. You may think you can fool the dragons by pretending to know what you don't, but that won't work. Dragons are wily creatures themselves. They can instantly see a lie or a "stretched" story. Then, without your being aware of it, the dragons will shift you into an illusory path that appears to you to be true. But you will have been sent into the mundane levels of magick. The only way to get back on track is to return to the place in the specific Ring where you stopped learning and started playing. This time, when you work your way up the path to the next Ring, you will be granted a true initiation for the Ring you are leaving, and you will be welcomed to the new Ring by the next level of dragon teachers.

To those who read for the joy of working magick with dragons, these Otherworld beings are willing to help you hone your magickal ability. They do not insist that you follow a spiritual path unless you wish to. Dragons are more aware of the right to free will than most humans are.

Since dragons like to work with intelligent, curious humans, they wanted this book to be written on two levels of understanding: the mundane and the spiritual. To those humans who discover and take the higher path, the dragons are ready to teach and escort you every step of your way. This "way" will culminate in important exterior and interior changes in all levels of your life. It also can help you peel away old façades and masks built during past lives. When these illusions are removed, your true spiritual self sends out brilliant waves of Light, revealing a new you—the person you were meant to be.

Dragon magick is actually more complicated than it seems at first. It speaks to humans according to whatever level of growth they have mastered. What one human magician reads and understands may not reveal itself to another magician. Certain categories of dragons will not appear to, or work with, humans who have not advanced beyond a required level. They do not put powerful dragon magick into inexperienced hands. And dragons are not tricked into thinking you are more powerful, responsible, or deserving than you are. You may lie about your magickal abilities to those around you, but you can't lie to a dragon. To a dragon, all your true motives, abilities, and plans are laid bare.

Dragon magick of the Five Inner Rings is very different in vibrational rate than other magick. Dragons weave their spells out of unusual currents of invisible energies. These exotic energies are connected to the Multiverse and its infinite worlds. It is rare for a human magician to have this knowledge and know how to manipulate the power to find, touch, and weave these currents. The magicians throughout the ages who have accomplished this feat have always had dragons as co-magicians. They also have had the good sense not to travel in the myriad of Otherworlds without a dragon as guide and protector.

Dragons also mold these invisible currents of energies into "keys" that allow them to pass through strange and wondrous gateways. These gateways open to other universes and worlds, the existence of which humans have barely dreamed. This is the Multiverse. Humans know only a very small amount about the Multiverse and the mysterious gateways opening into its infinite levels. We are a very young species in these realms of existence, while dragons have exchanged information with the beings of the Multiverse for generations past numbering. When it comes to working magick and gathering information, no creature is more knowledgeable and dedicated than a dragon.

The doorway to becoming an Apprentice, the first of the Inner Rings, stands open, waiting for you to walk through it. It will take commitment and hard work on your part to move through the Five Inner Rings. You will have to repeat some things many times before you get them right. Other tasks will come more quickly.

One of the reasons that it will not be easy to make your way through the Five Inner Rings is that you must fit these studies in and around your responsibilities in everyday life. Becoming a dragon magician does not give you the privilege of shirking the lessons and responsibilities you agreed to learn in the present human incarnation. Every lesson is part of a greater lesson. Every life is part of a greater life.

I wish you the greatest of adventures as you journey through the Five Inner Rings of mystical dragon magick. May your path be full of joy and excitement, and may the goal at the end, the goal found in the Fifth Inner Ring of the Dragon Mystic, be the crowning touch of illumination on your magickal, spiritual path.

Dragon Ring Code

All throughout the Multiverse
The power is there to bless or curse.
'Tis balance of darkness and of light
That holds the Web threads ever tight.
Black chaos dragons and those of Light,
Locked in balance that is right.
The dragons' code is very clear.
Each Ring should be for half a year.
From Apprentice to the Warrior guard,
The way to be Mystic is long and hard.
All levels explored, all truth laid bare,
The students' motives, pure as Air,
Must pass the test within the heart,
Before the Veil of Knowledge parts.
Dragon-trust he must earn, then wait
Until his teachers reveal the Gate.
Dragon magick, strong and old,
Requires the student to be bold.
Cast the numbers three times three,
For that is what the power will be.
No dragon spell is weak or small,
For dragon magick conquers all.

ONE

The Way of the Dragon Apprentice

FIRST OF THE INNER RINGS

When I wrote *Dancing with Dragons*, I knew I had too much dragon information to fit into one book. Besides, I was not certain how interested my readers were in the subject at that time. It turned out that the subject of dragons drew more interest than I had thought. The volume of e-mail asking for more on dragon magick kept growing. This book is my attempt to fill those requests.

I expected to begin this book as I did *Dancing with Dragons*—with discussions of the dragon species and their magickal abilities, front and center immediately. I thought that the dragons would want to begin instruction on the very first page. In fact, I didn't expect this book to be laid out as it is at all. But how can one argue with a dragon? The book is theirs; I'm just the typist.

When I finally managed to speak to Sairys[1], I asked if she would explain the reasoning behind this strange layout and the short delay in starting the lessons. Sairys informed me that the dragons wanted the beginning student to have certain knowledge before meeting the dragons—that these lessons required a different state of mind than the other book did. The students needed a slightly modified introduction to prepare their subconscious and collective unconscious minds for an entirely new, and very serious, look at themselves, the universe, and dragon magick. Only a true, dedicated student to dragon magick would walk the complete path from Apprentice to Mystic.

Then, in typical dragon fashion, Sairys presented me with a surprise. Since most of the knowledge I would be recording was new, even to me, I was to undergo the lessons of the Five Inner Rings as I wrote the book. Dragons have a sense of humor that is often very difficult to understand.

The Dragon Apprentice will be studying quite a few different subjects in this section. Besides becoming acquainted with the tools needed by the Apprentice, you will be introduced to magickal laws, the layout of the Otherworld and its Gates, co-magician

---

1. Sairys is the dragon of Air and the East, as described in *Dancing with Dragons*.

dragons, and dragon alchemy, among other interesting subjects. In other words, you will have a lot to think about and consider before you prepare to enter the next section, that of the Dragon Enchanter.

Take your time with each chapter. Let your mind absorb each presentation thoroughly before moving on. Practice meditations often so you can gain the most benefit from them. Good luck.

Principles and Laws of Magick

You stand at the threshold of the First of the Inner Rings. Now is the time for you to decide if you want to take the mundane path, learning simply the everyday types of magick, or if you are willing to accept the role of Dragon Apprentice and all the work it entails.

There is nothing wrong with studying the more materialistic type of magick. You can still apply it to all life around you to help yourself and others. This world is heavily populated with humans (sometimes called "mundanes") who have no belief in the psychic, magick, and the Otherworld. The word *mundane* means the everyday world, the material level. I don't use the word myself because, to me, it has a hint of prejudice about it. Nonbelievers in magick use their free will to make their choice not to believe, just as magicians use free will to make their choice. As universal beings, nonbelievers are worthy of help through herbal medicines and quiet spells and rituals to bind criminals, to make the nonbelievers' environment as safe as possible, and so on.

Because some people believe in magick, it doesn't make them better than other people. All magicians must work and live with the mundane world and karma. We are subject to the same universal laws everyone else is. Hopefully, we are wise enough to see the lesson in a life event sooner. By acknowledging the lesson and adjusting our lives and thought patterns to accept what it is and what it does to us, we don't have to pay the "penalty" all the way to the end.[2] A very wise magician will be studying and growing spiritually at the same time.

Mystical dragon magick is a spiritual, but nonreligious, path. The only oaths you will be asked to take are those that require you to acknowledge the existence of dragons and their magickal powers and to speak quietly, if at all, about the Multiverse and your study of it. This knowledge is not for those who chose not to walk the path of the Five Inner Rings. This request is very important to the work, and it is best for all if the

---

2. Many writers don't agree with me on this point of karma. However, it makes perfect sense that the Supreme Force (God and Goddess) takes no personal pleasure in the pain of repaying negative karma. Therefore, as soon as we see and accept the lesson embedded in a karmic event, the payment stops.

deepest magick, your experiences, and your results of working certain methods do not become topics of public discussion.

Before I explain in more detail about the Otherworld and the Multiverse, we need to take a closer look at what magick actually is. It isn't an illusion conceived by superstition or an unbalanced mind, nor is it a David Copperfield stage act.

Most beginning magicians are familiar with the definition of magick: by using universal energy drawn from outside and willfully channeled through you, and by molding that energy through your intent, visualization, and concentration into an event or desire, you can cause that event or desire to appear in your physical world. You don't say a spell and your desire falls into your lap. Nothing in life, not even magick, comes that easily.

Magicians and most Pagans in general do not recruit members. They believe that when a student is ready, that person will find the path to follow. When the deliberate choice is made to follow that path, all the teachers, books, and similarly minded friends the person needs will be there to help.

Whether someone believes in magick or not, it is very real. But it helps to believe in magick before you see or experience it. Then you will be less likely to dismiss a magickal spell's culmination as illusion or a freak one-time incident. Even if you think you know a lot about magick and how to do it, it is important that you keep an open mind to the possibility of learning something new.

Magick itself is both an art and a science. It is a science in that magicians are discovering things that do not violate scientific laws as we now know them but often appear to. Chemistry came about through the work of the Arabian and European alchemists. Many ancient herbal medicines led scientists to develop man-made medications that now control, or prevent, certain diseases among humans and animals.

Magick is also an art because it uses inner talents and mental "muscles" that scientists can't yet measure. Magick isn't pulling a rabbit out of thin air or tripping over lost treasure chests. It is mentally pushing against certain points in the flow of universal energies, carefully gathering separate strands from the Otherworld realm, and molding this ball of energy into the desire you wish to fulfill. By making small changes, the magician's opportunities to have that desire manifest become astronomical. Magick acts like a giant magnet, attracting what you want.

Trained magicians can learn to have greater control over their lives by using these techniques. By changing their lives, magicians also affect changes in their destinies. This comes about through interacting with the Multiverse on all its planes and according to universal magickal rules. Influencing parts of your future by having a hand in creating it is better than blindly accepting whatever happens.

Ancient magicians learned early in their training how to live in a Multiverse of many worlds besides this physical, material one. Magicians have exchanged magickal information with friendly Otherworld beings for thousands of years because this exchange benefited all. There is no way to know how long dragons and other fantastical creatures worked with human magicians before these beings fled the unreliability of humans and decided to permanently live in the Otherworld.

After their choice to move, these beings only made rare trips to this world. Therefore, magicians were forced to learn how to travel between the worlds and hope to find a reliable guide. This is as true of shamans and mystics today as it was centuries ago. Because of their ability to do so, shamans and mystics are still called Walkers Between Worlds, an apt description of what they can do.

A magician is responsible for whatever she or he does. The Multiverse (Goddess and God) put certain consistent rules about magick into place, just as it created scientific laws for every planet of the universe. You can avoid problems if you observe these rules.

Know yourself. This is the same motto once carved over the doorway to Apollo's temple at Delphi. In other words, don't allow illusions about yourself to cloud the reality of who and what you really are. If you don't like parts of your personality, don't blame others. Change what you don't like. You have free will. Obviously, you made some wrong choices, either in this life or another, and need to correct them. But never lie to yourself about these things. Lies come back at the most inconvenient times to haunt you through karma.

Never claim you are a master in anything. Someone will always come along to prove you wrong. Magicians who make it a point to brag to others that they are masters are best avoided. You will frequently find their teaching background questionable, their attitudes arrogant, and their information wrong.

Always be careful what you do and say, particularly when discussing magick with nonmagickal people. Talking about spells you do weakens them. By talking about a spell within the first twenty-four hours, you withdraw energy from your intent and concentration, allowing power to seep away. If another magician, for example one who doesn't want your spell to materialize, hears of your work, she or he can do a counterspell to make your spell null and void. Talking about a spell can sidetrack your determination. Intent and determination always control magickal results.

Take great care what you wish for. You might get it. This rule comes into play when magicians haven't made certain they are using the right spell ingredients or don't have the correct intent behind their wishes. Have you thought about your motive for doing a certain spell? Have you truthfully looked at all the positives and negatives that will come your way if your wish is granted? Is your spell so detailed that you leave no room in case something better comes along? Or have you been so lax with details that your visualization and intent wander off, turning the spell energy in another direction?

Never do magick to control another person. Using a person's name in a spell is *not* a good thing to do. The named person will subconsciously revolt against the control, eventually breaking free with obvious negative feelings toward you. If the person blithely goes along with your control, you may have just as negative an ending: a person who is a hypochondriac or won't get a job or help at home; an abusive, sneaking spouse; a person with a hidden criminal or mentally unstable mind. The list can be endless since even magicians rarely see the true characteristics behind the masks we all wear. Be careful what you use magick to get.

You are responsible for everything you create or cause to happen by magick. First, never do magick, even healing, for other people unless they ask you to do so. It is better never to do magick for another unless it *is* healing. You do not know fully the intents of the person asking you. Some people are too lazy to learn magick for themselves but are quite adept at using any such energy raised for them. Or these people are able to manipulate the energy into a negative path. If the spell turns out to be harmful in some way, or if it boomerangs, you are tied to the karma it creates along with the other person. This boomerang effect also can apply to your own spells on some occasions. You need to ground the remaining spell energy when you finish and set boundaries for how long the spell can last and how far the spell energy will go. This will be thoroughly discussed in the Enchanter Ring section.

Don't invoke anything you do not know how to banish. Some magicians get caught up in the rush of power they feel when doing magickal spells. Sooner or later, some of these magicians will feel they have enough knowledge and power to demand the presence of an Otherworldly being they've read about in some book. You may end up with a very negative, invisible companion who causes you no end of grief until you can find a more knowledgeable magician to banish the thing back where it belongs. If this creature is a very malevolent being, it can cause poltergeist activities and even attack you. Don't play at magick.

When you place yourself, by oath or otherwise, in a position to be called a student of dragon magick, you agree to become destined to fulfill a very meaningful purpose in your life. Your behavior, compassion, and use of magick will touch and influence all who are near you or cross your path, even if they never learn you are a magician. A meaningful purpose in life usually does not mean something spectacular either. It's all the little magick by obscure magicians that change and affect the Multiverse. All the work of the ordinary people in this world has far more impact on crucial events than one big-name personality.

Because of your oath to the Five Inner Rings, you may be called many times to silently use your magickal powers for a critical cause. Usually this call flashes into your heart and mind with such impact that you know the idea doesn't come from you. But be cautious. Never accept any advice that goes against your ethics or whose positive outcome is questionable. Primarily, these silent calls will be to minimize disasters, change the course of a possible war or invasion, to prevent massive riots and killings, or to build a wave of compassion, healing, and comfort for a large group of victims. However, being destined isn't something you brag about to others. You accept it with humility and a deep sense of duty to Earth, our universe, and the Otherworld. It isn't everyone who is chosen to be a dragon magician.

Magickal destiny and the appearance of "miracles" require our constant participation by free will. We can walk away at any time and avoid the heavy responsibilities. When we begin our magickal studies and learn how much dedication and hard work they will require, we can turn a deaf ear as we leave those studies behind. Avoidance also may come when we allow society and organizations to stigmatize us as weird or evil, thus discouraging us from learning. However, every moment of every day can be a decisive time for us, as it gives us another chance to help good magick happen.

No member of the Five Inner Rings is ever called a priest, priestess, guru, master, or any other nonsense name. There is no hierarchy. On occasion, a person is called by the title she or he has earned by journeying their way through the Rings. Even among those magicians, there will be no insinuations that one is better than another. Or you may call yourself a Daughter of the Dragon or a Son of the Dragon after you go through the initiation ceremony in this section.

No dragon magician represents any church or religion either. All magicians are on a private, personal, spiritual, but nonreligious path. Seeking spiritually is seeking to improve the soul. Religion today has come to mean belonging to an organization. All magicians of the Multiverse try hard to become an adept in magick, secret lore, mysticism, and ancient knowledge—not just for the sake of learning but to help others. This includes recovering forgotten Otherworld information. By this alchemy of sciences, the magician is subtly transformed spiritually.

Most magicians prefer to work alone, or perhaps two or three together. The group method would only become necessary if they all needed to work intently on the same spell, such as preventing an invasion of their country, averting another war, or eliminating the terrible consequences of some government deciding to use nuclear weapons. This method was effectively used during World War II by Witches and magicians in Great Britain.

However, magicians do take part in other Pagan activities, such as Renaissance fairs, seasonal celebrations, and gatherings for religious freedom. Dragon magicians are social beings, as all humans are—but not while they are seriously practicing magick.

Although magicians don't use pretentious titles to identify themselves, there is one important way to know where they stand on their magickal path. Any magician can be, and very frequently is, classified according to her or his magickal methods and intent. In wide, general terms, there are three kinds of magicians: white, black, and gray.

"White" magicians are usually very reluctant to work with their magickal powers. Many of them do not use magickal spells at all. Instead, they use poetry, song, dance, and positive thoughts, believing these to be in the best interest of all. They consider magickal spells to be a way to inadvertently harm someone. However, they do strong healing work and may use a minor type of thinking-spell for this. They truly believe that concentrating on and using positive words and phrases will make everything balanced. Although these are good words with positive action behind them, they do not prepare these magicians to deal with anything unpleasant. If "white" magicians find themselves in a testy situation that calls for a strong intent to repel or bind, they may get hurt. Not only do they not have the necessary training to protect themselves, they cannot believe that the "enemy" doesn't respond to their pacifist beliefs.

If this is your belief, it is basically a good one. Being kind, positive, and loving are good traits for all humans; it really is too bad that the Multiverse doesn't run on those ideas. For your own safety, however, please try not to get involved with dangerous magickal situations. You fulfill the role of healer quite well. There are never enough healers to go around.

The second category of magicians is called "black." These magicians primarily want power over others. They also don't want to be governed or judged by any laws, either human or universal. They are basically self-centered with little, if any, conscience when it comes to getting their way. Unfortunately, this is the world's typical stereotype of a magician, a Pagan, or a Witch.

The third category is that of "gray" magicians. These practitioners stand at the midpoint of magickal power, ready to do whatever needs to be done to protect all—usually without recognition or praise, which is the way gray magicians prefer it.

This path has been my choice since I was young. I later taught students, "If you find evil in your community, face it, trace it, and erase it. If you have any evidence of law-breaking, tell the police. Don't play fair. Just begin binding and tripping spells. Binding to keep the evil from hiding, and tripping so the evil ones are caught by their own errors. Karma is unlikely to accrue in this type of action, but if it does, it will certainly be less than if you knew about the evil and did nothing." Strangely enough, this attitude, which seems balanced to me, has brought me under fire several times from certain segments of the Pagan community.

When faced with stopping evil in any form, you can brainstorm for ways to work a spell in a positive mode. Tripping spells are very good for this, as they use the energy of the culprit to self-entangle and get caught by the police in circumstances that do not involve you at all. If negative spells are sent to you, you can return them to the sender without accruing bad karma. After all, the energy doesn't belong to you, and it is up to you to keep it or return it.

There is a universal rule in magick known as the Rule of Three. Simply put, whatever type of power you deliberately send out by strong intent or magick will return to you in three times the quantity, power, or energy. If your spells are positive, you will receive positivity in return. If the spells are negative and harmful, you may well get back three times three of the same energy. This fits perfectly with the law that like attracts like. It pays to think twice about the types of spells you send out into the universe and why you are doing them.

The dragons, too, have a code of ethics that covers both mundane and magickal, spiritual levels. As with all dragon teachings, each line of the code carries more than one level of meaning. Dragons will not point out the different meanings. You have to discover those on your own.

Dragon Ethics

1. Little seen gets more done.
2. Look for truth in the Heart of hearts.
3. A lie burns both the liar and the silent listener.
4. Be true to the responsibility of the balance.
5. Silence and magick: both are needed.
6. Honor your elders, for they carry important ancient knowledge.
7. Evil gives no forewarning and no pause for relief.
8. Dignity speaks well of a messenger.
9. You color your own light.
10. What happens to one stone reflects on all.

Please remember that the following short explanations of these ten ethical principles are relevant to this world level only. There is a deeper, more universal and spiritual meaning for each.

You can accomplish more in your studies and work if you don't waste time trying to impress your peers with your robe and wand. Let your life and actions speak for themselves. Those who want dragon magick without the work will not be impressed whatever you do. Those who are truly attracted to this path won't need to be impressed.

They will learn for themselves that the personal dragon center within you is called the Hidden Dragon Heart. It is a very powerful space. You can always find the truth there by calling upon your dragon teachers for aid and by using common sense to know how the energy of any situation or person feels to you. So don't be concerned with what other people think.

No lie ever escapes reward; when the truth finally is revealed, the listener who said nothing to expose the liar will share the liar's social punishment.

Everyone, magician or not, consciously or subconsciously, is responsible for keeping the balance of the Multiverse. If the beings on any world completely destroy the balance in their universe, chaos and destruction on all levels would occur like a line of dominoes, unless the Watchers and dragon magicians work quickly to repair the damage. Even if we knew the statistical accounting of the loss, we could not grasp such figures.

Not speaking about your magickal work keeps the spell strong, while talking about it draws away energy. The best magicians work quietly, without anyone knowing.

Elders of any culture on any world are valuable for their firsthand knowledge of many things; true history and ancient natural healing would be lost without our elders.

Never expect any negative-minded person or negative event to announce itself before it enters your life. Once at work, don't expect negativity to follow any code of ethics except its own. And those ethics will never be positive, or even the same, twice in a row.

Messengers never seem to carry a high percentage of pleasant or welcome news. Maintaining poise and dignity in the face of hostility reveals one's level of self-control. To walk away from such negativity with grace, the messenger learns how to use the ability to detach emotions. She or he also learns by intuition which people can handle the plain unvarnished truth, and which ones must be given a softer version.

Those people who can see or feel aura colors can easily recognize the type of person you are, the real you. All the exposed and hidden emotions and intentions leak into the aura around each person. Each color has a specific meaning. For magicians who are observant and listen to their intuition, it takes only seconds to determine what path a fellow magician follows: white, black, or gray.

Everything in the Multiverse is connected to the Web of Life. Everything in the Multiverse, animate or inanimate, is alive and connected. Therefore, everything and anything that happens on a world of any level usually causes a ripple effect of some kind on all the other worlds. An incident may occur on one other world, but the energy, positive or negative, will return to you in some way. Most of the time, we never know the complete results of something we do. Fortunately, this works with positive events as well as negative ones.

The Wiccan Rede is very similar to the dragons' ethical code, but much shorter: "If you harm none, do what you will." Don't deliberately harm anyone, including yourself. The succinct, but more detailed, code of the dragons can be applied to magicians of all paths.

Using magick requires commonsense thinking. If you use negative magick to get what or who you want, you will gain bad karma. If another magician or magickal group gets involved, you will likely start an avoidable magickal war. Before you decide on a spell to use, look at a problem from all angles, seeking positive methods of removing the irritant.

However, if there are extremely evil people, beings, or energy pools loose on any world-level (and such creatures do exist), it becomes the duty of all magicians to remove or bind them for the good of all worlds. Evil can, and does, move from world to world, level to level, throughout the Multiverse, picking up power as it goes. This does not mean magicians kill anyone. We use binding and tripping spells to get the negativity stopped and properly removed.

Yet, in the greater pattern of the Multiverse, we would not recognize Light without knowing Darkness. Light comes out of the Darkness—the blackness of the Void that is the source of all creative energy. So there is an actual purpose for every creature or occurrence. There is an eternal struggle to balance between Light and Dark. It is incorrect to say that either is wrong or evil, for they both fulfill a definite purpose in the Multiverse. This was recently brought to public attention by a series of articles released by scientists who have been studying dark matter for years. I will discuss that subject in the Enchanter Ring section.

Dark dragons are an example of the misconception of the Dark color and energy. These dragons are not evil. When their energies, efforts, and work are correctly coordinated with dragons of Light, they help provide the needed balance in the Multiverse. There are other examples of such creatures similar to Dark dragons, each type unique to a world and/or a level of the infinite Multiverse. They appear to be built-in guardians as well as necessary visual reminders of the need for negative energy.

Any creation birthed by the Multiverse must be half negative energy as well as half positive. Creation happens in no other way. Unless Light is appropriately mixed with Dark, there will be no middle ground, no understanding of either Dark or Light. Lacking proper balance, this universe, the entire Multiverse, and every world within it would spin out of control and destroy itself.

In every world and on every level, there also are beings, creatures, clouds, and currents that are live malevolent energies with negative, unfathomable agendas—creatures or energies only controlled by alert guardians of the Savage Heart clan. We have all come into contact with humans who revel in cruelty and who appear to have no

remorse or conscience. Fortunately, this type of human comprises only a small percentage of the total.

Chaos dragons are totally different from Dark dragons. Chaos dragons work only with the dark matter of the Creative Void. It is their duty to keep the pot stirred, so to speak. When a correct request is set into motion, by a magician or merely someone very intent on a goal, the Chaos dragons release the corresponding amount and type of energy needed to manifest that request. They also see that the manifesting energy bounces through the Multiverse to the proper destination without upsetting or changing other work along the way. Dark matter, which has just recently been verified by scientists, will be discussed more completely in the Enchanter Ring section.

Here again, we find balance through Multiversal laws and those who enforce them. Everything in this world and universe is mirrored in every other world and universe throughout the entire Multiverse. What we have on our planet has an equivalent of some kind on every other planet on every level of the Multiverse. What happens here, physically or magickally, affects one or more events or beings on other levels of the Multiverse. It may not occur immediately, but the event's energy will rebound, perhaps in lesser strength if the sender or receiver is knowledgeable enough to craft a spell or control visualization of a desire with caution. That is why magicians should take great care in how they word spells and how they concentrate their intent.

The positive and negative energies of each universe may appear in different shapes, events, and act in different manners, but they still are identifiable as positive and negative.

Since this is so, every area in the Multiverse is struggling to keep a balance of Light (positive) and Dark (negative). A loss or a bad misstep in one level of the Multiverse affects every other level.

Only a serious, dedicated student of dragon magick should walk the path from Apprentice to Mystic. It is a journey full of responsibility and selfless work. The dragons and other such exotic, wise creatures work hard to keep this sacred path clear and protected. These beings also are the only ones to teach their magick to humans and to the humanoids/beings who live on other worlds. Their students who stay the course are few, but just enough to help align all parts of the Multiverse. It is an unusual privilege for dragons to offer their great wisdom to us, considering that so many humans are classified as "unreliable."

If you feel the call to become a Dragon Apprentice, you are indeed fortunate. You have a rare opportunity to learn deeper magick from the masters of magick—the dragons. And you will gain a critical ability, for what you learn and practice in this world is easily carried with you into the Otherworld. Once you learn dragon magick, you are never without power.

Acceptance in Dragon Studies Meditation

Every magician needs to learn how to meditate. There are several important reasons that meditation is part of the Apprentice curriculum. First, learning to meditate teaches the Apprentice quite valuable traits necessary for successful magick: concentration, visualization, willpower, and patience. Because of the relaxation required for the body, the Apprentice also is likely to start receiving brief messages from the dragons and beings from the Otherworld. Dragons are excellent at telepathy, but other beings may send the message in a symbol code. Use common sense. Ask your teacher dragons to help decode each message. Never make any drastic moves or decisions based solely on messages from the Otherworld. If the message suggests anything that is against your ethics, morals, or better judgment, consider it a "bad" connection and refuse to accept further communication with the being in question.

Many people think that you must have no thoughts ever in your mind in order to achieve the correct meditative state. This is untrue, especially for Westerners. The great Paramahansa Yogananda pointed this out in his autobiography. He said his mission in the West was to teach people Eastern mysteries and ancient knowledge in a way they could understand. He was adamant that, since the West thinks very differently from the East, people in the West should allow their minds to follow symbols, pictures, or a "story line," so that we can find our way to the Divine Center. In dragon magick, the Divine Center is the same as the center of the Five Inner Rings. Same idea, different words.

Remember that the beginning and the ending of all guided meditations are done in the same manner each time. Refer to "Entering the Five Inner Rings," which begins on page 7, for the text of the beginning and ending of each meditation, including this one, and for additional information about prerecording and preparing for meditations.

You are standing at the bottom of a slope that leads upward to the crown of a hill. The slope is completely covered with huge boulders that look impassable. The rubble appears to be a maze of tumbled stones, a questionable pathway where one could easily become lost. To add to the problem, the Sun is sinking behind the hill. The deep shadows of the forest surrounding you make you uncomfortable, as if the forest hides dangers yet unseen. The summit of the hill seems to be the safest place around. You begin to thread your way among the boulders, seeking a way to reach the top.

"Hurry! You must reach the cave before darkness comes!"

You stop and look around you. Just above your head and to your left, a very small dragon hovers in midair, her thin wings making a humming sound as she holds her position.

"My name is Mirraglas," the dragon says. "Follow me, and I will get you to the cave in time."

You look below at the dark shadows under the trees and see stealthy, sly movements there. "Show me the way, please," you tell the little dragon.

Mirraglas quickly leads you along an intricate, tangled path up the hill. You glance up once in your climb and see that there actually is the narrow mouth of a cave near the crest of the hill. You move faster when you hear the slide of pebbles at the bottom of the slope. You don't look back. You have no desire to know what is there. You only know, deep inside, that when you reach the cave, you will be totally safe.

Panting from your quick ascent in the deepening gloom, you follow Mirraglas through the narrow cave opening. Instantly, a small fire ignites on a tall, flat stone at the back of the rough cave. The image of the fire is reflected hundreds of times in the quartz crystals that cover the walls in their jigsaw patterns. An eerie rustling ever so softly sighs through the cavern, along with a gentle air current that seems to come and go. You find yourself synchronizing your own breathing with this current.

"If you are determined and willing to be an Apprentice of the Five Inner Rings, you must go to the altar." Mirraglas flutters in front of you, a look of concern on her little dragon face. "But I cannot show you the way this time."

She turns and speeds away to a perch on one of the crystals.

When you look back at where you think the fire is, you are confused. You are not certain of the exact location because of the perfect reflections all around you.

You blink your eyes, but that doesn't reveal the true fire. The cavern seems to be filled with hundreds of flickering flames.

You look up at Mirraglas, who is watching your every move. You remember that you were directly facing the altar fire when the little dragon fluttered before your face. You stare straight ahead until you find what you are sure is the original fire. Ignoring all the reflections around you, you slowly make your way, step by step, your gaze never losing sight of the flames as they dance and tremble in the slight wind that comes and goes through the cave.

Hesitantly, you reach out one hand to grasp the flat stone while you run the other hand above the fire. You flinch when you feel the blistering heat.

"So, you have come at last." The deep voice comes from above the altar where the rock ledges and wall are covered with shadows. "I wondered if you were brave enough to climb the hill and intelligent enough to find the true flames."

The scratch of claws on rock and the slide of scaled, leathery hide just beyond your sight quickly bring up the mental idea that you are not alone in the dark with just one small dragon. The slight wind is now erratic in its movement, as if many large dragons are gathered around you.

You peer up at the rocks and shadows until you finally make out the huge head of a dragon staring back at you. You realize the dragon was there all the time. You just hadn't been observant. The long neck with the triangular head is lifted high into the shadows near the roof of the cavern, yet the glittering eyes see you clearly.

Very carefully, you look around you on all sides. Here, you catch a glimpse of other pairs of large eyes reflecting the firelight. There, you see an enormous foot barbed with sharp claws. Overhead, you hear a quick whish as another dragon stretches and refolds its mighty wings.

"If the sponsors and teachers of this human are present, come forward now."

You hold your breath, wondering if you will be rejected before you even begin your studies. You give a sign of relief when you feel heat from dragon bodies close to each side and behind you. One gives a gentle puff of air against your neck.

"We will work with this human," says a deep voice above you. "We will sponsor her (him) as an Apprentice of the Five Inner Rings."

"So let it be recorded." The first dragon reaches a clawed hand out of the darkness and lays an open book beside the fire. The cover of this book is worn at the corners, the edges of the parchment yellow with age. You lean forward and see that each page contains a long list of names. The dragon's other hand reaches out to hand you a feather quill.

"Do you take oath to diligently learn the ways of the Apprentice of the Five Inner Rings? And do you take oath to keep silent about any knowledge you are *taught within those Rings? I, Aldram, Keeper of the Book, ask for your truthful answer."*

Now is the time for you to make a very serious decision. If you don't feel comfortable giving this oath, tell the dragon this. You will immediately be returned to your physical body without harm. The dragons will work with you on a mundane level to learn magick.

If you answer yes, take the pen and sign your name to the bottom of the list in the book. One after the other, your sponsors take the quill and sign their names in a strange script below yours.

A low humming of many dragon voices fills the cave as the last dragon lays the quill beside the book. Smaller dragons of every size gather around you, laughing in happiness. You hear some of the larger dragons leave, but your personal sponsors now let their invisibility shields dissolve so you can see them. You feel excitement fill your mind as you think about learning the secrets of the Five Inner Rings.

"It is time for you to return to your world," Aldram says as he gathers up the book and quill. "Mirraglas will take you home. You will meet with your teachers again, soon enough. You are now a Daughter/Son of the Dragon."

The small dragon flies just ahead of you, leading you toward the back of the cave. You pass many huge, shadowed figures that you know are dragons, but you cannot see them clearly. Mirraglas perches on the top of an archway, pointing with her small clawed hand for you to go through into the bright light beyond.

Code, Color, and Other Items of the Apprentice

Each of the Inner Rings has its own special code and color. The code of the Apprentice is "To be called is to be destined. Know yourself well." There are no such things as destinies greater than others. We all have an important part to play in this life, and with the dragons. By knowing yourself well—truthfully looking at all your abilities, warts and all—you are less likely to place yourself in any magickal danger. You also are more likely to listen to your dragon teachers and guardians.

A true blue color, the hue of calm emotions and the psychic, marks the Apprentice level of the Rings. This color can be displayed in clothing. However, the Apprentice will also want to get two feet of half-inch blue ribbon. At this point, the ribbon can be draped over the shoulders when meditating. Later, especially when reaching the Mystic level, this colored ribbon will be incorporated into a magickal project that will have lasting memories for you of your journey through the Five Inner Rings.

Symbols play an important part in every dragon magician's life. Even though the older dragons are very adept at telepathy, the very young dragons find it easier to communicate with humans through the use of symbols. The dragon teachers of the Inner

Rings chose a specific written symbol as an identification sign for the students of each Ring.

For the Apprentice, the master teachers decided to use an elvenstar, or a star with seven points. Seven has been considered the most sacred of numbers for at least three thousand years. To the ancient Egyptians, it meant eternal life and perfection. Today the elvenstar is called the mystic star, or elf star. Tracing its design with one finger has much the same effect on the subconscious mind as does tracing or walking a labyrinth: an ease in contacting and studying with spiritual teachers of the Otherworld.

The symbol of the elvenstar, or elf star, is shown on page 204.

Certain stones also are considered to be symbols for the ranks of the Inner Rings, and a crystal point is thought to be so important that it is required of all students. This quartz crystal point can be worn as jewelry, carried as a pocket stone, or left in your sacred space to generate energy. It does not need to be clear or perfect in shape. Some of the best crystals I've used have fractures, inclusions, mists, veils, and other "flaws." Choose a crystal that feels good in your hands; don't choose it due to the way it looks, how big it is, or how much it costs.

Other stones that will be of use to the Apprentice are amber, amethyst, aventurine, and moss agate. The Apprentice may use small tumbled chips of these stones for magickal and ritual use. Amber does come in several colors, but at this point I recommend that the golden-reddish-brown amber be used because of its versatility. This color of amber is also less expensive and easier to find. Although you don't need to buy every stone listed in each section of this book unless the stones have a vital use for you, you really do need those four stones: amber, amethyst, aventurine, and moss agate. When laid out on your altar cloth, they represent the four Element dragons. The personal crystal point also is a necessity.

As an Apprentice, you should handle your stones often in order to become familiar with the different feel of their energies, the colors of the stones themselves, and what they say to you personally. Yes, all stones "speak" to humans if we take the time to listen.

Golden-brown amber helps to clear mental confusion. If used with a crystal in meditation, amber can aid in opening the Akashic Records, or the stories of your other lifetimes. Since dragons live a very long time, it is quite possible that your present dragon teachers have worked with you before.

You can find amethyst in clusters, geodes, and points. It can be a very pale purple or a very dark purple, or any shade in between. This stone increases the activity in the right, or creative, brain, especially in developing psychic talents. At the same time, it can help you see through illusion of any kind.

Green aventurine attracts unexpected adventures, something every Apprentice should expect. Dragons delight in revealing the unexpected. It is also a prosperity and good fortune stone.

Moss agate is a beautiful white or almost transparent gray, with moss-shaped inclusions in various colors. It is one of the most powerful healing stones, and it gives a strong clarity of thought and intent in magick.

The Dragon Enchanter section of this book contains a much longer list of stones, their meanings, and the type of dragon connected with each stone. This list can be helpful if you are interested in learning more in-depth knowledge about a particular stone.

Magickal Clothing in General

The type of clothing worn by a student of the Five Inner Rings should be comfortable, in a style you like, and should make you lay aside the everyday and put on your magickal personality. Women may wear trousers and tunics, while men may choose to wear wizardly gowns. Or the student can wear one type of clothing one time and another set of clothing the next. You may even decide to tailor your clothes to match the Inner Ring in which you're studying. It is a personal choice. The only rules here are that clothing for special rituals be comfortable, and ritual clothes are not to be worn as everyday garments. Good places to get clothing ideas are Society for Creative Anachronism (SCA) meetings and Renaissance fairs.

Most magicians of the Inner Rings eventually end up with capes, dragon jewelry, a headband of cloth, metal, or leather, a leather belt (even for women) hung with pouches and bags, and at least one specially decorated robe. Mystics frequently wear an embellished gown or tunic and trousers under their robes, which are open down the front and have long full sleeves. Enchanters, shamans, and healers usually carry a shoulder bag filled with jars, smaller bags containing their necessary supplies and stones, and their altar cloth.

Apprentice Ritual Tools

Magicians of all kinds tend to gather a wide variety of tools for both magick and healing. Or they do so simply because they like what they find. You can easily guess how long a magician has been practicing by the pack-rat coziness of her or his sacred space or ritual room. The energy in such a place seems to attract people, whether or not they believe in magick.

There are a few essential items that an Apprentice must have as soon as it is possible to find, make, or purchase them. These items are likely to be used all your magickal life—or, in the case of the Dragon Hoard, until you wear it out or fill it up, making it necessary to replace the book. No tool has any power except that which you channel through it. The actual power source is you and your connecting link to everything in the Multiverse.

You will need a three-foot square of cloth, decorated or plain, to place on the floor, or on the ground if you don't have an altar. A fringed fancy shawl makes a nice cloth if you prefer something decorative. A low table or even a chest also works well. If you have a permanent altar, you would cover it with your cloth.

A very good astrological calendar is a must for any serious magician. This calendar must show the four Moon phases accurately and show which sign the Moon is in on any given day.

If possible, it is advisable to have a small cupboard, box, or chest of drawers in which to store your magickal materials. Very small bowls or geodes to hold sea salt and spring water are necessary to cleanse a ritual area. Check a toy store for tiny dish sets for children. Even if you do have a fairly accurate sense of direction, you should get a small compass so you can find true north. Frankincense or patchouli sticks or cones are also good for smudging yourself and the area if you can't find small bundles of sage.

Please remember that the number of such tools you acquire, or don't acquire, has nothing to do with your ability to perform dragon magick. The presence of tools is to get the left brain to work with, instead of against, the right brain. Tools are merely channels for the archetypal, universal energy that magicians direct through themselves.

At this time, the most crucial tools for an Apprentice to make, or put together, are two books: one called the Dragon Hoard, the other called Dragon Secrets. Although beautiful bound, blank books exist on the market, these are practical only for Dragon Secrets, which is a journal and record of your daily experiences, showing how your life and view of your life changes as you progress through the Rings.

The Dragon Hoard is a collection of rituals, spells, results of magickal spells, and such. Therefore, it is better that the Apprentice buy a three-ring binder and a set of index tabs for this project. The binder can be any color, covered with cloth and glued-on objects, or it can have a design painted on it. I suggest the use of a three-ring binder because it will make it easy to write on pages outside of the binder, copy and replace messy pages, and increase the total number of pages as you progress through the Rings.

On the very first page of Dragon Hoard and Dragon Secrets, you should write: 'This book of secrets is written by the hand of [your magickal name].' You will choose your name when you enter the Enchanter Ring. Sometimes this sentence is 'These secrets are in the hand of [your magickal name].' These are your personal books and may be decorated any way you wish. This sentence may be written in the dragon alphabet or any font that appeals to you. You can write it with brightly colored markers, ink, or paint. You can also add colorful designs around this statement.

The tabbed index pages will help you quickly find what you need in the Dragon Hoard. The first section should be marked Rituals. The second most important section is Spells, followed by Herb Secrets, Stone Secrets, and Dragon Names (which will include notes on the qualities and powers of each dragon you meet).

The last section is simply called Results. After you have kept proper notes in this part of the Hoard for a time, you will realize its value. In the Results area, you write a brief name and reason for every spell you do, such as "Finding Lost Objects, misplaced library book." Under the spell name, write down the ingredients you used, what the Moon phase was and in which zodiac sign, the day of the week, the actual date for the season of the year, and whether the spell did or didn't work. Also include your personal feelings about the spell before and during its performance. This record will help you determine why some of your spells work and others don't. The reason may be as simple as wrong ingredients or as complicated as your feelings about doing the spell—or the feelings of anyone watching, if you allowed anyone to watch.

It is also your choice what kind of pen you use to write this all out. Quills are not required, nor are they practical. Regular writing pens work much better. Just be certain that the ink isn't the kind that smears, for you will get water droplets on pages at times. Black ink is best. You will find that your blue Apprentice ribbon makes an excellent bookmark, and using it thusly ensures that you know where the ribbon is.

The Dragon Lore book can also be a small ringed notebook, or choose a blank bound book with a decorated hard cover. There are many spiral-bound books with beautifully sculpted covers. However, these can be expensive, and the number of pages is often scant. So I suggest you browse through a bookstore that carries blank journals. You should try to write some comment in this journal every day, even if it is only the date and local weather. It is useful to dig deeper into your feelings and attitudes here, positive or negative. These musings will later show you how far you have traveled in your personal life and in your dragon studies.

If you have a bad pattern of habits that keep recurring, you will be able to see this in your journal. You then will need to set goals to break the habits and replace them with positive action. Being human, we all need to work on perfecting ourselves.

All this being said, the Apprentice doesn't need everything listed. Neither does the student of any Ring. All each student is required to have are the vital tools she or he will definitely need for a particular level.

Understanding the Otherworld and the Gates

What makes the Otherworld so difficult to understand and believe in is that it occupies the same space as the Earth plane, yet it is elastic in nature. There is no linear thought or any concept of time there. Time itself is a human-conceived idea. Dragons and Otherworld beings can move quickly about the Otherworld and the Multiverse because they are not hampered by any preconceived idea of space or time.

All teachings say the two worlds interpenetrate each other but have different vibrations, which makes this interpenetration possible. I could never find a satisfying scientific explanation for this until a military friend talked to me about the tachyon (a subatomic particle) theory of quantum physics. This theory makes perfect sense of the dual occupation of space. I am not a fan of quantum physics, or of any similar scientific ideas, as I am primarily a right-brained individual. However, I will try to explain this in a way everyone can understand.

Like electrons, tachyons can't be seen. We know of their existence only by the manner in which they make other things behave. For a very long time, scientists believed that nothing could travel faster than the speed of light. Then quantum-physics scientists spent thirteen years specifically studying the strange appearance and disappearance of electrons, the very real possibility of a negative density, and strange swirls of energy movement. Just as with electrons, which we can't see, physicists had to accept another and nearly opposite theory of tachyons, which we also can't see.

Because of vibrational differences, the two areas (worlds) occupy the same place. On occasion, an individual tachyon shows itself in our world. Thus, both worlds need each other to exist. And the wonder of it all is that both fields exist at the same time in the same space. This is the exact same story, without the fancy scientific words, that shamans and mystics have told us for thousands of years.

Tachyons cannot travel slower than the speed of light, while electrons cannot exceed that speed. When tachyons gain energy, they get slower. When they lose energy, they gain speed. No one is certain what the top speed of a tachyon is. All scientists know is that electrons seem to appear out of nowhere, and then they eventually disappear back into the nowhere. Although no one has concretely identified the source of electrons, it is quite possible they are produced in the tachyon field or realm, exist in our universe for an unknown period of time as our blood cells do, and then are reabsorbed back into the tachyon field to be recycled.

As an ultra-swift particle, tachyons have some very different features, unknown before (or at least unaccepted) in our universe. A tachyon travels faster than light. Unlike the electron, the tachyon gains energy when it slows and loses energy when it speeds up. It can also go forward or backward in time. In other words, in the tachyon realm there definitely is no such thing as time, nor are there any barriers to visiting any area of what we call time.

The tachyon field is extremely dense, but it can't be measured because it is a negative state. In other words, it mirrors the positive universe in which we live. It also creates, sustains, and energizes our physical universe. Its energy is potentially omnipotent, yet it is

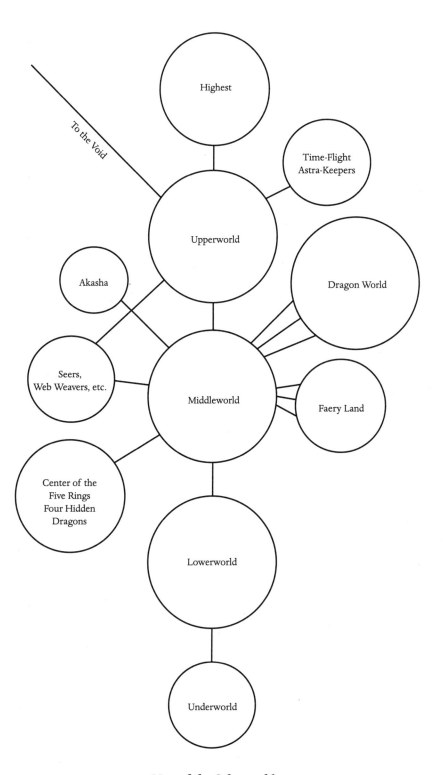

Map of the Otherworld

harmless to biological organisms. When an imbalance of positive energy appears in our universe, the tachyon field flows into the breach, nourishing all living organisms until balance is regained. The nervous system and brain of any creature comprise a highly sophisticated antenna and receiver that has learned to absorb, process, and transform tachyon energy into "food" for thinking, movement, and creativity.

We are looking at a symbiotic theory in which neither universe could exist without the other. As energy flows from one universe to the other (and it does this all the time), there are swirls of perpetual but gentle movement. Psychics, healers, mystics, and magicians have learned how to tap into this energy. Even more exciting, these people have discovered how to temporarily travel to, and gain information from, this interpenetrating universe, the Otherworld. The logical explanation for two worlds in the same space is that each vibrates at a different frequency. Therefore, to move our essential astral bodies from this world to the Otherworld, we must learn how to temporarily change our vibrations to match the Otherworld's—and then change the vibrations again to return to this world. The Dragon Apprentice now should begin to understand the seriousness of her or his studies. Unprepared or unbelieving humans who find themselves suddenly in the Otherworld could suffer mental imbalances from their experiences. The Apprentice's only reliable guides are her or his dragon teachers and friends.

Added to this amazing cosmos, there are a multitude of gateways to yet more worlds and realms. Some gateways are fixed and don't move, while others appear and disappear from one level of our Otherworld to another level on no particular schedule. If we consider these worlds beyond, and we must, there is not just one universe but a Multiverse of worlds and realms for us to explore. All universes would be in pairs—positive and negative—and all with gateways to yet more worlds.

There are many gates to the Dragon World in our Otherworld. Most of these gates are in the Middleworld, along with the gateways to Faery Land and many other exciting but strange realms. Your dragon teachers will introduce you to the Middleworld and its gates first, as this area is the easiest to understand and relate to.

Refer back to number 10 in the dragon code of ethics: "What happens to one stone reflects on all." This can be applied to the Multiverse as well as our universe. Since both worlds mirror each other, what a dragon student or any person does, or thinks hard enough on, in this world will be manifested in the Otherworld before bouncing back, full-grown, to this world. That is why magicians tell students to concentrate on, visualize, and claim as real whatever they want their magick to do. If the tachyon field, or Otherworld, can create electron particles or rebalance our universe as needed, its energy and ability to manifest something is as easy as blinking.

However, to ensure greater rates of success, the dragon magician must learn to prepare for the desired manifestation by performing spells with certain ingredients, movements, and words that resonate in a special way. Understanding this portion of dragon information is a huge step for a new Dragon Apprentice.

Magicians and shamans have always known there are other worlds because they do, and did, visit them to find new healing power, get a clear look at the future for their people, and work with Otherworld beings to prevent disasters.

The Otherworld is usually described as being of three levels: the Middleworld (which is a kind of alternative, time-space world to this one); the Upperworld (a high spiritual level), and the Lowerworld. The Lowerworld is not an evil place, nor is it a prison for evil people. It is merely a level of the Otherworld that has a different kind of vibration, as do all the other levels. However, I have discovered two more levels, which add sensible depth to the Otherworld.

The Upperworld has a very high, refined spiritual vibration. Here the traveler finds all the ancient deities from every culture. This level is the home of the dragon Kaudra and her special cave. One may also see many angelic messengers coming and going between all levels of the Otherworld from an unseen level far above this one.

This highest upper level, the Highest, isn't visited by humans or beings from other worlds. It is the dwelling place of the Goddess and the God, and the Supreme Creative Source (or whatever name you apply to the force and thought behind the existence of everything). Only archangels, angels, and a very few dragons enter this high area. They act as messengers for the Goddess and the God.

The Goddess and the God, also called the Lady and the Lord and the Great Mother and Great Father, intermediate for the Supreme Creative Source. Their visible forms are connected with the Source at all times. They and the Source are actually inseparable, for they are all three one abstract Being who is beyond our comprehension. Although all creation everywhere in the Multiverse is constantly connected, the Goddess and the God are so entwined with the Source that they have identical vibrations. They *are* the Source projecting itself in female and male images, so that humans may understand the abstract better.

Between the Goddess and the unseen Source, but closer to the Lady, sleeps the oldest dragon alive. She is so old that not even dragons remember her original name. She is known only as "She Who Lives Within the Greatest." This ancient dragon has a constant telepathic link with the Goddess. On rare occasions, she will exchange thoughts with those who stand at the only Gate to the Highest. Her misty form wavers in and out of sight as she balances her existence in the vibrations between the Upperworld and the Highest. When this dragon does open her eyes, she reveals their gleaming silver color.

The Upperworld is a level of great beauty and wisdom. Here the traveler will find all the cultural deities who were ever worshipped on our world, each pantheon in its own area. These pantheons will communicate with anyone, as long as they are treated with respect. They continue to exist through the energy supplied to them by human thoughts and worship. Because of the renewal of interest and practice pertaining to certain ancient cultures, some pantheons have a stronger physical form than others. There is a Shining Ones Shrine for each set of the ancient Earth deities, where one can ask to speak with the gods and goddesses of that pantheon. Although there are also deity shrines for other worlds in the Multiverse, these aren't open to those from Earth.

Every level except the Highest and the Underworld also have Gates that lead to side areas or other levels. Most of these Gates are stationary, while a few are called "wandering" and are not considered safe to enter.

The Upperworld has four such Gates. The Travelers' Gate is decorated with a spiral design. It takes you to any level of the Otherworld except the Highest and the Underworld. The Web Gate, marked with a cobweb painting, leads to the special side area of the Web Weavers. (See the diagram on page 39 of the Otherworld levels and the Gates).

Encircled by twelve stars and the twelve zodiac signs, the Zodiac Gate opens into the side area of the Time-Flight and Astra-Keeper clans. The Dome of Multiversal Stars is a sacred workplace with an enormous, very complicated metal structure inside the domed building. This structure shows the actual placement of all planets in all inhabited galaxies on all levels of the Multiverse. When a rebirth of a soul is approved by the judges in the Lowerworld Hall of Justice, these two groups of dragons determine the appropriately matching birth time, place, and conditions of birth for each soul. This new chart will be influenced by whatever karma is necessary for growth.

The Void Gate with its ominous black circle is used only by Chaos dragons. If the Chaos dragons want to speak with you, you won't go to the Void. They will come to you.

All levels of the Otherworld, and the side areas attached to them, have a number of sacred places to find peace, to reflect on your life, and to consider whatever is in your thoughts. Some in the Middleworld reconnect you with Earth energy to keep you from "losing" yourself and becoming too "spacey." A few in the Lowerworld offer safe places to reflect on any past lives with which you are familiar.

These sacred sites can appear as monolithic, moss-covered stones, standing singly, in circles, or in the shape of ancient tombs—two or three as uprights with a slab stone for a roof. Some are huge, irregularly shaped boulders with roughly chiseled steps leading upward to a "chair" for contemplation. Other sacred sites are tiny streams or wells that trickle into small carved stones. These basins can be used for scrying, as with a crystal ball or dark cup of water. It isn't unusual for spirit guides and animal allies to meet you in these sites. Some of these stones will be crystal-filled geodes—the open cavities large and deep enough to sit, stand, or lie down in.

One of the sacred sites in the Upperworld is the crystal cave found near the Gate to the Highest and protected by the Kaudra, a dragon with glittering crystal scales. Kaudra belongs to the Web Weavers; these powerful female dragons are part of a category of seer dragons. Inside her huge cave, with its shadowy chambers, is a huge, transparent, bubble-like crystal known as the Dream Chamber. The Dhuaar, or High Council of the Multiverse, meets in the Dream Chamber to ensure that the members' thoughts are not influenced by vibrational "chatter." The High Council is convened to discuss events and happenings of vital importance to the balance of the Multiverse.

Many side chambers of this cavern contain meditation seats, small shrines, counselor benches, and thrones. If the God or the Goddess appears, they sit on the throne with archangels and angels standing beside them. When Kaudra considers you worthy and ready, she will send you into the empty Chamber to be cleansed and to open your path to your highest spiritual connections.

The Garden of Wisdom and Solitude, enclosed by a high hedge, is an endless garden of all cultures. It has a multitude of shrines, temples, gazebos, and flower-covered shelters to explore. Paths lined with every known flower lead to small streams, waterfalls, fountains, and little bridges over ponds. You may meet other students here from throughout the Multiverse.

The Shrine of Remembrance is an important sacred site for spiritual growth and the removal of some kinds of karma. Here you can ask the attending angel to see and speak with deceased friends and loved ones. However, you may find yourself facing someone you didn't get along with in life. If this happens, that phase of your life has a barrier that needs to be removed by forgiveness. When both of you ask or give forgiveness for whatever wrongs were done, that spirit will leave. If it doesn't, ask the attending angel to send it away. Sometimes you don't know why there was a problem between the two of you. If the person doesn't truthfully forgive you, then at least forgive that person, so that energy can forever be removed from your future lives.

The Path of Return Light is a multidimensional open-roofed building of black marble. It exists on every level of the Otherworld except the Underworld and the Highest. If you stand on, or walk across, the bronze medallion set in the floor, you will be returned at once to your physical body. Of course, you can return at any time simply by thinking of your body. The medallion in this building appears to make your return easier, although actually it is a little slower because, at the same time, it rebalances your astral energy centers, called chakras.

The Temple of Beginnings and Endings is a little-used temple near the Void Gate, used by the Chaos dragons. No one visits the realm of these powerful dragons. If they have something to communicate to you, they find you. This Temple is where they teleport you, either during your sleep or while you are exploring the Otherworld. I have seen the inside of this Temple, but I've never been called there.

The most delicate and simple of the Upperworld sacred spots is the Temple of All-Healing. Constructed of very pale pink stone, the façade supported by pillars of a darker pink, this healing place is filled with celestial music of the most soothing sounds. Plain comfortable beds fill all the rooms. In the center of each room is a large crystal in a basin of pure spring water. A variety of healing angels and spirit guides work on anyone who asks for healing within this building. No one is refused, whether the illness is physical, mental, emotional, or spiritual.

The Middleworld is a fantastical level that is the dwelling place for elves, faeries, unicorns, and other mythological creatures—in addition to presenting the human traveler with a variety of possible ways our world could have gone. Animal allies are sometimes discovered on this level.

The Web Weaver area also has direct access to the Middleworld. The Web Weavers have the authority to send you to the dragon clan they believe will best help you. This clan of Star-Moon dragon lineage (see "Categories of Dragons" in section 3 of this book) works with the present and future potential happenings in the Multiverse. Its leader is Aia Cardys. The clan can be reached through the Web Gate in the Upperworld or the Mysteries Gate of the Seers of the Merkabah. This Gate has an image of a hooded figure holding a sword. Their series of different architectural palaces contain a sacred spot in an alcove of each building, an alcove that gradually helps you build your psychic abilities during meditations.

This side area, which sits between worlds and time, is also the place that holds certain other groups. The scenery changes in each group's territory here. The Seers of the Merkabah live in a volcanic cave in snowy mountains.

The Teachers' Gate, with its five different wands, leads to your choice of the co-magicians or the Ring Initiators. The co-magicians occupy a mountain-ringed valley. The Ring Initiators live in caves at one end of this valley. Aldram, Keeper of the Book, spends most of his time here with the Initiators, although he also has a misty, cloudlike dwelling near the Void. Aldram keeps his vast collection of ancient scrolls, books, and visually programmed crystals in the Void castle.

The Seers of All Time, including Tiamat, have several elaborate castles on the cliffs beside a great sea. This all-female group is composed primarily of very ancient, powerful deities from Earth's history, with a few powerful ancient seers from other worlds. You can reach them by using the Ancient Seers' Gate, decorated with a crystal ball in which one can see constantly moving images. Tiamat, the Great Mother dragon, spends most of her time in the Middleworld, guarding the Gate of Balance.

The Akasha Recorders live a quiet, almost solitary existence in their small side realm, keeping the Akashic Records up to date and advising the judges who oversee the rebirth process. You can visit the Temple of Akashic Records by going through the Past Lives

Gate with its design of a large decorated book. Inside this Temple, you will find assistants ready to find your personal records, so you can determine what part of your past still affects your present life—and could affect your future unless you make changes.

The Sacred Spirit Gate of rainbow colors leads you back to the Upperworld, where the Goddess sits inside the Gate to the Highest. If you go through the misty Dream Gate, you will again be in the Upperworld near the dragon Kaudra.

There are three different Dragon Gates, all of dark wood, bound with elaborate iron hinges and decorations. Each Gate opens in a different area of Dragon World, a fascinating area where dragon families spend their leisure time and hatch their eggs.

There is one large sacred area in Dragon World that is quite extraordinary. This is the triple ring of monolithic stones, called the Circles of Distant Truths. From the outside, these stones look and feel rough, appear splattered with lichen and moss, and are cold to the touch. When you walk between the stones and stand inside a ring of stones, though, the view is very different. The monoliths become almost translucent, providing you with a slick surface that shows you a portion of ancient dragon history or some virtue or truth that could enlighten you. Unless your co-magician dragon accompanies you, however, you are unlikely to understand what you see and hear. Still, the mere fact of walking around each ring of stones brings a peacefulness, healing, and guidance for whatever positive path or goal you are attempting to reach. The more you study and work with dragons, spirit guides, and angels, the more information you can gather within these stone rings.

The Gate of Wondrous Things hides an antechamber with three more Gates. The inner Gates are engraved with strange symbols that humans seldom see. All three of these Gates open into a section of Faery Land—one Gate each to the elves, the human-sized Fae, and the Small Folk, who interact so much with humans.

There are three sacred places within Faery Land, places that defy description, except to say they are nature-based and very powerful. These are the Palace of the Seelie Court (the Fae), the Palace of the Unseelie Court (a branch of the Fae), and the Palace of the Elf King and Queen. Time spent in Faery Land can reconnect you to the nature spirits and the deep Earth wisdom they have.

The Rings Gate, with its pattern of five concentric circles, takes students to the side area of the astral school, the space of the Five Inner Rings. Although the four Hidden Gates of Wisdom are close by, you won't be able to use these at this time, for they are found in the center of the Five Rings. Only Mystics who have passed through their initiation are allowed to travel these paths. Each Gate is guarded by one of the Four Hidden Dragons and leads to a separate Mystery School.

The last permanently fixed Gate is the Gate of Balance near the Sacred Well of Balance. This half-white, half-black portal goes to the Lowerworld, where the Lords of

Light and Dark dragons wait beside the other end of this well. Both the Gate and the wellspring are connected, with power flowing in both directions. The great greenish gold dragon Tiamat is found near the Middleworld end of this Gate. Through Tiamat's guidance, you can see through all the illusions you have built around yourself. Only truth can be seen in this mystical well and in the eyes and thoughts of Tiamat, the Great Dragon Mother of Earth.

Some Gates in the Otherworld are not fixed, but move from place to place without notice or on any schedule. These are termed "wandering" Gates. Eight of these unnamed Gates in the Middleworld should not be used without the company of your co-magician dragon. There is no visual method to tell positive wandering Gates from negative wandering Gates, although the dragons have some way of discerning which is which. It is therefore safer not to enter any wandering Gates by yourself.

The Grove of Shadows and Twilight can be rather frightening when you first venture into this mass of tall evergreen trees. The paths often wander in circles but never reach the same place twice. This is where you will first meet your Shadow Self, the darker side of yourself. (See section 3, "The Dragon Shaman," for more information on the Shadow Self.) Establishing communication with the Shadow Self will be important later, when you retrieve pieces of a shattered soul. However unsettling this forest is, it is a sacred grove where you can meet and talk to the "darker" deities of Earth's pantheons. These are *not* demons or the devil. They have important duties to fulfill in keeping balance. They also have valuable information about life, personal balance, self-acceptance, and gaining true self-confidence without ego inflation.

In an out-of-the-way place in the Middleworld, you will discover a compound of many different types of temples. This is the holy area of the Temples of Ancient Ways. Every spiritual path that did, or does, exist on Earth is represented here by instructors and counselors in their religion's temple. Teachers of the old religions outnumber the modern ones. You can speak with any of the instructors, either about possible changes to your personal path and studies, or to learn something new.

The Gardens of Healing are similar to the healing gardens in the Upperworld. Set in a serene, beautiful variety of gardens are buildings that represent different types of healing powers, both old and new. You can ask for a personal healing or instruction in a healing method.

The Lowerworld is a level of vibrations heavier than those in the other two levels. However, this does not make it evil. Ancient underworld deities live here, such as the Crone with her cauldron of rebirth.

The Lowerworld's heavier atmosphere recognizes the vibrations humans experience when they go through a dark night of the soul. When they face traumatic changes in their lives and must look back at both the good and the bad, they go through the

Crone's rebirthing ritual. Her Sacred Cauldron of Rebirth not only sponges clean the conscious minds of reincarnating souls into actual physical bodies, but is used for the soul rebirth of initiates.

This great black Cauldron, hidden away in a shadowy cavern reached by twisting underground tunnels, helps the tormented minds and hearts of physical travelers who are faced with traumatic life changes and are in great need of healing from painful personal losses. Four shallow black bowls of ever-burning, leaping fire burn at each of the four directions, making strange jumping shadows dance on the cavern walls. These flames reflect the silver designs on the Cauldron and radiate an awesome power.

This is also the site of the Karmic Councils. Most deceased humans awaiting reincarnation occupy this level, although they are free to visit any level you can. It is possible that you could meet any of your ancestors at any time during your journeys, particularly in the Lowerworld. However, you are certain to meet some of them at the Shrine of the Ancestors. This onion-domed building sits in a garden laid out in geometric patterns.

All the incoming and outgoing souls are brought to the Hall of Justice and Rebirth. Those who are returning are told what karmic debits and/or credits their recent life accrued for them. Anyone, even a traveler, can speak in their defense. Those souls preparing to be reborn discuss their upcoming life with the Council. Some are willing to take on the duties that allow other humans in their "new" family to work out problems. That doesn't, however, mean that those people will use the advantage. Other souls accept their new life plan with resignation, while still others are in total rebellion. If the rebellious souls present the Council with valid reasons for their disagreement, such as "This plan didn't work before" or "The people involved have changed for the worse and are no longer receptive to help," then the Council may postpone the rebirth for a time of reconsideration.

The Lords of the Light and Dark dragons can be found near the Sacred Well and the Gate of Balance. Using this gateway will return you to Tiamat in the Middleworld. These dragons can be helpful in pointing out subtle imbalances you have and suggesting methods to rebalance.

Often, the souls being reconsidered use the Glory Gate, near the Hall of Justice, to go to the Upperworld until they are called again. There they talk with the dragon Kaudra. They also can visit all the sacred places of that level, while they search for the truth of their long path through a number of lives. Also, they can seek help from the Goddess, the God, any elder dragons, or angels in their quest to find truth.

The third Gate in the Lowerworld is the Journey Gate. This is a wandering Gate usable only by Dragon Warriors, Dragon Mystics, and the dragons themselves. It will take you to any desired designation.

There is only one level below the Lowerworld—that of the Underworld. There are no side areas to the Underworld, and only the Prison Gate leads in and out of this heavily guarded level. The Underworld is a type of maximum-security prison, created to hold truly evil beings and energies. The souls kept confined here revel in murder, torture, and any other negative deed they can do.

When the dragon student reaches a certain level, she or he is brought here, accompanied by at least two experienced dragons. One of these will be a Moosha, or a Warrior of the Savage Heart clan. Here you will see fights to the death between rival Underworld groups. They destroy each other, only to have the body parts rejoined and life returned to each. Their vile, destructive attitudes clearly show that they have no desire to change.

On rare occasions, Rogue dragons will batter through the walls from outside and allow the escape of some inhabitants. Most of the escapees will be caught in short time because they are so self-centered that they won't join the Rogue groups. At the first warning of an attack on the Lowerworld, the Warrior dragons spring into action. The bands of Rogue dragons (also known as the Annihilator's Offspring) are similar in thought to the beings imprisoned in the Underworld. They are an enemy that lurks everywhere in the Multiverse. The Warriors hunt them at all times, trying either to destroy or imprison them. The other, and more deadly, enemy is the Annihilator, a huge, sentient mass of evil that also roams the Multiverse. However, the Annihilator seeks to destroy everything it meets, even the Rogue dragons. You will learn more about the Annihilator in section 4, which is about the Dragon Warrior.

The Underworld, in spite of its constant evil, does have two sacred places. The Temple of Despair provides a refuge and counseling for those prisoners who have become enlightened enough to truly seek help. No one is ever turned away from the Temple of Despair. When one of the Underworld beings reaches the doorway to this Temple, she or he sees the two mammoth guarding pillars of stone. One is called Hammer and Anvil, the other Fire of Truth. The deep truth of their being is judged as that entity passes between the two stones and into the Temple. If there is no repentance, Hammer and Anvil sounds like a deep tolling bell, its warning tone echoing throughout the Underworld. The worthy creatures are welcomed by Fire of Truth, with its sounds like crystal bells. The worthy repentants are met by priestesses and taken to the Inner Chamber of the High Priestess. Here in the Inner Chamber, also a sacred spot, the candidate is spiritually cleansed, then escorted to the Hall of Justice.

Some candidates visit the Temple of Despair frequently in order to meditate in the cleansing calm before they are deemed sincere enough in mind and spirit to be taken to the judges. The priestesses make certain these beings understand that they will have a heavy karmic burden when they are reborn.

Gates to other fabulous places can be found on all three middle levels. From each of these new worlds there are gateways to yet more realms. These gates and realms continue in an infinite number. However, these particular gates are difficult to distinguish from the wandering, unsafe Gates. You will need one or more elder dragons to help you if you wish to use these unmarked Gates.

My description of the Otherworld is more of a road map than a travel guide. It is impossible to write about everything you can find on the levels of that realm. The joy of finding something new lies around the bend in any Otherworld path.

Ritual for Attracting Your Guardian Dragon

This is a serious ritual, for you are asking a guardian dragon to help you in your daily endeavors and make itself known to you in some way. Prepare your mind to be open and accepting of the new companion. Don't rush into performing this ritual or hurry through it, expecting a guardian to pop out of thin air. Dragons and magick work in their own ways and in their own time.

Even though the guardians, or any dragon, can become visible, they rarely make their presence known in this manner. "Visible to you" means visible to anyone else in the vicinity. It would be very upsetting to find yourself seeing perhaps only a dragon's head in a room with you while the rest of its body was outside the house. Not only that, but what would the neighbors or your family say, assuming they thought to say anything at all before they started shooting? All the arguments in the world about being ready to "see" a dragon doesn't mean you actually would be ready. So be patient after performing this ritual.

Ingredients: An altar cloth and two small bowls, one containing sea salt and the other containing water.

Preferable day: Thursday, a Jupiter day.

Carefully spread your altar cloth on the floor or ground so that one of the sides faces north. Set the bowl of salt on the left side of the cloth in the west, and the bowl of water on the right in the east.

Kneel by your cloth, facing north. Hold your left hand over the salt and your right over the water at the same time. Say:

> *I call upon the positive powers of the universe to fill this salt and water.*

Take the bowl of salt and stand. Moving clockwise around your altar cloth, sprinkle a few grains of salt at each directional point: west, north, east, and south. Set the salt back on the cloth. Take the bowl of water and repeat the actions you performed with the salt.

Drape your blue Apprentice ribbon across your shoulders while you kneel or sit cross-legged facing the northern direction. Say:

> *I am safe within the powerful ring of the Dragon Apprentice. As I sit within this sacred space, I invite and call for my guardian dragon to be here with me. I offer you loyal, warm friendship. May we walk the path together through the Five Inner Rings to the mystical center.*

Close your eyes and relax your body. Let your thoughts drift where they will, without any certain expectations. Within a short time, you will feel a light touch on your skin, a breath on your neck, or the very distinct feeling that you are no longer alone in your sacred space. For some reason dragons prefer to stand behind you. The older teachers rarely let you see them, while the tiny young ones can scarcely stay in one place for any length of time.

Don't expect the physical manifestation of your guardian dragon, for that rarely happens. Instead, the dragon will appear behind your closed eyelids. You may glimpse the entire body or just a friendly eye with eyelashes. Her or his thoughts will flash through your mind. You can distinguish the dragon's thoughts from your own by the wording, tone, or content. Although you may not get the dragon's name at this time, mentally send out thoughts of greeting and friendship. In return, your guardian dragon will surround you with a warm sense of friendship, like a hug. From this point onward, you and your guardian dragon will be inseparable.

Slowly open your eyes and place the palms of both hands on your altar cloth. Say:

> *I thank all dragons who were here with me during this ceremony. I especially thank my guardian, my friend and companion from this day forward. I release the*

> *excess power of this ritual into the Earth. May this ceremony harm no one, but bless*
> *the Multiverse with love and healing.*

This is an excellent time to sit for a few moments so you become familiar with your guardian's vibrations. The gender of your guardian has nothing to do with yours; a female guardian may choose to help a man simply because the two can work well together.

Pour out the water into a potted plant or onto the ground. It is full of healing energy with vibrations that exactly match those of the Earth. Put away the rest of your ritual items until they are needed again.

Don't be surprised if you feel the presence of very tiny dragons soon after your guardian arrives. The guardian often appears to baby-sit younger siblings. The very young ones are exuberant, full of mischief, and seem to be in constant motion. One of their favorite dragon games is to move an object you need to another place where you know you didn't put it.

The guardian dragons have usually matured beyond such "childish" games. However, if you ignore your guardian and don't try to make contact each day, your personal dragon may just join the tiny creatures in their mischief-making. Remember to keep the bond between you and your guardian dragon strong. This can easily be done by a few minutes of mental conversation each day.

Since dragons age very slowly compared to humans, I still have the presence of Tinsel and Rudy, mentioned in my first dragon book. They are still a delight. Nip and Tuck visit from time to time, but the beautiful Nesta now guards.

Respect Names for Dragons

You should never call any dragon by its name unless you have been given direct permission to do so. To do otherwise is considered to be very rude, as is calling a dragon by just its clan name.

Female dragons hold any position a male dragon does. They are to be held in the same high regard, just as the Daughters of the Dragon are as much respected as the Sons of the Dragon. There is no visual way to distinguish a female dragon from a male. In other words, coloring, size, and manner of speaking are not gender distinctions, as they often are among humans or other Earth creatures.

The following is a list of respect names, which will keep you out of possible trouble when meeting and communicating with any dragon:

Chasah: Name for a leader of any clan. Meaning "leader" or "guide," this respect name
    is used whether the dragon is female or male. It is quite common for females to lead
    clans.

Mon-Tah: Your teacher/co-magician, unless given permission to use their name.

Moon Gutash: Star-Moon clan members, except their young.

Moosha: Name for all Gate guardians, who are members of the Savage Heart clan. The name means "warrior."

Mot-Tah: Other teachers and co-magicians.

Star-Gutash: Star-Born clan members, except their young, who you are not ever likely to see.

Tad Ekam: Name for any Chaos dragon.

Tah-Soor: Any older dragons you meet.

Tah-Soor-Izoris: The Elders and very important dragons you meet.

Tika: A general child-name for the small and guardian dragons of any clan.

Ritual for Attracting a Co-Magician Dragon

As you learned in the discussion of the Otherworld, the co-magician dragons are a clan of specially trained dragons who work with students throughout the Multiverse. Remember to call your personal teacher by the respect name of Mon-Tah until she or he tells you otherwise.

Ingredients: Altar cloth; a small bowl or geode of sea salt and one of water; a seven-pointed star (can be drawn on paper); and pieces of amber, amethyst, aventurine, and moss agate.

Preferable day: Sunday (Sun) or Monday (Moon).

(Beginning of ritual)

Carefully spread your altar cloth on the floor or ground so that one of the sides faces north. Set the bowl of salt on the left side of the cloth in the west, and the bowl of water on the right in the east. Place the stones on the cloth in front of where you will sit.

Kneel by your cloth, facing north. Hold your left hand over the salt and your right over the water at the same time. Say:

> *I call upon the positive powers of the universe to fill this salt and water.*

Take the bowl of salt and stand. Moving clockwise around your altar cloth, sprinkle a few grains of salt at each directional point: west, north, east, and south. Set the salt back on the cloth. Take the bowl of water and repeat the actions you performed with the salt.

(End of beginning)

Drape your blue Apprentice ribbon across your shoulders while you kneel or sit cross-legged facing the northern direction. Say:

I am safe within the powerful ring of the Dragon Apprentice.

Hold the quartz crystal in one hand with the other hand cupped over it. Say:

> *This crystal destroys all negative energies around me and strengthens my personal shield. It helps me to communicate clearly with all dragons. Its powerful beams of pure energy will attract the right dragon to work with me on dragon magick, a dragon who will teach me what I need to know to progress through the Five Inner Rings.*

Lay the crystal in the center of the cloth with the point facing north. Pick up the amethyst and hold it in your hands. Feel its vibrations against the palms of your hands.

> *This purple stone of spiritual and psychic wisdom will help me to be sensitive to the dragons and all of the Otherworld. It will break any illusions so that I always see the truth.*

Put the amethyst at the northern edge of the cloth. Take the amber in your hands and repeat the sensitizing process.

> *Amber was formed millions of years ago when this planet was young. It holds many secrets of history. It can show me the way to the records of my past lives, the Akashic Records. Amber also can help me to read, understand, and apply the knowledge I learn from those lives.*

Place the amber on the eastern edge of the cloth. Hold the aventurine between your hands while you feel the chill of adventure creep up your back.

> *Green stone of sudden adventures, of unexpected methods of gaining more knowledge, I honor your connection with the dragons. Dragons, too, love adventures and the discovery of new Gates and worlds.*

Place the aventurine on the southern edge, directly in front of you. Pick up the last stone, the moss agate. Look carefully at the strange but beautiful moss-like inclusions in the misty stone. Say:

> *Help me to develop strength in thoughts and intent, so that my magick will be of benefit to all worlds. Teach me discernment between needs, desires, and merely frivolous thoughts. I feel your great healing power, and I ask that you heal whatever is out of balance in me, for I seek a co-magician among the dragons. One or more that can be teachers, guides, and guardians. For I wish my ultimate goal to be the center of the Five Rings.*

Put the moss agate on the western edge of the altar cloth. Close your eyes and breathe evenly until your body relaxes and you feel the presence of your personal guardian dragon.

Carefully center your thoughts on the intent of gaining a co-magician dragon to help you. Don't visualize what you think she or he will look like, but focus instead on the qualities you think you need for balance. These qualities can be patience, observance of surroundings, knowledge that will help you work through all the Rings, awareness of the need to expand through visits and adventures in the Otherworld, and other similar traits. In other words, you need a dragon with qualities that balance what you do not have within yourself. Keep your intent firm, yet friendly, as you send out a mental call for a dragon to fill your need for a co-magician.

Relax, focus, and keep calling mentally until you feel the presence of a larger dragon just behind you. This is the time to exchange greetings and names, to begin to learn about each other. Although your guardian dragon, and the smaller ones, may be mottled and not just one color, your co-magician dragon will be of one specific color. The co-magician may not be at all what you expected. She or he may not even give you a name at this first meeting. Do the best you can to be friendly because you are not likely to be given another co-magician dragon.

When you and your new co-magician are finished, slowly open your eyes. You may catch a glimpse of dragons around you from the corners of your eyes. However, if you try to look directly at them, they will fade away.

Place the palms of both hands on your altar cloth. Say:

> *I thank all dragons who were here with me during this ceremony. I especially thank my guardian, my friend and companion from this day forward. And I give special thanks to my new co-magician dragon who will teach me and take me places and to other teachers in order to further my knowledge of ancient wisdom. I release the excess power of this altar into the Earth. May this ceremony harm no one, but bless the Multiverse with love and healing.*
>
> (Ending of ritual follows)

Pour out the water into a potted plant or onto the ground. It is full of healing energy with vibrations that exactly match those of the Earth. Put away the rest of your ritual items until they are needed again.

Dragons of the Elements

Remember, European dragons are physically, mentally, and emotionally different from Eastern dragons. You will find yourself working closely with both kinds as you work your way through the Five Inner Rings. Even though the colors, reactions, knowledge, and activities as teachers can be very different, the dragon co-magician and other teachers will help in every way possible.

Element dragons usually match the colors described by many cultures for the corresponding directional point. East is for Air with the color of yellow. South is for Fire and red. West is for Water and shades of blue, while North is for Earth and goes all the way through soil colors to the dark green of ancient forests.

The Asian studies of dragons are the only ones to mention the Four Hidden Dragons of Wisdom. These great dragons exist in the center of the Five Rings and protect the four Hidden Gates to higher areas of Mystery School study. The Four Hidden Dragons guard theses four Gates.

Air dragons are led by Sairys (pronounced *sair'-iss*). These dragons are in all shades of yellow. Air is in the eastern part of the circle or square of a sacred place. Air dragons belong to a family whose subspecies include those of wind, storm, and weather. Sometimes, they join with dragons of fire and volcanoes, seas and other waters, mountains and forests, even chaos. No one element works totally alone, whether in the physical world or magick.

Fire dragons come in every shade of red, orange, and golden-yellow. Led by Fafnir (*faf'-near*), these dragons are related to the subspecies of desert and arid regions, sometimes with those of chaos and destruction. They belong to the south and are connected with all kinds of fire, including sunbeams, volcanoes, and lightning. Subspecies of this element are desert and arid-region dragons, including dragons of volcanoes, destruction, and chaos.

Water dragons are found in the west. Their leader is Naelyan (*nail'-yon*). His duty is to oversee dragons of the seas, springs, lakes, ponds, and rivers. Water dragons are shades of blue. They help balance emotions, compassion, peace, and intuition. In their negative traits, they work in floods, rainstorms, whirlpools, lack of emotional control, and any kind of harmful water. The Water subspecies are those of all the seas. Water dragons frequently work with those of wind, storm, weather, mountains, forests, and destruction.

The north belongs to the Earth dragons and their leader Grael (pronounced *grail*). These large dragons have mostly clear, dark green scales, interspersed with shimmering scales like gemstones. It is the northern dragons' duty to oversee the mountains, land in general, minerals, gems, caves, and the Moon and moonbeams. Since these are the most placid of the species, they stir up disruptive energies

when they do become angry, which cause massive earthquakes. Earth dragons often work in conjunction with the subspecies of Fire, volcanoes, destruction, and chaos. They are closely related to those of the mountains and deep forests, the desert and arid regions.

In the center of the cast circle are huge, powerful dragons that balance all the elements, so none gains control over the others. These are two white (Light) and two black (Dark) dragons. Dark is not the same as Chaos, which I will discuss later. These center dragons are not always the same ones with each cast circle. They are constantly alert to any universal imbalance.

Although Light and Dark dragons appear to keep things running smoothly, that condition does not mean the same to us as it does to them. These dragons follow a higher guidance of the greatest kind, far beyond our ability to understand. Universal laws will not allow static conditions to exist for any length of time. Everything is in motion; nothing stays still. If there is no growth or change, whether it be creature or condition, that part of the universe is recycled into a more productive form. To humans, this may appear as destruction, when actually it is the process of eliminating stale energy and allowing growing energy to take its place. We are such a tiny part of the Multiverse that we can't grasp the concept of the bigger picture.

A magician learns to skillfully blend Light and Dark as needed with other elements. This is the gray magician I wrote of earlier. No magician can understand and work with Light if he is not aware of the power of Dark. This is why your guardian and co-magician dragons had you experience the energy balance earlier.

Dragons of Light, of the spirit, handle positive currents of magickal energy. Their primary duties include the Sun and daylight, any spiritual growth, the balancing of karma, and helping the magician to develop psychic guidance. These dragons exist in a strange bubble where primordial matter is constantly being sent to blend with Dark energy.

The dragons of Dark control negative currents of energy and weave this into the positive stream of energy handled by the dragons of Light. Dark dragons are usually a shade of gray or black. They rule over the Moon and stars, dreams, psychic guidance, balancing karma, and seeking the truth. They, too, live in an isolated bubble of primordial matter, from which they send negative energy to blend with Light.

In a later chapter, I will detail the dragons of Chaos and Destruction and how they differ from the dragons of Dark.

With the four main Element dragons are four more, of even greater power and position. These are the Four Hidden Dragons. These are the same dragons who guard the Four Hidden Gates in the center of the Five Inner Rings.

No one can enter the Four Hidden Gates without permission of the guarding dragons, for each Gate leads to an ancient compound of Mystery Schools. In these four Mystery Schools, the Dragon Mystic specializes in deeper aspects of dragon magick.

The first Gate is guarded by Durka. This path leads to the Northern Mystery Schools. Durka has the European dragon shape of a heavy, broad body. The triangular head sits at the end of a long, sinuous neck. His snakelike tail ends in a barbed tip. His two leathery wings are long and strong. Ridges of thick, sharp-edged scales frame the eyes, which are golden with rims of greenish-yellow. His claws are steel gray. Durka is covered with scales colored in swirls of green shades, from pale green to almost black.

At the second Gate lies Hun-Tun, her scales a kaleidoscope of shades of yellow-gold and orange. Although her body resembles a very thick, long snake, she has two small front feet with black claws. Her scales change colors and patterns when she moves. The two small wings on her back by her back legs have diamond patterns. Her head is long and narrow and merges with her body, which has no neck. Her eyes are a piercing, glittering black. Three red strips run parallel to each other from the tip of her nose to the end of her pointed tail.

Im-Miris of the third and Southern Gate reminds one of the dragons of Babylon and Chaldea. He has a thick body and head with the blunt muzzle of a huge canine. His four paws have four dark red claws. His two front feet are shaped like lion paws, while the two back feet are reminiscent of huge bird feet. He has two wings with featherlike scales. His all-over coloring is a mixture of rich desert hues, brick red, and deep sparkling brown. His scales resemble short, fine hair, but are actually hard and semi-shiny. His neck is short like that of an animal, and his glittering eyes are bright red.

The Gate to the Western Mystery School is watched by Gark-Yin, an azure-blue Eastern dragon with gold edging on her scales. Red thread-thin whiskers wave from above her eyes and around her nose. Her long, slender body has four legs with four dark gold claws on each foot. These legs are small in proportion to her body. There is no discernible division where her neck joins her body. Her head is wide and blunt. Long, feathery antennae rise from the top of her head, like those of a moth. These antennae are colored in a beautiful pattern of gold, azure blue, and pure red, twisting and turning as she senses the air for changes in vibrations, especially in the emotions and mental thoughts. She has no wings. Her golden-brown eyes are watchful but compassionate.

There is one other type of element that doesn't have a place within a cast circle, but which has a strong influence over everything. This is the element of Storm, which is controlled by the Storm-Bringers clan. The leader of the Storm element dragons is Charoseia. As expected, their color is a stormy gray.

I consider Storm to be a separate and distinct element, not to be confused with the Storm dragons. The energies of the element of Storm lie between the traditional four elements and the Void. Storm is an elusive but dynamic element that can block and redirect any elemental powers if a far deeper "balance" becomes necessary. Storm is a catalyst, a substance that creates great changes in other beings or events, but isn't changed itself. The Storm element bursts into action when massive cleansing and rebalancing are needed, or when a speedy intellectual, mental, or spiritual awakening becomes vital. The recipient of this action may be a person, planet, or galaxy.

With humans, this intervention usually happens when a person goes through a dark night of the soul, with its deep depression and despair for the future. Drastic changes are vital, but the person can see no solutions. The element of Storm steps in, taking decisions out of our hands and control. When the clouds lift and the lightning stops, we find ourselves and our direction in life changed in a manner we never expected. Of course, it is changed only if we accept the cleansing.

The Storm element, and the entire Multiverse, work on the principle that all is done for the greater good. Any sentient beings involved in this can be changed and can work with the change or be destroyed by it. No being, world, or situation can become static and continue to exist. If any species, group, or world can't adapt to changes in the environment, it becomes extinct. Only the adaptable with willingness to accept change will survive.

All stones and other magickal ingredients have correspondences to elements. Storm-element stones can create transformative changes on a gigantic basis or rebalance any human chakra or aura. However, such stones should be used only for short periods of time because of their harsh swiftness. Don't use them in healing unless you are prepared for a huge transformation that may not be to your liking. The same applies to spellwork. Storm-element energy affects both the recipient and the magician, should she or he need changes. Radical shifts in life are certain to happen when working with the Storm element.

Now that you have discovered, and hopefully are working with, the dragons of the elements, it is proper timing for you to open your magickal life in a meditation to any dragons who want to meet you.

Welcoming Other Dragons Meditation

Use the meditation opening from page 7.

(Beginning of meditation)

Drape your blue ribbon across your shoulders. Breathe slowly and deeply while you visualize yourself standing in the stone courtyard of a mighty castle without walls. Everywhere you look there are dragons of all sizes. There are also other humans with blue ribbons across their shoulders. You recognize that they too are students of the Dragon Apprentice Ring.

Suddenly, your guardian dragon appears by your side and urges you to mingle with the crowd of dragons and other apprentices. Your dragon nudges you with an elbow, indicating that you should introduce yourself to several larger dragons nearby. You laugh at such a humanlike gesture and, for reassurance, take your guardian's hand as you approach what you instinctively know are co-magician dragons.

You introduce yourself and your guardian, bowing your head politely to the older dragons. One by one the co-magicians lower their heads to look into your eyes. You are so intent on noticing the different colors and shapes of those eyes that you forget to be afraid. You are amazed to see that dragons have eyelashes, even though their scales and long tails remind you of the reptilian family. You realize that there is a lot about dragons you haven't learned yet—and may never know.

You wander through the crowd of dragons and apprentices, stopping here and there to talk to someone. It doesn't take you long to learn that several apprentices are from Earth. Other apprentices who resemble humans are not human at all, but are from other worlds and levels of the Multiverse. You are pleased to discover that those who are definitely not humanlike can communicate by telepathy.

Before long you become aware of the low humming noise in the background. It is the telepathic speech of the larger dragons. You recognize the sound from the ritual that accepted you into dragon studies.

Each co-magician goes to her or his apprentice, places a hand on each side of the student's head, and whispers "Listen."

You are puzzled as to what you should hear until you finally notice chords and strains of harmonious music. This music comes toward you, then drifts past, as if it is floating everywhere in the air.

"You are hearing the music of the Multiverse and all its worlds," your dragon tells you. The co-magician sighs at a discordant tone that is quickly gone. "A world that is not in harmony with the rest of the Multiverse," the co-magician explains. "Some worlds are only a little out of tune, while the music of others is very harsh to the ears."

The apprentices are released to enjoy juice and cakes set on several tables. You eat quickly and go back to introducing yourself to the older dragons. You want to know as many of them as you can. You discover that each co-magician dragon has an individual personality, just as humans do—another fascinating fact to think about later.

The co-magicians move themselves into a long line, their personal students standing before them.

"Welcome, Apprentices," the dragons say in unison. "May you prove worthy of learning the ancient dragon magick."

"Thank you, and welcome to you," the Apprentices answer. "We are honored by your presence. We will strive to be worthy."

As the dragon magicians begin to hum again, a number of bright doorways appear around the Apprentices. You are drawn to enter the portal near you.

End the meditation with the ending meditation on page 8.

(End of meditation)

Basic Personal Protection

Very few people actually come under authentic magickal attack. Most trouble comes from ill-wishing, jealousy, and envy, primarily from non-magicians. However, if enough of these negative vibrations build up in your home or in your personal aura, you could find your life not going the way it should. You may suddenly become clumsy when you weren't before. You may experience a string of small accidents, mistakes, and misunderstandings that eat up your time and money. On a few occasions, you may well find yourself in immediate need of aural protection from the directed hostility of another person. There are a few quick magickal tricks you can use to protect yourself.

The fastest protection is to immediately visualize yourself totally surrounded by brilliant white light. This light encases you inside a globe that negativity cannot penetrate. This will give you time and opportunity to put distance between you and your attacker.

If you must remain near the attacker, for whatever reason, the next best way is to visualize yourself wearing shining blue armor that covers every part of your body. By wearing armor, you can physically move your protection with you without having to constantly think about it.

The third method is to be constantly prepared by wearing a consecrated good-luck charm of your choosing. Some magicians like to wear a crystal—sometimes held by a dragon's foot, other times held by an entire dragon. The crystal itself will work alone as well. Any charm that has meaning to you can be used this way. Consecrate the charm by passing it through the smoke of frankincense incense, then swiftly through the top heat of a candle's flame. Follow this by sprinkling the charm with water and touching it to the Earth, or a bowl of earth. This fills the charm with the powers of the four elements.

The best protection, however, is to take care not to place yourself within the presence of a known troublemaker or put yourself in situations in which there is bound to be conflict. Be observant at all times. However, there are times when you cannot avoid the problem. Use one of the above personal protection techniques, plus a Look Elsewhere spell.

The Look Elsewhere spell is very simple and uses the same basic techniques as the protection method. You make no eye contact with anyone. You move slowly and smoothly along the path you must travel. All the time you are doing these things, you mentally focus on a direction away from yourself and strongly think "Look over there! Something interesting is in that direction."

Dragon Ride Meditation

Use the meditation opening on page 7.

(Beginning of meditation)

You walk across a stone-paved courtyard of an ancient castle. The first light of dawn has turned the sky to a rosy pink, a promise of another beautiful day. You climb a set of stone stairs built into the outer wall. Waiting above you, wings slightly spread, is your co-magician dragon, the new rays of the Sun glistening on his green and gold scales. The dragon bends one knee to help you grab the harness strap and pull yourself to sit on his shoulders between his wings.

Your dragon turns his head and looks at you with a twinkle in his eye. "Would you like to fly around the world today?" he asks.

As soon as you are comfortably in place, an invisible bubble of warm air surrounds both the dragon and you. You realize this bubble provides you with protection from the cold, airless skies, as well as acting as a safety net should you fall off the dragon.

You tell him yes and tighten your hands on the harness as you feel the muscles bunch beneath you. With a mighty flap of his wings, the dragon soars off the castle wall, his wings catching the thermal air currents and lifting him far off the ground.

You catch your breath at the wonder of being so high in the air, the patchwork fields spread out below you. A line of trees marks the edge of the dirt road, while low shrubbery lines the banks of a canal that uses water from the river just beyond the castle.

The dragon banks to the left and levels off, flying to the southeast with confident lifts and pops of his powerful wings. The variation of the western states of the United States lies like a modernistic painting on the ground below you. The green of pine-covered mountains gives way to the summer bleakness of high desert plateaus as the dragon moves swiftly from the Pacific Northwest south to Arizona and New Mexico. The stacked red rocks, the ancient dwellings built high in the side of cliffs, the breathtaking depths and twists of the Grand Canyon are stunning.

"I want to see more!" you call to the dragon. "I want to see the Mississippi River and the Atlantic Ocean and the ancient places in the Far East." Your words are nearly silent within the strange surrounding bubble, but your dragon hears you.

"If I take you to those places," the dragon answers, "you must answer one question at the end of the ride. If you answer correctly, I will grant you the right to move to the studies of the next Ring. If you fail the test, it will be put to the Council of Elders whether you repeat the Apprentice studies or are sent to learn on only the mundane levels."

Your desire to see the world from this amazing angle overrides your fear. "I agree," you say.

The dragon finds an air stream that sweeps up the Mississippi River from the Gulf of Mexico over to the Great Lakes in the north, and sails the invisible current with outstretched wings. The scenery soon all looks much the same from your angle, so you try to discover something different in the land below. It takes you several tries before you get a complete idea of what looks like an electrical system laid out across the ground below. In some places, the flickering current runs in rather straight lines, while in other places it seems to have been damaged at some time and rerouted itself around those areas.

"Look with your inner psychic eyes," the dragon tells you. "You will see the energy lines within the Earth."

When you switch your attention, you easily find the lines. They pulse with energy like blood flowing through a body. Volcanoes and other places glow bright where the energy reaches the Earth's surface.

"Look below. The Great Wall of China." The dragon shields the two of you from human sight while he skims above the ancient wall. You feel the ancient vibrations of blood and war emanate from the stones below.

"Where else would you like to go?" The dragon rides a spiral of heated air right through a surreal landscape of clouds.

You tell the dragon what you would like to see, and he takes you there. (Give yourself all the time you need to explore these places from a dragon's-eye view. When you are ready, return to the castle where you started.)

"Did you enjoy our journey?" the dragon asks. You answer him. "Now, I will ask the one question you promised to answer. The answer will determine whether you go through the Gate into the Enchanter Ring. What tools do you need to have power to cast a spell?"

You answer the dragon, and a lighted door opens in the castle wall.

Use the ending meditation on page 8.

(End of meditation)

Only you and the dragon will know if you answered correctly. The answer is that the power comes from within you. Tools have no power in and of themselves.

Dragon Alchemy

When you mention alchemy, nearly everyone thinks of the fraudulent magicians of the Middle Ages, who tried to make rich men believe they could turn lead into gold. Actually, alchemy is not a study of metals and the attempt to produce gold. It is an ancient secret of spirituality that perfects a human's balance of body, mind, and spirit. By bringing all levels into balance, the dross (lead) is subtly changed into higher vibrations until it reaches perfection (gold). Alchemy was studied not only by Europeans, but by the Arabs and in the Far East also.

The practice of alchemy was the very beginning of the present science of chemistry, but only because of a misunderstanding and misinterpretation of the ancient spiritual transformational processes. The original teachers and practitioners of this art called themselves philosophers and sages, not alchemists. To protect this knowledge, they wrote it down in terms of the planets, metals, laboratory experiments, and strange symbols. There were nearly as many mysterious symbols in the books as there were words. The most fundamental keys to alchemy were passed from teacher to student and never written down. This practice of using symbols and double meanings was quite common with all knowledge that came from Atlantis and Lemuria.

The dragons taught the physical, magickal, spiritual practice of alchemy to people on faraway planets before they came to Earth and taught it to humans. The remnants of the original teachings were preserved in the ancient text called the Emerald Tablet. Since the scrolls were found in one of the temples of the Egyptian god Thoth, the knowledge was attributed to him. Unfortunately, most modern translations of the original forty-two complex books, or scrolls, have been reduced to a few pages.

It wasn't long after the introduction of alchemy to Europe that the untaught, self-appointed alchemists degenerated into what were called "puffers"—quacks. The convincing ones cheated many people before being caught and imprisoned. The only good thing to come from the physical side of alchemy is that, by the late Middle Ages, the chemical blending experiments evolved into a primitive science that would yield modern medicines, tinctures, perfumes, and similar substances. These alchemists became a guild with laws for apprentice training—and a council within the guild that judged charges against alchemists and decided who was worthy to become an apprentice.

This physical, material use of alchemy was a healing remnant remembered from Atlantis and Lemuria. The dragons knew it would play an important part in future history. However, they worried about the temptation to turn chemical medicine into gold before they actually proved the medicinal worth. Reading about the total and partial failures in medicine today, the dragons were right to worry.

However, the magickal and spiritual sides of alchemy were overlooked by the populace during the time of the fraudulent puffers and the rise of the medical chemists. By this time, the dragons had long ago moved to the Otherworld as a permanent home, only appearing to and teaching certain people on this plane.

Since the magickal and spiritual sides of the science were not likely to elicit monetary returns, that part of the teaching was safe until Christianity and the witch-hunts began. The books of alchemy then became reduced to even more mysterious symbols and metaphors, and were forgotten by all but a very few.

Both magickal and spiritual alchemy taught the use of planetary powers, mixtures of the elements, and the goal of the Philosopher's Stone. Spiritual alchemy was the highest goal, but the elder dragons were wise enough to know that human magicians needed to see a theory work, and to know how it worked, before visualizing how the same theory worked on the spiritual level.

Testing Your Energy Balance

This exercise will help you, your guardian, and co-magician dragons understand where your strengths and weaknesses with energy might lie, and help you establish an unbending trust with dragons.

Begin this mental challenge by finding a quiet place, the same kind of area you need for a meditation. Surround yourself with white light and relax your body. When you feel ready, visualize a wide, very long board balanced on top of a golden pyramid. This board and fulcrum sit in a place where the only light is what glows from it. One side of this area is brilliant white. This light dims to a bright gray as it nears the fulcrum over which the board lies. From the center point on, the light continues to dim until only darkness exists at the other end.

Your co-magician dragon motions you to stand on the board at the point directly over the pyramidal support. When you stand on that place, you become aware of how each physical movement you make one way or the other affects the balance of the board. Slowly, you become aware that your thoughts also affect the balance of this strange board.

You hear your dragon explain by telepathy what the board is and what you are to do. You are presently standing at the calm pivotal point of Multiversal energy. You feel safe and comfortable standing where you are. The brighter end of the board exudes an attraction of absolute calm, but that power feels as if it is less than the power where you are. You look at the dark end of the board and feel its allure of deep power. Strangely, the power at that dark end also feels less than the power where you are.

Your dragon instructs you to move slightly toward the dark end of the board. You feel the temptation of taking up that dark energy, but you remember your lessons about positive and negative energies. The dragon again motions with a hand to slide gently, that you will be held safe. You take a deep breath and, by willpower, you make yourself slide toward the negative polarity. You relax when you feel the dragon's astral hold on you. You go only a short way before you stop. Carefully note all you feel about the negative energy. If anything happens, take note of that, too, for it will help you understand if you are out of energy balance at this time.

Make yourself return to the balance of the pivotal point. Relax a few moments before sliding toward the bright, positive end of the board. Again, your dragon's hold keeps you from moving far into that beguiling brilliance. It has a different power temptation to offer you. Again, note your feelings and any happenings.

You move back to the center and step down from the board. Were both extremes uncomfortable to you? Did you feel best balancing in the center, or slightly to one side or the other? What did your feelings and any happenings mean to you on a personal level? Your co-magician dragon will now explain to you how to rebalance yourself if needed. Only you and your dragons will ever know the outcome of this exercise.

Dragon Apprentice Ritual

Ingredients: Altar cloth; small bowls with sea salt in one and water in the other; your altar stones. Have a chosen piece of jewelry, or even a belt buckle, on the altar cloth before you.

Preferable Day: Full Moon

Use the ritual/ceremony opening on page 52.

> (Beginning of the ritual)
>
> *Close your eyes and relax your body. Feel the solid walls of a great cave come into being around you. You clearly hear the humming of a large flight of dragons as they greet you for this ritual. You feel the warmth of their bodies around you and hear the rustle of folding wings.*
>
> *Open your eyes and say:*
>
> *"Greetings to all of dragon-kind. I have come to ask that you let me pass into the Enchanter Ring. I have held true to my promise as a Dragon Apprentice."*
>
> *You sense the presence of Aldram, the Keeper of the Book, the ancient dragon who took your apprenticeship oath when you started your studies. You hold out both hands, palms up. You feel the light touch of dragon skin as Aldram lays his hands over yours.*
>
> *"Do you take oath to learn the ways of the Enchanter of the Five Inner Rings?" Aldram asks you.*

In reply, you chant:

"I give my oath to learn the ways that an Enchanter spends his (her) days. To learn the spellcraft power to mold into a need that's spoken bold. To help, not harm, the Multiverse, while blocking ills and spiteful curse. Leaf and blossom, candle bright, all magick uses in the night, I will learn for the good of all. Dragons, be with me when I call."

You take your piece of jewelry into your power hand (the hand you use most). Tighten your fist around the jewelry as much as you can while holding that hand over your head.

Every hour is dragon power!

Touch the jewelry to the center of your forehead, then over your heart.

"I willingly take up the studies of the Enchanter Ring. I will do my best at all times, and will not speak of Enchanter arts to those not of that Ring."

Sit quietly for a few minutes.

Use the ending of the ritual on page 54.

(Ending of the ritual)

The Way of the Dragon Enchanter

 SECOND OF THE INNER RINGS

Dragon Enchanters study the art of magick. They learn how to prepare correct herbal mixtures and combinations of essential oils to use in spellwork, plus they are taught how to actually perform the spells themselves. Improving your life by using magick isn't wrong, unless you are doing it at the expense of others, such as through control or intimidation. There is more than enough positive energy in the Multiverse for every being to be prosperous, healthy, and loved. No matter how much positive energy you use, no one else will have to do without. Also, the fact that you desire and work toward filling your life-cup to overflowing, with events and people that make you happy and complete, isn't a selfish goal and doesn't make you a "bad" person. If you perfect your magick by manifesting good things for yourself, you will have all the practice necessary to help others.

I rarely recommend doing spells for others, because it usually ends up with the other person being unhappy in some manner about how the spell manifested. However, knowing human compassion and the desire to help friends and loved ones, I recommend two things. First, don't do healing spells unless the person asks or gives permission. You may need to offer help using words they understand and respond better to than "magick spells." I often say I will light a healing prayer candle, which gets a positive response.

Second, if you want to help someone on a more physical level than healing the body or mind, you are probably better off doing the spells in a general way, without telling them. If someone is looking for a job, for example, you could tell them, as a friend, that they should be alert to all opportunities. Then you do a spell for them to find the right job as soon as possible. This way, you don't violate their personal free will or their opinions for or against magick. They also can't come back later to gripe to you about "missing the mark" on what they wanted or about the manifestation not appearing when they wanted it to.

The last time I did a spell for someone else, the woman in question refused a job offer as not good enough. She threatened to put an ad in the paper that I was a farce, that the spell didn't work. However, she didn't take advantage of the opportunity given her, and she wanted what she wasn't qualified to have. I said, "You go right ahead and place an ad. I don't mind at all." I hadn't asked for payment, and I generally rely on karmic balance if trouble arises. The woman didn't run an ad and didn't return. I no longer do spellwork for others at all. If a person wants such help, I believe it's better if they learn how to do their own spells.

Becoming an Enchanter also requires the student to learn to withhold judgment (and sometimes a burning urge for revenge) in order to raise the correct energy to power a spell. These feelings may arise when others are interfering in your life and telling you what you should or shouldn't want. Your full intent has to be on the spell's purpose if it is to properly manifest for your good. Without your emotionally uninvolved concentration, the spell either won't work at all or will produce a result you don't want.

Remember: you are responsible for what you create. Concentrated thought in spellwork can change parts of the future (and that includes tomorrow). Those changes are seen in the results that occur. You certainly don't want the opposite of the spell intent to appear.

This Ring also introduces the student to the healing arts through magick. The Enchanter primarily uses spellwork for healing an imbalance on the physical level, while the Shaman concentrates on spiritual healing of shattered souls. However, no magician ever recommends that any person take any herbal mixtures or stop seeing an orthodox doctor. Magickal healing is far different from, yet complementary to, orthodox medicine. Since the medical community doesn't accept magick at this time, you don't want to cross the legal line into dangerous territory.

The dragons pointed out that healing in the physical includes more than just repairing a sick human body. The physical areas for humans include love, prosperity, employment, and a myriad of other everyday desires and necessities. If a person feels a need in the physical area, and it remains unresolved, she or he will not be able to raise the desire to reach for spiritual growth. Thus the Enchanter can work magick for a wide range of interests and needs other than just bodily illness.

Becoming a competent Dragon Enchanter will develop closer ties between you and your dragons, between you and dragons in general. Dragons are very attracted to magick in all forms, perhaps because they are such experts in this ancient art. Magicians will find that any time they change awareness from physical to astral, they will discover dragons close around them at all times. Some dragons will come and go, while others will be constant companions.

Learning to be an Enchanter is not an easy task. You will delve deeper into the fields of magickal herbs and the uses of essential oils than you ever have before. You will learn to make waters, washes, mixtures, and powders. You will see how the dragons, through natural planetary powers, can affect magick, and you will learn about the mysterious element that isn't quite an element, but has the ability to affect everything.

The dragons will expect you to be diligent in your studies. Dragons do not like sloppy magick. They also are quick to point out that the magician who learns magick just to have power over others is a tyrant. True dragon magicians desire power only over themselves. Dragons have no use for tyrants, nor will they reveal secret information to such magicians. Instead, dragons will see that path is full of problems and misinformation.

So, welcome to the Enchanter Ring. Approach your new studies with an air of expectation about discovering new things, as you will find new knowledge around every corner.

Code, Color, and Other Items of the Enchanter

The code of the Dragon Enchanter is "Magick is both an art and a science. Always treat it with respect."

Too many people new to magick are not careful with their spell preparations, their use and/or selection of certain spells, or their actions during a spell. The ingredients of all spells can be substituted with others if you choose those with identical or similar correspondence and purposes. The same applies to the oils. However, be certain you know what you are doing. The wrong ingredients can turn the spell from its original purpose.

It is a great temptation at first to concentrate on spells for love, revenge, and control. Little thought is given to the ethical side of dragon magick. New magicians try to convince themselves that doing that spell this time won't hurt. These types of spells are bound to backfire somewhere along the line of daily life. If you seriously think about it, life is tough enough with daily karmic decisions without deliberately stepping outside the ethical boundaries.

New magicians also seem to disregard their actions when practicing with ritual tools. One of the most common offenses, and dangers, is the waving around of your wand and pointing it at others. A wand is not a toy. It becomes charged with universal energy by use during magickal work. Although you will not see a beam of energy come from the tip when you swing it around, I assure you that energy does shoot from there like a laser beam. The damage it can do to the aura of others will not be visible immediately. However, within a few days the person with whom you were "playing," and perhaps you yourself, will feel the astral results through illness, extreme tiredness, and/or a sudden cycle of ill luck. Treat your ritual tools with respect. They are filled with magickal power that can harm as well as help.

The Enchanter's color is a true green. Green is the color of growth, prosperity, and good magick. You will need to purchase two feet of half-inch green ribbon. As the Apprentice also does, you will drape this ribbon across your shoulders while working or meditating, and you will use it to mark a section of the Dragon Hoard. I hope you are working on your ritual book, the Dragon Hoard, and writing each day in your journal, the Dragon Secrets.

The symbol for this Ring is an upright triangle, meaning the top points upward. This represents the traits needed to be an Enchanter. The two bottom corners of the triangle symbolize compassion and knowledge. They are the firm foundation of the top point, which is healing magick. The triangle also refers to body and mind on the lower points and spirit at the top. It also can represent the rule of three in spellwork; what the magician sends out in magick is returned in three times the power. This is definitely a rule to think about if you are tempted to place a curse on someone.

You can also add more stones to the ones you already have to place on the corners of your altar cloth. If you feel the need, you can always add more than one of the same stone.

If you can't afford to purchase the stones listed for each Ring, work with the stone colors instead. This method isn't as fine-tuned as using a specific stone, but it is better than not using stones or spending money you don't have to spare. Stone colors are discussed later in this section.

I want to recommend a few more stones by name that will help any dragon student in spellwork. Rose quartz is a part of the quartz crystal family. A very compassionate stone, it is useful in spells for removing sorrow, when working for children, or magick to find true love and friendship. It is very good for healing deep emotional wounds that show up in the patient's aura.

Fluorite has beautiful layers of alternating purple, green, clear, and sometimes pink. It has qualities similar to amethyst. It can affect the emotions, and the stress that causes upset emotions, as well as any imbalance in mental attitude. Wearing fluorite jewelry or holding a piece of this stone will increase concentration and inner harmony, and it is excellent in helping with studies. One of its strongest powers lies in the fact that it will ground excess energy, whether it be physical, mental, or magickal energy left over from a spell. Frequently, fluorite will increase the inner sight so the user can make a better mind-visual connection with the dragons.

Although onyx comes in several colors, it is best known in black. It is most useful in black, too, as that color of this stone will create calmness and absorb all negative vibrations within its vicinity. Black onyx also helps in resolving past life problems, balancing karmic debts, and facing challenges in this life.

Hematite is a silvery-gray stone that has blood-red dust when cut or scraped. Use it as a worry stone to dispel stress and negativity. If you have modern jewelry with "marcasite" in it, you are wearing hematite. This stone reflects negative vibrations away from you before they even get close. It works well with other stones, even in jewelry. Because of its shiny, reflective surface, a moderate piece of hematite can be used as a scrying stone, similar to a crystal ball.

Lapis lazuli has long been a sacred stone in many cultures, including ancient Egypt. It is a beautiful dark blue stone, usually having small gold flecks or tiny marks of white calcite. The energy of this stone is of very high strength and quality. You will have to work to raise your mental, emotional, and spiritual energies to connect with it. Besides balancing and clearing the chakras, lapis will help attract a good job, develop your psychic powers, and empower communication with your spiritual guides and the dragons. Dragons are very fond of this stone. If you are still subconsciously carrying unnecessary emotional baggage, from this life or a past life, carrying or wearing lapis will cut the ties.

Each stone that you acquire for magickal or personal use can be cleansed of unwanted vibrations at any time by passing the stone through the smoke of frankincense incense or smoldering sage. This is the safest method, unless you are certain that the stone you want to cleanse can be safely held under running water. Some stones, such as calcite, will dissolve in any liquid. Placing a stone on a crystal cluster for a week also cleanses the vibrations.

You definitely need to cleanse your stones if other people handle them. Plus, you should cleanse them after any magickal use. The stones should have only your vibrations on them. In this manner, they become attuned to you and work better when you perform spells. If you use incense, you also can purify yourself by using your hands to wave this smoke over your body.

Purifying something doesn't remove its natural vibrations and properties. When you "cleanse" something, you return it to its original unaltered state. Banishing negativity is a form of cleansing, since you forcibly remove negative vibrations and return the object or person to their original state. In this case, though, you need to concentrate on sending the removed vibes into the Earth for a thorough purification.

There are two other stones that are beautiful and helpful, but are also rather expensive. Aqua aura is man-made: a quartz crystal is coated with a microscopic layer of gold. This melding layer creates a power object with unique magickal qualities. It not only soothes and relaxes the emotions, but it also calls up serene energies and directs away stressful ones. Mystic fire (also a man-made stone) has a heavier layer of gold bonded to white topaz. This produces a very strong energy that can be used when in the Otherworld. Its energy can also backfire, however, if the sender isn't well trained in the Warrior Ring.

Enchanter Ritual Tools

Clothing for all the Rings is discussed in section 1, the Dragon Apprentice section.

The power in every tool you use for spells and rituals is the power you placed within it, or direct through it. All the tools attract the attention and focus of the linear left brain, so the creative right half can work unimpeded. Besides, a special outfit, plus magickal tools, really puts you in the proper mood and atmosphere, helping you to switch from the mundane mode to pure magickal, Otherworld thinking and actions.

If you have not acquired a wand yet, now is the time to do so. It doesn't have to be large, fancy, or expensive. You can purchase it or make it. You may find a fallen tree branch or an appropriate piece of driftwood to use as your first wand. Often a piece of doweling or copper tubing is easily made into a wand, depending on your creativity. Small stones may also be glued to the sides of the wand. If you find small dragon charms, those would be welcome additions.

Or there is another way to make a really fascinating wand. Purchase a clear glass or plastic tube about the diameter of your little finger and about fifteen inches long. Plastic is perfectly acceptable, and unbreakable. Using a dry-clear, strong glue, attach a quartz point to one end. Allow it to dry for a couple of days before proceeding. Fill the tube with whatever tumbled stones you like, perhaps checking their meaning, by color if necessary. When the tube is packed, glue a tumbled "balance" stone to the remaining open end. Let it dry thoroughly before using.

A quartz point can be clear quartz, amethyst, citrine, or smoky, as these all are found in natural points. However, you can also use a shaped point of rose quartz, snow quartz, or any other powerful stone. The "balancing" stone needs to be the alternate energy—such as black onyx, obsidian, or even a very dark smoky quartz.

Most magicians I know collect a number of wands during their magickal lifetimes. Some wands project a vibration that is good for all spellwork, while others make it known that they are most powerful only in certain types of magick. You will find the same to be true with pendulums and tarot decks.

If you make your wand, you might consider putting a crystal point in one end and wiring a small piece of black onyx, obsidian, or another meaningful stone to the other end. Flexible copper wire (not too thin) and quick-drying jeweler's glue are very helpful in putting together a wand. Besides, the copper wire adds to the stones' powers. If you are a person who seems to attract shocks by static electricity, I suggest you wrap leather thongs tightly around the wand where you will hold it.

A good wand will amplify and enhance your magickal energy, but it won't make you Merlin or Morgan le Fae. A wand can help you strengthen and open your inner eyes and ears so you see and hear Otherworld magickal realms all around you. However, it is up to you to study and practice, to become comfortable using all your magickal tools if you wish to grow magickally and spiritually. A wand merely helps direct your stream of magickal power like a laser instead of a shotgun blast.

To consecrate your wand to your magickal work, you will need to perform a small dedication ceremony. This is best done during the Full Moon, or when the Moon is waxing (growing larger). Check your astrological calendar if you aren't certain of the right day. Begin with the opening ritual from page 52.

Place the wand in front of you on your altar cloth. Sprinkle it very lightly with a few drops of water from the dish and say:

> *I ask the dragons to cleanse this wand with spiritual energy.*
> *Wand of power, I welcome you to the Five Inner Rings.*

Slowly wave the wand through the incense smoke, or wave the smoldering sage bundle over it.

> *Mighty dragons, strong and old,*
> *Fill my wand with power bold.*
> *Teach me its uses, right from wrong,*
> *And make it bright with dragon-song.*

Slowly wave the wand through the smoke again. Then perform the closing ceremony on page 54. Leave the wand where the light of the Full Moon will shine on it for at least two hours this night.

As an Enchanter, you will need to add a few more valuable items to your other working tools. A small metal cauldron or bowl is necessary for burning herbs, papers, and sometimes other items mentioned in a spell.

Also put a yard or two each of white, green, red, and black cotton cloth in your workbox for making poppets, sachets, and power bags. You will need to include several small spools of different colors of thread, a needle, scissors, black and red markers, and two feet of thin cord or yarn in the colors of each Ring. A short nail is useful for carving on candles. The colored thread will be used in sewing poppets, and in knot magick and web weaving spells.

You will use small jars with tight-fitting lids to store your herbs. It isn't necessary to buy more than one-quarter ounce or half an ounce of herbs at a time. This way you will have a rotating fresh supply when needed.

Although later you can use a coffee-bean grinder to pulverize your herbs, you should begin with an old-fashioned mortar and pestle. Mortars made of marble or heavy ceramic are best, in my opinion. The metal ones are too slick to pulverize the herbs.

Whichever type you use, you should know that there are certain herbs that simply cannot be powdered, whatever you do. Even an electric grinder has trouble with them. Some of these are bay leaves, gums, resins, and woods or bark from trees. Bay leaves are best cut into small pieces with scissors. Try to buy any wood or bark already ground; sandalwood comes in a powdered form. Frankincense, myrrh, and dragon's blood are notorious for sticking together in a mass or ball when using a mortar and pestle. Try to purchase these powdered or in very small pieces. However, you may have to settle for what are called "tears," or small pieces. If you are patient and slowly add other herbs to the resins as you grind, you will have less trouble. Also, the odor is so fragrant that it makes the effort worthwhile.

Of course, if you purchase ground herbs, you will only need a bowl and wooden spoon to create your herbal mixtures. In this case, any chant to be recited while grinding herbs would be said while mixing them.

See the lists of herbs, oils, and candle colors in the "Magickal Mixtures" part of this section. These lists will help you decide which all-around items you can stock to use for spellwork. If you're serious about your studies, you should keep an assortment of candles, oils, and herbs at all times. It isn't necessary to have every listed item, however.

Another object for the Enchanter is a sturdy shoulder bag and smaller drawstring bags in which to carry jars of herbal mixtures, stones, the altar cloth, your wand if small enough, a deck of tarot cards or divination stones, and any other supplies necessary for a spell. This shoulder bag can be of leather, decorated or fringed, or of any very sturdy material. This is highly useful in keeping your work secret if you need to go elsewhere to do your magick. Using a shoulder bag leaves your hands free for your walking staff or to do the usual things associated with travel. At this stage of training, though, I don't recommend traveling to do spells elsewhere. It's best to only use your personal outdoor power spot or the altar cloth in your room. The dragons agree on this.

If you prefer a different kind of incense burner than the ordinary one, fill an abalone shell with a layer of sand and burn cone incense. Frankincense, or a blend of frankincense and myrrh, is an excellent all-purpose incense to use, either sticks or cones. The strongest-smelling incense, and the one most likely to put a lot of smoke in the air, is the herbal-resin type burned on charcoal. The least smoky is the stick incense. If you have allergies, and can't breathe smoke without coughing, you may wish to put a few drops of corresponding oil on a cotton ball instead of using incense.

Placing shells on your altar, such as the conch, cowry and augur shells (the long, twisted ones like unicorn horns), will help you draw upon the vast powers of the oceans and the Water element for certain spells. A small container of soil, tree leaves, stones, or plants can represent the Earth element. Incense represents Air, while a lighted candle is for Fire.

It also is a respectful gesture to the dragons to have small dragon statues on your altar, along with a bowl into which you can put gifts of stones and jewelry. Dragons do like to have their stashes of shiny baubles, even if they aren't precious materials. It is the show of respect and friendship that counts. If you find drawings of dragons with either the Eastern phoenix or panther, be aware that these fabulous creatures work well together. Sometimes a phoenix or panther will appear with your dragons to help you in your work.

Choosing a Magickal Name

Taking a magickal name is a way of telling your subconscious mind and the Otherworld beings that you are serious about magick and working in the Multiverse. This name helps you create a magickal personality that changes your outlook and actions whenever you are working with the dragons and spells. At first, nonmagickal people will only catch a tiny glimpse of this hidden personality. As you grow stronger in your studies of dragon magick, the personality will merge slowly with your everyday persona, until only those people on magickal paths will see that side of you.

There is a reason for keeping this name secret from most people. To know someone's magickal name can aid another person in tracking down your unique personal vibrations, thus giving them the power to hurt you by spellwork, if they are negative. This taboo about names can be traced far back in any culture's history.

Using this name during magickal work creates an astral body of energy that enables you to connect with the Otherworlds. Through this astral body, you can explore the Multiverse and experience firsthand the technique of molding Multiversal energy to manifest.

The biggest question about this subject is, how do you choose a name? You may discover a name during dreams or meditations. A name may appeal to you because you associate it in some manner with dragons and their attributes and abilities. Your guardian and/or co-magician dragon may suggest one. If the name does not feel right to you, keep looking. Only accept a name you like.

You may use one name if you work with a magickal group and another secret name you never share except with the dragons. If you decide not to work with the group, do a short ceremony and sever your vibrations from that first name, still keeping the secret name.

One method of deciding on a name is to use the meaning of your present name in some way. For example, Iris means "rainbow," Elizabeth means "chosen one," and Byron means "bear." Or you can make a name by connecting separate groups of sounds that appeal to you, such as Men-Ken-Tek. Usually, magicians prefer to adopt names of animals, insects, plants, or the elements. You can have one name, such as Bear, or you can combine two names, as in Sun Bear, Willow-Star, or Crystal Butterfly. But don't try to look important by using four or five names strung together. That looks and sounds pompous and arrogant. Starlight Heather is much better, and more dignified for an Enchanter, than Eagle Goldensky Star-Shooter.

Think long and carefully before choosing your special name. Strive to be unique, at the same time letting the sounds and meanings fit you. You can avoid following the ordinary crowd if you don't use three or more names together. You can be different if you don't use the ever-popular Merlin, Wolf, Moon, Hawk, or some deity names. Give your creative imagination free rein. Make a list of all the ideas that come to your mind. Let the list of names simmer in your subconscious mind until one or two stand out from the rest. Then choose the one that really speaks to you, not the one you think will impress others.

Choosing a name that has the same numerical value as your everyday name or birth date is helpful for some people. Using the chart below, add together all the values of all the letters of your present name. If necessary, reduce the final number to just a single numeral by adding together any double digits—unless the numeral is 11, 22, or 33, which are considered powerful numbers. Read these three double digits under the meaning given for 11. If working with your birth date, simply add together the numbers of the month, day, and birth year.

For example, if your total name number is 35, add those together to get 8. If your birth date total is 13, add together those numbers to reach 4. Then add up the value of the letters in your magickal name and see if they match.

The total of your name is called your Expression number, while the total of your birth date is your Life Path.

1	2	3	4	5	6	7	8	9
A	B	C	D	E	F	G	H	I
J	K	L	M	N	O	P	Q	R
S	T	U	V	W	X	Y	Z	

1: Independent and a natural leader with great ambitions. You do not work best in work groups. As you are quite opinionated, people either like you or dislike you, with no middle ground. At times you can be self-centered and a bit of a bully. Your criticism of others causes a loss of friends. When correctly applied, your determination can lead to great success.

2: You work best with a partner, not alone. You like groups and love to solve problems. Although you are cooperative and sympathetic, there are good and bad sides to being sensitive. You may be oversensitive to conflicts and hostile work conditions. However, even with good intuition, this number is reluctant to make decisions for fear of being wrong.

3: Your expression of optimism inspires others. You are creative, artistic, and skilled verbally, but you often lack self-discipline and order. You make good plans and conceive great ideas, but you often have trouble putting them into use. You see life and ideas in pictures, not words. You take any criticism very hard, which makes you moody and cynical.

4: You make slow but steady progress on all work because you are methodical and an organizer. Sometimes you take on the work of others, merely to be certain the details of the plans are logical and followed. Besides, you are a workaholic. Although your stamina will help you reach goals, you tend to nitpick when you're tired.

5: You insist on freedom, change, adventure, and new things. These demands may get you into trouble because you resist boundaries and laws. Open-minded, you sometimes try to push ideas onto others. Although you are clever and a quick thinker, your life is usually unorganized, and you get bored quickly. Your gift of gab may be limitless, but you need self-discipline to be successful.

6: Friends, family, and truth are very important to you, as is a stable life and a circle of congenial companions. Although highly creative, you need to guard against using that skill in unethical ways. You can show bad behavior, domestic tyranny, and always demand your own way. You are good at reconciling opposite points of view when faced with your behavior. Success will come through helping others.

7: You probably began life with many hard experiences to learn. With your analytical mind, you are interested in everything from science to mysticism. This builds the inner strength to go in any direction you want. You don't handle stress well, but you cut off others to be alone. Distant and aloof most of the time, you can become unfaithful, dishonest, and cruel. Restore harmony and balance.

8: Highly competitive, you enjoy challenges and have a bulldog tenacity when it comes to succeeding. You need to have sympathy for others because you aren't a tolerant leader. Therefore, life gives you some hard tests. Beware of becoming stubborn, intolerant, or overambitious.

9: Extremely idealistic and compassionate, you want to transform the world, whether the world wants to be changed or not. Sometimes, this works against you, and you feel used and persecuted by others who don't believe in your cause. You aren't a particularly good judge of character. Whatever opposition faces you, you are always ready to accept new cycles of life. You need to learn responsibility for what you do.

11: You attract powerful ideas and psychic information, but you need to control this flow of energy for emotional peace. Because you had to stifle your enormous sensitivity as a child, you are now careful sharing feelings. You do your best when helping others find solutions to problems. You need to become more selective about where you place your time and energy.

◎   ◎   ◎

These meanings of the numbers are my own interpretation. There are many excellent numerology books available that will give you other meanings. If you are interested in selecting your magickal name by this method, you will be able to expand your search easily in this area.

It isn't necessary to have a numerically correct name. I've had three names in my life so far, and none are numerologically correct. I liked them personally, and they fit my personality at the time they were chosen. Your new magickal name should please you and draw a positive response from the dragons. This name will denote the real you as an active astral magician.

You may decide to change your magickal name if you pass a major transitional point in your life, or if you change direction and no longer work or associate with the same magickal people. However, think as long and hard about changing names as you did in the first choosing. Don't force a change in your magickal life—unless you have grown far beyond the original name, too many people have found out your name, you leave a group, or you have passed through great life changes or cycles. The last reason is ordinarily the reason magicians change their secret name. Changing your magickal name is a type of formal initiation that can also change you.

A new name may not appear for a time, leaving you feeling in a void. This time is actually a rest period, letting you readjust to creating a "new you." Several names may come to mind before you find the right one. Sometimes, altering the spelling or sound of the old name is enough to set up an entirely new energy pattern. You could change Star-Shooter to Shooting Star, or Knight to Night, or Iris to Sirhis.

Whenever you decide your name, for the first time or as a change, do a simple ceremony at your cloth altar. Light a white candle and the incense of your choice. Set out your stones in the usual places on the altar. Sit quietly for a few moments until you feel yourself in the presence of your dragons. Then say:

> *I am now [magickal name]. I am a dragon magician and a friend of dragons.*

Continue to sit quietly so the dragons can communicate with you if they wish. It is very possible that the dragon Aldram, Keeper of the Book, will appear to record your new name in the book you signed when you entered your dragon studies. When you are finished, thank the dragons and clean your altar as instructed before.

Now is an excellent to make notes about the ritual and your feelings during and after it.

Dark Energy of the Universe

There has always been a difficulty when trying to explain that everything, animate and inanimate, is created, and first exists, in a beyond-the-Otherworld place called the Void, or the Great Dark Sea, in legends. This Void is of the Otherworld realms, yet separate. All is created out of the energy of that Void before it can manifest on any world on any level of the Multiverse. Many magicians like to have some sort of plausible explanation of Otherworld happenings and don't like to take much on "blind faith." Yet they learned, as long ago as the beginnings of human history, that magick simply didn't work unless they accepted and applied that theory. In 2006, scientists finally released the valuable information that they had found proof that invisible dark matter does exist in our universe.

The cosmos, as we know it, is composed of atoms and electrons that make stars, planets, air, and life. However, these visible objects are only a tiny fraction of what exists in the entire universe. Scientists said there had to be another, different source (type) of gravity, or stuff, or else galaxies and clusters couldn't hold together. Unsure what this invisible something is, they decided to call it "dark matter." Doing so "explained" the unseen gravitational force to the scientific community. Dark matter can't be seen. Actually, scientists don't know what it is either. However, it produces a blue color representing the edges of its gravity fields. This can be calculated by how the light from each background galaxy is distorted in telescopes.

Using NASA's Chandra X-ray Observatory, scientists found a bullet-shaped cloud produced by cosmic winds. They deduced that this cloud and winds were created by a high-speed collision of two clusters of galaxies about 6.3 billion years ago. The phenomenon of dark energy beats out gravity, causing the universe to expand at a faster pace than thought possible. This collision apparently caused normal and dark matter to separate. Thus, normal matter moves at its slower rate of speed, while dark matter, which doesn't interact with normal matter in its ordinary form, continues to go at its usual rapid pace.

Dark energy, similar to but not exactly like dark matter, also went its own way, creating massive pools throughout our universe. We can only theorize whether the same happens in other layers of the Multiverse.

After years of study, scientific observers released a report dividing the universe into 5 percent normal matter, 25 percent dark matter, and 70 percent dark energy. We would call normal matter "positive energy" and dark matter "negative energy." This means that the remaining 70 percent called dark energy must be an enormous tachyon field, or the Void in magick and legends. There is a constant movement of electrons back and forth between the material world and the Void, or tachyon area. It is theorized that the migration of electrons takes a tail of dark matter with it when entering the Void. The dark energy mysteriously seems to mix the dark matter and electrons, releasing a new stream of electrons back into the material universe.

This is an elaborate scientific "theory" that tries to explain what magicians have known for centuries: magick mixes positive and negative energies in the Otherworld's Void to manifest what is desired in this world. It's nice to know we now have the backing of scientists, in a way, although they don't use the same words we do. As has been the case since science came into its modern shape, they are just now beginning to accept a few of the things magicians have known since humans did the first spells in tribal shamanistic ceremonies. And even dragon magicians haven't learned all that the dragons have to teach us.

Magickal Mixtures, Spells, Amulets, and Talismans

Now that you will be preparing for, and then doing, spellwork, the dragons want to repeat some important information on magick.

True magick is about transforming or changing the world, or at least re-creating your personal future in the world. Ethical principles should govern your choices in life and your behavior, though. You are responsible for using magick properly. Actions have consequences. Clean up your mistakes and make them right. Evil allowed to exist harms all, but take great care how you define evil.

All things appear to move through time and space in circles. Every circle, however, is actually a spiral that is part of a larger spiral, which is also moving. The pattern of movement is rather like an open helix, like a DNA molecule. Everything on every level moves in a similar fashion while connected to everything else in a gigantic multiple universal web. This web connects this world with our universe, then to the Otherworld, and from there with the Multiverse.

If you know the true name (the exact vibrations) of a person or thing, you have complete control over it. This makes you responsible for what you create with your knowledge. If you use it negatively, you will be paid back in kind. The same applies to using it positively. If you brainstorm over the way to do a spell, you can find positive ways to respond to the most negative events.

Like attracts like, yet everything contains its opposite. Female bodies have male hormones as well as female, and vice versa. The same applies to every stream of positive or negative energy. This is to create a harmonious balance, and it is a clue to what ties all in the Multiverse together.

Energy is magnetic in that a certain quality or vibration tends to attract energy of the same quality and vibration. Strong, continued thought is a quick, light form of energy. Therefore, a form will follow any powerful idea. We always create something first by our concentrated thoughts and intentions. This blueprint then magnetizes and guides the physical energy into that form, eventually manifesting it on the physical plane. Whatever you send out into the universe will be reflected back to you. Whatever we think about the most is what we attract. If we believe in something very strongly, expect it on the deepest levels of our being, and imagine it vividly, it will manifest.

Carl Jung believed that one of the principles of magick was what he called active imagination, or daydreaming. He taught that active imagination was a way to access the collective unconscious, or superconscious mind. This level of mind connects each person to everything that has ever happened and will happen, as well as to every person who has ever lived. Thus, we tap into the Multiverse's infinite power through archetypal imagery. Certain symbols, images, and religious patterns unite us all.

Give your spells a reasonable amount of time to work—several days to a month at least. If nothing happens, revise the spell or your intent. If still nothing happens, release the desire for the manifestation. Sometimes we hold onto spell energy, and the spell can't manifest.

Also include a prevention statement that will keep the spell from rebounding on you or anyone not connected with the spell result. Use words such as: "If this spell is blocked, or rebounds, send its energy safely into the ground to be made neutral. Never shall it return to harm me or mine."

Never specify exactly the way a spell should work out. Be intent on what you want the result to be, but not on how that result will manifest. By visualizing a specific way the spell will end, you will either hinder the spell or disintegrate it altogether. The best way to really know if you are focusing on the right idea is to write out exactly what you want the spell to do, but end it with the words: "This or better. Make it so." Doing this gives the dragons more options to direct the spell's energy. It also gives you an opportunity to work on the wording until you get it right. You could even decide that your desire isn't what you want at all, and redo the entire spell.

Grounding is needed at the end of all spellwork and rituals. Grounding means to put your body and spirit in contact with the Earth in some way. You must balance and replenish your energies and release the remaining spell power from your body. You should also place a time limit on the spell, with an order to dissolve into the Multiverse at the end of that time.

Herbs

The use of magickal herbs is not a new science, but rather it has come down to us with the herbs' traditional values from the earliest cultures of humankind. Magick has many uses for herbs. Gums and herbs can be burned as the sole incense ingredient in special mixtures, or in conjunction with ready-made incenses. This burning fumigates a room or space with the herbal power.

After rubbing candles with oils, you can roll the candles in crushed herbal mixtures to increase their potency. Poppets, or cloth dolls, constructed for healing, prosperity, fertility, protection, love, and so forth, are stuffed with cotton batting mixed with appropriate herbs. Mixtures of herbs, a few appropriate charms, leftover candle wax, perhaps a few strands of someone's hair can be put into leather or cloth charm bags or a magickal box. Sometimes these charm bags and boxes are made for someone else's goals, but you can make them for yourself.

Whatever magick you use, it is safest not to use it to control another person. If you do, you are certain to get an emotional or financial leech or someone who wants nothing to do with you. This causes no end of trouble. Control is best avoided.

Small amounts of herbal mixtures can be tied in cheesecloth and used in bathwater also. An old fashioned tea ball, a small container with a screw-on lid with holes in it, works just as well. This bath method helps you absorb the herbs directly into your body. Just be certain that you have no allergic reactions to them.

I have chosen the easiest herbs to find, some of which can be found on your kitchen shelves, in the local grocery store, or at a New Age shop. Before you waver over the following list, please understand you don't need them all. There is no need to buy all of these herbs or oils at the moment.

Choose up to ten herbs that you think you will use and that cover a wide range of correspondence to spell results. Wait until you determine what spell you want to use, and then purchase the ingredients you need. That way, you have a fresh supply on hand. If you decide to do a spell that requires something you don't have, use a substitute. As long as the herb or oil corresponds to your spell, it is okay to make a substitution.

You may never need all these herbs and oils, so be patient. Herbs and herbal mixtures should be disposed of in three years—bury them or add them to your compost bin.

My interpretation of the magickal uses of herbs and oils may not match those of other writers. Each magician may experience different results.

To get a harder "kick" from herbs, match the spell use to an element, a planet, and/or a zodiac sign in addition to the correct Moon phase. Additional information on this subject comes later in this section.

Although I have tried to omit any herb that is poisonous, follow this rule: *never ingest any herbal mixture unless you are a trained, certified herbalist.* Also, be alert at all times for any allergic reactions you may have to certain herbs. Several spells, not in this book, call for powdered yellow dock root; be warned that this herb leaves a permanent stain on anything it touches.

You can determine which dragons will be of most help to you by knowing under which ritual influence a spell falls, or which element or planet has the most effect. Planetary dragons and their ritual/magickal meanings are in the corresponding subject title later in this section.

Allspice: Happiness, spiritual wisdom; banishes negativity. Planet: Mars; Element: Fire.

Angelica: Protection against evil spells or enchantments. You can carry the root for a protection amulet and burn the leaves to purify and exorcise negativity from a home. Planet: Sun; Element: Fire.

Anise: Protection, purification, averts evil thoughtforms. Keeps away nightmares. Planets: Jupiter, Mercury; Element: Air.

Balm of Gilead: Use the buds. Protection, manifestations, sharpens the mind. Planet: Saturn; Element: Earth.

Basil: Protection and exorcism, banishes fear and calms. Planet: Mars; Element: Fire.

Bay laurel: Stops interference from others, protects. Reduces physical stress. Planet: Sun; Element: Fire.

Bergamot: Also called *bee balm, monarda,* or *Oswego tea.* Good health, friendship, attracts good luck. Planet: Jupiter; Elements: Fire, Water.

Betony: Protection against evil spirits and spells. Purification. Planet: Jupiter; Element: Fire.

Boneset: Binding, tripping spells. Planet: Saturn; Element: Earth.

Caraway: Carry it in charm bags for protection. Add it to other charm bags to attract love. Strengthens the memory. Planet: Mercury; Element: Air.

Catnip: Courage, love, happiness. Planet: Venus; Element: Water.

Cedar: Use dust, if possible. Purification, exorcism, protection. Planet: Jupiter; Elements: Fire, Water.

Chamomile flowers: Good health, calmness, peace, luck in gambling, gaining a marriage proposal. Brewed into a tea, this herb is good for relaxation and helps with sleep. Planet: Sun; Element: Fire.

Cinnamon: Confidence, grounding, attracts anything you desire. Cassia bark has the same odor and qualities as cinnamon. Planet: Sun; Element: Fire.

Cinquefoil: Protection. Strengthens what is called the "five lucks"—love, money, health, power, and wisdom. Most frequently made into an oil to anoint candles. See page 93 for more information on blended oils.

Clary sage: It resembles ambergris in odor. Love. Planet: Moon; Element: Water.

Clove: Banishes evil, gains desires. Planet: Sun; Element: Fire.

Dragon's blood: A resin. Removes hexes and attracts good luck. Use for protection, money, love, and good luck. Although this may be a bit more expensive, a little goes a long way and is worth it. If you feel a desire to use dragon's blood ink to write out symbols on paper, you can make your own ink. Put one-eighth teaspoon of powdered dragon's blood resin in a small bottle with one teaspoon of alcohol solvent. Shake vigorously before using. Planet: Mars; Element: Fire.

Fennel: Usually sold in the form of seeds. Protection from evil influences. Used for strength, courage, and long life. Planets: Mercury, Moon; Elements: Earth and Air.

Frankincense: Exorcises, protects, and purifies. Raises spirituality. Planet: Sun; Element: Fire.

Ginger: Love, money, success, power. Planets: Mars, Sun; Element: Fire.

High John the Conqueror: Also called *bethroot.* You can carry a piece for extreme good luck in all matters. Success, prosperity, very good fortune. Planet: Sun; Element: Fire.

Juniper berries: Happiness, spiritual blessings, attracts love and psychic development. Protects against thieves. Planet: Sun; Element: Fire.

Lavender: Love, money, helpful spirits, calmness. Banishes negativity. Planet: Mercury, Jupiter; Element: Air.

Lemon verbena: Drives away evil. Repels a suitor you don't love. Planets: Venus, Jupiter; Elements: Air, Fire, Water.

Low John: Also called *galangal.* It can be carried whole as a good-luck charm. Its odor is similar to ginger. However, don't eat it! Knowledge, psychic development, good luck. Planets: Mars, Jupiter; Elements: Fire, Water.

Marigold flowers: Also called *calendula.* Add to pillows for psychic dreams. Use in fluid condensers to cleanse. Planet: Sun; Element: Fire.

Mugwort: Protects, strengthens divinatory powers; connects with spiritual teachers. Planet: Venus; Element: Air.

Myrrh: Purifies, protects; increases spirituality. Planet: Sun; Element: Water.

Nutmeg: Gambling, luck, love, prosperity. Buy this herb ground, or you will have to grate it. Planet: Jupiter, Mercury; Element: Air.

Orris root: Also called *Florentine iris;* use the ground herb. Has a scent like violets. It strengthens the odors of other ingredients. Helps divination; attracts the opposite sex. Love, faith, wisdom, and valor. Planets: Venus, Sun, Jupiter; Elements: Water, Fire, Earth.

Patchouli: Breaks up any spell. Helps defeat enemies. Money. Planets: Sun, Mars; Element: Earth.

Pepper, red: You also can use black pepper. Beware getting this around your face and eyes! Use it for protection. Planet: Mars; Element: Fire.

Peppermint: Purification, love, psychic ability. Connects with spiritual teachers. Planets: Venus, Moon; Element: Air.

Pine: Burn crushed, dried needles to purify a room. Fertility, purification. Planet: Mars; Element: Earth.

Rose petals: Love, happiness, spiritual blessings. Planet: Venus; Element: Water.

Rosemary: Grounds, exorcizes, banishes negativity, cleanses. Planet: Sun; Element: Fire.

Rue: Repels negativity; attracts the right love; gets things moving. Planets: Sun, Saturn; Element: Fire.

Sage: Purification, protection, wisdom. Planet: Jupiter; Element: Earth.

Sandalwood, yellow: Protection, exorcism, spirituality. Purchase this wood powdered. Planets: Moon, Mercury, Venus; Element: Air.

Savory: Love, sexual attraction, dreams, creative inspiration. Planet: Venus; Elements: Earth, Air.

Thyme: Strengthens psychic powers, purification, repels nightmares. One of the herbs loved by faeries. Planet: Venus; Element: Air.

Verbena: Repels psychic attack; attracts love; reduces stress. Purification, good health. Planets: Venus, Mercury; Element: Water.

Yarrow: Helps to gain confidence. Keeps couples happily married. Helps with divination by cleansing the environment. Planet: Venus; Element: Water.

Although a single herb can be as useful, a combination ordinarily has a stronger influence on a spell's vibrations. Use whichever method appeals most to you. However, it is helpful in your training to know how to make herbal blends.

If an old herbal formula says to use "one part" of an herb, it means that you set your measurement against the largest amount and work down. So if the largest "part" you decide is one tablespoon, all lesser amounts are calculated against the tablespoon. If I plan to reuse this kind of spell, I write down what quantities I used. The only vague measurement I'm comfortable with is a "pinch." That is very plainly the amount you can pick up between your thumb and forefinger.

Later in this chapter are a few samples of herbal combinations with spells for different types of magickal spells. After working with these for a time, you will understand how to devise your own combinations and write your own spells to suit your personal needs.

Always pass your wand over all spell ingredients on your altar before each spell. While moving the wand, concentrate on what this spell should do. This action seals the ingredients to the spell energy for which they will be used. Since an herbal mix, powder, or oil blend has more than one magickal use, it is best to put only the exact amount you will use in a spell on the altar. In this way, the remainder is free of other vibrations and can be used in other spells.

When making herbal mixes, oil combinations, herbal powders, and any other mixture according to an element, always cleanse the ingredients with your wand before combining the ingredients. Concentrate on the element involved in each of these.

After each spell, when the candles or any ashes are cold, dispose of them in the garbage along with any herbs used—that is, unless you put the herbs and wax into a charm bag or dragon wish box.

Some magicians believe the remains should be buried in the ground, which is impossible for most people to do. Besides, in a short time, a magician could have the entire neighborhood dug up and "polluted." That's definitely not a way to be a good neighbor or keep your magickal practices private.

A charm bag is simply a small bag or piece of cloth in which you put leftover herbs, candle wax, and stones in order to continue the spell energy for a longer period of time. The charm bag is often tied shut with a piece of red yarn. Sometimes, this bag is called a medicine bag. However, this bag can be any color and can be made or purchased.

The dragon wish box is a small decorated box in which you can store the same items, along with magickal symbols written on paper. Often, you may have more than one box on or nearby your altar. One may contain slips of paper with the names of people who request healings; another box may have similar papers with names of those who need a material need met. The third box will most certainly be for your own needs.

Blended Powders

Magickal powders consist of herbs and/or oils blended carefully with unscented talcum powder. If you don't have, or can't find, inexpensive talc, you can always use baking soda. Most powders are sprinkled lightly around the house, in the mailbox, or in a circle around a candle or photo during spellwork. A few can be used on the body of the person for whom the spell is done, by dusting lightly with a large puff. Money powders can be sprinkled in the purse or wallet and on what money you have to make it increase.

To make a powder, grind the chosen herbs into a fine consistency, like dust. Mix them with one-fourth cup of talcum powder in a bowl while adding a few drops of oils. Store the powdered mix in a sterile, labeled jar with a tight lid.

You will be instructed on how to use the following powder blends in certain compatible spells later in this chapter.

EARTH POWDER WITH CHANT

Finely grind together one-half teaspoon each of patchouli, pine needles, fennel seeds, and sage. Mix with the talc and add five drops of patchouli oil and one drop of pine oil. Chant while grinding:

> *From your mountain caverns deep,*
> *Rise, Earthen dragons, from your sleep.*
> *Lead me to riches, purpose true.*
> *Give me endurance. I call on you.*

AIR POWDER WITH CHANT

Finely grind together one teaspoon lavender flowers with one-half teaspoon each of lemon verbena, mugwort, and thyme. Mix with the talc and add five drops of sandalwood oil. Chant while grinding:

> *Dragons strong of cloud and wind,*
> *Help me a new cycle to begin.*
> *Quicken my mind, renew my life.*
> *Grant me joy free from strife.*

FIRE POWDER WITH CHANT

Finely grind together one teaspoon marigold petals with one-eighth teaspoon basil and one-half teaspoon betony. Mix with the talc and add two drops of cinnamon oil and one drop of rosemary oil. Chant while grinding:

> *In your cavernous, fire-filled hall,*
> *Echoes the request I now call.*
> *Stir my blood with opportunities bold,*
> *To create new changes from the old.*

Water Powder with Chant

Finely grind together one teaspoon orris root, one teaspoon yarrow, and one-fourth teaspoon each catnip and bergamot. Mix with the talc and add five drops of rose oil, one drop of verbena oil, and five drops of myrrh oil. Chant while grinding:

Calm water, moving water, deep hidden lakes,
I call now upon the elusive water drakes.
Whisper your dragon secrets straight to my heart,
Lift my spirit higher as mysteries you impart.

All-Purpose Powder with Chant

Grind together until fine one-fourth teaspoon patchouli, one half-teaspoon mugwort, one-eighth teaspoon allspice, and one teaspoon lemon verbena. Mix with the talc, and add one drop of sage oil, five drops of sandalwood oil, one drop of bay oil, and four drops of myrrh oil. Chant with grinding and mixing:

O great dragons, wondrous, wise,
Powers of Water, Earth, Fire, and skies,
Light and dark ones, join me here
To fill this mixture with energy clear.

Essential Oils

Several small bottles of certain essential oils will also be required, as well as capped empty dram bottles. All of the herbs, oils, and candles should be stored out of sunlight in a cool, dry place.

Some Enchanters believe that only pure oils should be used, not synthetics. However, some oils, like absolute rose, are prohibitive in cost. Other oils, such as musk and civet, are taken from live animals. I've never noticed any discernible difference in good synthetic oils and the "pure" ones. So I refuse to purchase ultra-expensive oils or those taken from animals. I suspect any lack of action of a synthetic lies in the mind of the Enchanter, not in the product. If you don't expect something to work, it won't.

Use a drop or two of the straight oil, or more if oils are mixed together in a sweet almond oil base, to anoint candles. Rub the oil from the wick to the end to attract something, and from the end to the wick to repel something. Take care when using straight oils, however, for some people are allergic to certain oils of that strength. And *never* ingest any of the oils or herbs. They are not meant to be eaten in magickal spells.

Later in this chapter there are several formulas for mixing two or more essential oils into a larger base of almond or virgin olive oil. By mixing the oils in this manner, you strengthen the energies of each oil, as well as getting more use out of the more expensive ones. Remember that if you can't afford, or don't have on hand, an oil called for in a spell, then substitute another with the same meaning or correspondence.

Amber: A man-made oil, not the stone. Happiness, love. Planet: Sun; Element: Fire.

Ambergris: Attracts high spiritual vibrations. Purest love. Clary sage resembles the odor of ambergris. Planet: Venus; Element: Water.

Bay: Protection, visions, divination, exorcism, purification. Planet: Sun; Element: Fire.

Bayberry: Prosperity, protection, controlling a situation. Planet: Jupiter; Elements: Earth, Fire.

Bergamot: Money, happiness. Planet: Jupiter; Elements: Fire, Earth.

Carnation: Healing, strength, protection. Planet: Sun; Element: Fire

Cedar or Thuja: Removes hexes. Good fortune, wealth, contentment. Attracts good spirits and repels negative. Planet: Jupiter; Elements: Fire, Earth.

Cherry: Peace, harmony, happiness, wealth, good fortune. Planet: Venus; Element: Water.

Cinnamon: Money, energy, protection, problem solving. Planet: Sun; Element: Fire.

Clove: Stimulates creativity. Drives away disease and evil influences. Planet: Sun; Element: Fire.

Cypress: Blessing, consecration, protection, repels negative vibrations at funerals. Cypress wood and actual essential oil could be dangerous, so clean your hands thoroughly after using. Planet: Saturn; Elements: Earth, Storm.

Frangipani: Love. Planet: Moon; Element: Water, Air.

Frankincense: Protection, purification, exorcisms, visions. Planet: Sun; Element: Fire.

Gardenia: Peace, love, harmony, healing, protection. Helps with marital problems. Planet: Moon; Element: Water.

Heliotrope: Wealth, protection, peace, harmony, aids psychic development. Planet: Sun; Element: Fire.

Honeysuckle: Money, psychic abilities, love, stimulates creativity. Planet: Jupiter; Element: Earth.

Hyssop: Increases finances; purifies. Planet: Jupiter; Element: Fire.

Jasmine: Love, money, psychic dreams and protection, astral travel. Helps attract and hold a lover. Planets: Moon, Jupiter; Elements: Earth, Water.

Lavender: Healing, love, exorcisms, peace. Planets: Mercury, Jupiter; Elements: Air, Fire.

Lemon: Repels negative spirits, thoughtforms, and spells. Planet: Mercury; Element: Air.

Lilac: Wards off evil. Helps to recall past lives. Stimulates mental powers. Planets: Moon, Mercury; Elements: Air, Water.

Lily of the Valley: Gives both spiritual and emotional peace. Planet: Mercury; Elements: Earth, Air.

Lotus: Protection, purification, good fortune, harmony, blessings, astral travel, visions. Planet: Moon; Element: Water.

Magnolia: Harmony, psychic development, meditation. Planet: Mercury; Element: Air.

Musk: Attracts the opposite sex. Prosperity, courage, determination. Planet: Saturn; Element: Earth.

Myrrh: Breaks hexes; helps psychic development. Protection, healing, meditation. Planet: Saturn; Elements: Earth, Storm.

Orange (Neroli) or Orange blossom: A women's oil to attract men. However, the scent can be repulsive if too much is used. Love, attraction, marriage proposals, balanced emotions. Planet: Sun; Elements: Water, Fire.

Patchouli: Love, protection. Use for a peaceful separation. Wards off evil. Planets: Mars, Saturn; Elements: Fire, Earth, Storm.

Peppermint: Stimulates creativity. Money, energy, life changes. Planets: Venus, Moon; Elements: Water, Air.

Pine: Protection, purification, exorcisms. Planet: Mars; Element: Earth.

Rose: Love, fertility, artistic creativity, health, balance. Planet: Venus; Elements: Water, Earth.

Rosemary: Protection, energy, exorcisms, determination, common sense, courage, repels nightmares, helps prophetic dreams. Just smelling this oil often cures headaches. Planets: Sun, Moon; Elements: Fire, Water.

Sage: Finding wisdom and truth. Purification. Planet: Jupiter; Element: Earth.

Sandalwood: Raises the vibrations. Cleansing, visions, protection, finding past lives. Planets: Mercury, Venus, Moon; Elements: Air, Water.

Strawberry: Helps in acquiring wealth and good fortune. Planet: Jupiter; Element: Earth.

Vanilla: Mental powers, sexual love, restores energy. Planet: Jupiter; Element: Fire.

Vervain: Removes hexes. Money, love, protection, good fortune, purification, stimulates intellectual creativity. Planets: Venus, Mercury; Elements: Water, Air, Earth.

Violet: Luck, love, protection, finding solutions, wards off evil, gives peace in marital problems, love, good fortune. Attracts faeries. Planet: Venus; Element: Water.

Wisteria: Unlocks the doors to the Otherworld. Opens the higher consciousness. Divination, astral travel, psychic work. Planet: Moon; Element: Water.

Ylang-ylang: Love, harmony. Soothes marriage problems. Attracts the opposite sex. Planets: Venus, Moon; Elements: Water, Earth.

Blended Oils

Blending essential oils into a base of jojoba, cold-pressed almond, or extra-light pure virgin olive oil is a fascinating project. Personally, I prefer almond oil for its smoothness and general absence of odor. You will need a very small glass measuring cup (like a shot glass); a toothpick; eyedroppers; rubbing alcohol to clean the droppers between using different oils; a stirring stick; and sterile, labeled, one dram vials with tight caps. Check that you have all the ingredients, or correct oil substitutions, and any specific instructions on timing. Label the vials before filling them, because any dripped oil will make it impossible to write on the label when you are finished. Also remember to date the bottles.

Start with small batches of the chosen blend, using just a teaspoon of the base oil. If you mix the blended oils in a measuring cup with a pouring spout, it will be easier to fill small vials when you are finished. No spouted measuring cup? Fill the little bottles by using an eyedropper. Add the essential oils, one drop at a time, to the base. Just remember, it's better to add another drop of an essential oil than to get too much the first time and have overly scented oil.

Make at least two blended oils that fit most of the spells you plan to do. If you need others at a later time, you will know how to mix them. It's always easier the second time to know which essential oils you prefer to mute, by adding less, and which you wish to emphasize, by adding more.

After blending all the oils together, hold the filled measuring cup in both hands and repeat the appropriate chant given with each blend. Concentrate on pouring the correct intent into the mixture. Fill and cap the vials. Store them in a dark, dry place out of sunlight and heat.

If you haven't used up the mixture after three years, check the odor of the oil. If it is rancid, or the scent is nearly gone, pour the oil down the drain. You should dispose of all outdated herbs, herbal mixtures, powders, waters, and blended oils at the end of three years. Essential oils last longer, but are ordinarily used before that deadline.

If you have blended oils on hand, you can make a candle spell more powerful—and do it with ease without having to wait to mix oils. And having blended the oils yourself, you'll know exactly what is in the blend and what the timing was when you made it. Of course, you can use a single essential oil on your candle if you wish. If you are undecided about this point, discuss using one or a blend with your dragons. They have far more knowledge on this subject than humans.

Herbs, oils, stones, planetary dragons, and Moon phases will require the most study in this section.

CINQUEFOIL OIL

This oil is very difficult to find on the market. It is easier to make your own. Put two ounces of the herb into a sterilized jar and cover with almond or jojoba oil. Let it sit in a warm place, out of direct sunlight, for at least two weeks. At the end of this time, strain the oil through a coffee filter, squeezing the oil out of the herbs as much as possible. Discard the herbs. Pour the oil into small, labeled bottles with tight lids.

DRAGON'S BLOOD OIL

Grind about a quarter to half an ounce of dragon's blood resin into as fine a powder as possible. Stir this into a sterilized jar containing a cup of almond or jojoba oil. Label the bottle and put on a tight lid. If the powdered resin is fine enough, you won't need to strain it through a coffee filter. Shake the jar well before using. It is good in spells to break curses, banish unwanted spirits, attract wealth and happiness, or give protection.

HIGH JOHN THE CONQUEROR OIL

It can be difficult to find this oil, also known as *jalap*. You can make your own by chopping a small root and adding it to a pint or less of almond or jojoba oil. Do this on a Full Moon, and let it steep until the next Full Moon before using it. If you decide to pour the oil into smaller containers, put a piece of root in each bottle. Label and cap tightly.

Also called *bethroot*. Use this oil in spells for success, prosperity, and very good luck.

LOW JOHN OIL

Low John oil, also called *galangal*, can be hard to find as well. To make this oil, follow the above instructions for making High John oil.

Its odor is similar to ginger. However, don't eat it! Use in spells for knowledge, psychic development, and good luck.

VAN VAN OIL

I decided to include the traditional formula for Van Van oil, since you are certain to run across it in spell books. This blend of oil is used to attract luck, love, and prosperity, as well as repel negative magick of any kind. It is a blend of five wild Asian grasses: lemongrass, citronella, palmarosa, gingergrass, and vetiver. All of these can be purchased as oils. However, gingergrass oil is extremely difficult to find. Van Van oil can also be purchased ready-made.

To make your own Van Van oil, add equal portions of the grasses to a sterilized jar and cover with jojoba oil or safflower oil. You can add patchouli for extra power. Let this mixture sit in a warm place, out of sunlight, for at least two weeks. Strain through a coffee filter into another vessel, then squeeze the soaked herbs to drain through the filter, too. Discard used herbs. Pour the oil into small labeled jars with tight lids.

EARTH OIL BLEND WITH CHANT

Add one Balm of Gilead bud and three drops of patchouli oil to one teaspoon of almond oil in a sterile, labeled bottle. Chant while holding the bottle:

> *Powers of stone born in bones of the Earth,*
> *By will of Earth dragons, your spark does leap forth.*
> *This mix is now powered with Multiverse song,*
> *While dragons lock in their power so strong.*

AIR OIL BLEND WITH CHANT

Add four drops of sandalwood oil and three drops of lavender oil to one teaspoon of almond oil in a bottle. Chant:

> *Whirling like leaves at the end of a storm,*
> *Air dragons blow energy into this bottle so warm.*
> *This mix is now powered with Multiverse song,*
> *While dragons lock in their power so strong.*

FIRE OIL BLEND WITH CHANT

Add five drops of frankincense oil, one drop of juniper berry oil, and a pinch of powdered dragon's blood to one teaspoon of almond oil in a small bottle. Chant:

> *Fire dragons leaping in dances of power,*
> *Fill this bottle with fiery energy this hour.*
> *This mix is now powered with Multiverse song,*
> *While dragons lock in their power so strong.*

WATER OIL BLEND WITH CHANT

Blend three drops of rose oil and seven drops of myrrh oil with one teaspoon of almond oil in a bottle. Chant:

> *Calm as a pool, or wildly riding the sea,*
> *Dragons of Water, empower this for me.*
> *This mix is now powered with Multiverse song,*
> *While dragons lock in their power so strong.*

ALL-PURPOSE OIL BLEND WITH CHANT

Add two drops of patchouli oil, one drop of peppermint oil, a pinch of dragon's blood powder, and five drops of bergamot oil to one teaspoon of almond oil in a small bottle. Chant while holding the bottle:

Earth and Air, Fire and Sea,
Bless this bottle with your energy.
This mix is now powered with Multiverse song,
While dragons lock in their power so strong.

Fluid Condensers

Fluid condensers aren't that difficult to make. Following are the directions for making condensers for Earth, Air, Fire, Water, and an all-purpose condenser. Later, as a Mystic, you will prepare a condenser to use strictly during scrying or divination.

Add several drops of the proper condenser to any herbal mixture, powder, or candle oil to increase that element power in the spell.

Use the same method to make each fluid condenser. Put the proper herbs in a ceramic pot and cover with pure spring water. Heat slowly until the water begins to boil. Put on a tight lid and reduce the heat to just a simmer. Continue to heat for fifteen minutes. Remove and strain out herbs. Carefully squeeze liquid from the herbs back into the pot. Reheat the liquid in the pot with the lid on until it simmers. Cook until the liquid is half the amount it was. Cool with the lid on the pot. Strain through a coffee filter and then pour into labeled bottles.

It is preferable to use bottles with eyedroppers as lids. This makes it easy to use the condenser fluid.

EARTH CONDENSER

Put five Balm of Gilead buds and equal amounts of savory, verbena, and boneset in the ceramic pot and cover with pure spring water. Heat as directed above.

When bottled, chant:

Earth powers here, in my hand,
I thank your mighty dragon band.
I trust their wisdom and their power
That helped me make magick in this hour.

AIR CONDENSER

Put equal amounts of lavender, lemon verbena, mugwort, and savory in the ceramic pot and cover with pure spring water. Heat as directed above.

When bottled, chant:

> *Wild as Storm, or soft as summer fair,*
> *This bottle holds the power of dragons of Air.*
> *I trust their wisdom and their power*
> *That helped me make magick in this hour.*

FIRE CONDENSER

Put equal amounts of angelica, bay leaves, chamomile, and marigold flowers in the ceramic pot and cover with pure spring water. Heat as directed above.

When bottled, chant:

> *Fiery removal of blocks far and near,*
> *Fire dragons empowered the condenser here.*
> *I trust their wisdom and their power*
> *That helped me make magick in this hour.*

WATER CONDENSER

Put equal amounts of rose petals, verbena, and yarrow flowers or leaves in the ceramic pot and cover with pure spring water. Heat as directed above.

When bottled, chant:

> *Water dragons, subtle yet bold,*
> *Energize this bottle that I hold.*
> *I trust your wisdom and your power*
> *That helped me make magick in this hour.*

ALL-PURPOSE CONDENSER

Put equal amounts of sage, peppermint, betony, and catnip in the ceramic pot and cover with pure spring water. Heat as directed above.

When bottled, chant:

> *Four element dragons, powerful and wise,*
> *Of Earth and Water, Fire and skies,*
> *I trust their wisdom and their power*
> *That helped me make magick in this hour.*
> *These four with me have magickally formed,*
> *The fifth, and most powerful, Storm.*

Waters and Washes

Many of the older spells, especially those from the southern states, call for such things as Florida water, war water, angel water, and holy water. You can easily make these yourself to have on hand if you should need them. I don't care for the waters that require high-proof vodka, and instead I substitute something else. That's just my preference.

For some of the waters there is more than one way to make them. I've only given one example each time.

ANGEL WATER

For true angel water, you cannot omit or replace the crucial ingredient—the leaves of the myrtle tree. The myrtle grows only in North Africa, on the Mediterranean coast, and along the southern Oregon coast. Although all the ingredients can be purchased as oils, it is preferable, if possible, to make an infusion. At least use myrtle leaves and rose petals. Put a cup of each of these into a ceramic pot and cover with spring water. Bring to a slow simmer. Cover the pot, remove from the heat, and let sit until cool. Add a dram of neroli (orange blossom oil). Strain through a coffee filter into a sterilized, labeled bottle. This is generally used in love spells.

HOLY WATER

Although many magicians, not all of them new to the practice, think this means only holy water from the Catholic Church, that isn't necessarily the case. History and tradition give a number of ways water can be considered holy: rainwater collected on Summer Solstice, May Eve, Spring Equinox, Autumn Equinox, Winter Solstice, Halloween, New Year's Day, or one's birthday. Also, rain falling during a Full Moon or a lunar eclipse can be holy. However, pure spring water with a little salt added, along with a quarter cup of rose water, is said to be holy water in Pagan circles.

Holy water is sprinkled for cleansing, purification, blessing, healing, banishing, and empowering objects.

If you can't collect at least two gallons of rainwater, get the same amount in pure spring water. Add two tablespoons of salt, along with a quarter cup of rose water (made or purchased), to each jug. Some even add a pinch or two of powdered dragon's blood resin. Place the jugs on your altar between two white candles. Light frankincense or white sage incense, then the candles. Pass the incense around each open jug, visualizing dragon power pouring into the water. Put the jugs back between the candles and tightly cap, then label them. Then the jugs on the altar until the candles burn out. Store the water in a cool, dry place, out of light.

FLORIDA WATER

There are many versions for making Florida water. All of them are extremely powerful for protection and cleansing.

- 2 cups of 90 proof vodka
- 2 tablespoons rose hydrosol
- 16 drops essential oil of bergamot
- 12 drops essential lavender oil
- 6 drops essential oil of orange flower water

- 3 drops essential oil of rosemary
- 2 drops essential oil of jasmine
- 2 drops rose attar

Mix all these together in a large container, and store in a tightly closed jug. Add to mop water when cleaning your house, especially the ritual room. If you have carpets, instead pour a little in a spray bottle and mist every room. External use only!

War Water

This is used for protection; it is an aggressive spiritual cleaner. It is also used to return any curse to its sender.

Collect rainwater in a jar while there is a fierce thunderstorm going on. Put nine to eleven rusty nails in the jar. If you can't get rusty nails, put either cut or plain iron nails in the jar. Put a lid tightly on the jar, opening it once daily to let in oxygen. In about ten days, the nails will begin to rust. Add enough water to fill the jar. Store the jar in a cool place. When the water is needed, strain out as much as you need at that time. Add more water and replace the lid. You can keep this going for years.

However, if mold or bacteria form, throw it all away, including the jar, and start a fresh batch.

If you use much of war water for returning curses and exorcisms, you might want to keep a second, much stronger, batch available. Kick it up by adding a half-teaspoon each of black and cayenne pepper to each jug. Be aware, however, that both peppers will burn if accidentally rubbed near the eyes.

Candle Colors

If you haven't done so, purchase a variety of colored candles and several sturdy metal candle holders. See the list given later in this chapter for the candle colors and their meanings.

If you burn votive candles in glass holders, carefully remove the metal plate on the bottom of the candle before anointing and burning. When this metal gets hot, it often cracks the container. Take hold of the wick with one hand while you carefully remove the metal with the other.

If the spell requires that you burn a candle for a short period of time, then extinguish it and light it again later. You will need to trim the wick before the next lighting. This will prevent heavy smoke and soot from going into the air. It is traditional and more in keeping with the magickal atmosphere you created to use a candle snuffer instead of blowing out the candles. Or you can quickly pinch out the flame with your fingers. I use a snuffer if possible, but I refuse to pinch out a hot flame. Some ridiculous ideas have arisen about blowing out the flame, including that you will kill faeries, blow away the spell's energy, or lose your luck. None of these are true.

For candle magick, have a cloth or paper towels ready to clean your hands after using an oil. If you are burning more than one candle at a time, and each requires a different oil, be certain to clean your hands between oils.

Also have a lighter at hand to light the candles. Most Enchanters do not like to add the smell of matchstick sulfur to the spell vibrations. Nor do they like the odor of the fuel used in small lighters. However, there are now candle lighters that are easy to use and leave little odor behind. If there are children in your household, the candle lighter is safer to have around.

Some spells call for you to engrave symbols or names on the candle with a nail. Do this before applying the oil. If you are using a seven-day candle in a glass container, write the symbols or names on a piece of paper. Slip the paper under the candle container and burn the paper when the candle goes out. To oil such a candle, simply put a few drops of oil on the top and spread it over the top with your fingers.

If you want to use the glass container again, let the remaining wax at the bottom of the jar cool completely. Put very warm water in a pan, and hold the container bottom down in the water. As soon as the remaining spot of wax begins to melt, use a long knife or spoon handle to loosen the edges. Then simply dump out the old wax. Next time you need a container candle, purchase the free-standing, tall pillar candles in the needed color. Just make certain the candles aren't the big thick ones that won't fit the glass. Etch the symbols and/or names on the candle and apply oil before you stand it in the old container. This process can be repeated many times. Out with the old. In with the new.

If you wish, you can either roll the oiled candle in the appropriate powdered herbs or sprinkle a ring of these herbs around the candle in its holder.

Several candle magick spells are given in this chapter. If you study them closely, you will be able to write your own spells using the proper colors and ingredients for whatever intent you have in mind. There are no rules that say you can't write spells or rituals to suit your personal needs.

Although you can scratch any symbol or writing on a candle, it helps to use a different alphabet and to use symbols that especially coordinate a full meaning into one design. The shaman symbols are good for this, as are the planetary signs and the rune symbols in the graph.

Black: A very powerful color that requires care when using it. Absorbs and removes all negative vibrations; binds negative forces; reverses, uncrosses, protects, releases, breaks up blockages, moves stagnant situations. Creates confusion and discord among your enemies.

Blue: Take care if you use royal blue, for it's a strong color. Use it for happiness, loyalty, psychic power, and expansion. Light blue is used for truth, inspiration, wisdom, understanding, harmony, good health, and protection on the mental/emotional level.

Brown: Use this color when wishing to communicate with the Earth elementals. Attracts money, financial success, study, and employment. Use to concentrate, balance, overcome a financial crisis, strengthen ESP and intuition, and fulfill basic material needs.

Gold, or very clear light yellow: Helps with great fortune, intuition, understanding, divination, fast luck, and financial problems. It attracts higher influences (such as dragons), knowledge, money, and healing.

Green: This hue is associated with abundance, fertility, good fortune, material gain, wealth, success, renewal, marriage, healing, and communication with nature spirits. It also balances an unstable situation.

Indigo: This purplish-blue, almost black, color belongs to Saturn. It helps with meditation, and it neutralizes another's magick. It also balances karma and stops gossip, lies, or undesirable competition.

Magenta: This color is burned with other colors to make things happen very fast, It is burned alone for quick changes, spiritual healing, and exorcisms. It is a very dark but clear red with a deep purple tint to it. This color could be called cranberry or maroon.

Orange: A vibrant, powerful color: be certain you want major changes in your life before using it. It helps with adaptability, encouragement, attraction, sudden changes, prosperity, creativity, change of luck, success, energy and stamina, and mental clarity.

Pink: This color can banish hatred, depression, and negativity. It is also associated with pure true love, friendship, affectionate romance, spiritual awakening and healing, and family love.

Purple: The powerful energies from this color can be difficult for beginners to handle. It helps with success, idealism, higher psychic ability, wisdom, progress, protection, spirit contact, greater knowledge, success in court cases, and business success. It also removes jinxes and hexes.

Red: Can be used to protect against psychic attack or to conquer fear or laziness. Associated with energy, strength, physical desire, passionate love, courage, willpower, and good health.

Silver or very clear light gray: Neutralizes any negative situation and repels destructive forces. It helps to develop psychic abilities and helps with victory, stability, and meditation.

White: When in doubt about a candle color, use white for its highly balanced vibrations. It raises vibrations and destroys destructive energies. Use for greater attainments in life, contacting spirit helpers, balancing the aura, confusing enemies, childbirth, purity, truth, sincerity, and power of a higher nature.

Yellow: It helps with intellect, imagination, power of the mind, creativity, confidence, attraction, concentration, mental clarity, knowledge, commerce, medicine, counseling, and healing.

Even after you become more skilled with magickal spells, you will find that sometimes you just don't get results, or you get the wrong results. Your failure may well be caused by one of the reasons given in the following list:

1. You are trying to force another person to do something against his or her will or ethics.
2. Your intent and concentration aren't strong or clear enough.
3. Your emotional energy isn't 100 percent behind the spell.
4. You are asking for too many things out of one spell.
5. You aren't allowing enough time for the results to manifest. Manifestation can take from a couple of weeks to six months, depending upon the results you want and the number of possible people involved for this to happen.
6. You think or talk about the spell. You have to release any connection to the magickal energy for a spell to work.
7. What you want isn't for your highest good. Be very happy if this last reason is why your spell didn't work. Ninety-eight percent of the time, magick will manifest what you ask for, even if the manifestation ends up making you miserable.

Spells, at Last!

All spells and rituals should begin by welcoming in your dragon helpers with the Welcome Dragons Chant. After the spell itself is finished (although an entire ritual may not be), chant the Charm of Making. If you begin by inviting your dragons to help with the spell and end with a statement of manifestation, you are setting into motion a powerful surge of cosmic dragon energy that is certain to bring about your desire.

If you have cast a circle, you will need to thank the guardian and "cut" the magickal circle, sending remaining energy into the Earth. Later in this section, an entire ritual is provided, should you decide you want to do one. However, you will probably find that you only do full rituals for a few important issues and use shorter spells for most of what you do in magick.

WELCOME DRAGONS CHANT

When you are ready to perform your spell, stand before your altar and open your mind to the dragons. Chant:

Dragons, welcome to this space, not of time and not of place.
Help me make magick strong tonight. Clear out the darkness. Create new light.
Draconis!

CHARM OF MAKING

By glow of Sun, the power's begun.
By moonbeam's light, the spell is right,
To create desire by Earth and Fire.
Water, Air, make magick fair.
Powerful Charm of Making, creative magickal undertaking.
By Storm, be formed!

HALT EVIL SPELL

Time: Waning Moon.
Ingredients:

- 1 tablespoon patchouli
- 1 black candle
- metal holder
- saucer
- 1 sharp knife
- ½ teaspoon verbena
- ¼ teaspoon lavender blossoms
- 2 tablespoons salt
- ⅛ teaspoon peppermint leaves
- 1 sliced lemon

Use during a waning Moon to break any negative spells or to remove any bad spirits or vibrations from a building. This spell is good for the times you feel under attack in your home and aren't sure why, or aren't sure what or who is behind the attack. Often, the negativity simply is a buildup of thoughtforms from other people, personal negative events or problems, or spirits who drop in unannounced and who don't have anything to do with you. If you follow this spell with a good sage smudging of the entire house, you should feel a positive atmosphere immediately.

Chant the dragon welcome.

104

Grind the herbs to a fine powder while chanting:

> *From whole to dust, these herbs will go, to stop all negative power flows.*
> *This is my will. Then make it so.*

Stir in the salt, saying: *One, two, three, four; evil is gone forever more.*

Oil a black candle from the end to the wick with a protection oil of your choice. Place the candle in a holder on your altar and light it while thinking about the vibrations that must leave.

Put the lemon on a saucer, slice it crosswise into five slices, and arrange the slices around the saucer so they don't overlap. Sprinkle the herbs and salt over the lemon while saying:

> *Bitter taste and blackened heart. Return to sender. Now depart!*
> *Whether you be from Air or Earth, I take away your power and worth!*

Chant the Charm of Making, and leave the candle to burn out.

Check the lemon slices daily. If they dry out, the spell worked. If they mold, you need to repeat the spell. Throw away the moldy lemon, wash the saucer well, and use a new lemon in the repeat spell.

When the lemon is dried, throw the slices, the herbs, and any remaining candle wax into the garbage.

Conquer in Court and Legal Matters

This spell works equally well to win court cases, sway judges to your cause, or remove all curses or negative thoughtforms.

Time: New Moon.

Ingredients: 1 indigo candle; 1 magenta candle; holders; frankincense incense stick; metal bowl; two small bags or squares of white cloth with red thread to tie closed. One tablespoon each of vetavert and bergamot; patchouli oil.

Light the incense and the candles, and lay out your other ingredients on your altar or workspace. Grind together High John the Conqueror root (small piece) and a tablespoon each of vetavert and bergamot. Add a drop of patchouli oil or a condenser. As you blend the mix, chant:

> *See that my case is just and fair,*
> *Judges of Earth, Fire, Water, Air.*
> *All legal challenges find success for me.*
> *No harm will come. I am found free.*

Divide the herb mixture, putting half in each bag or cloth. If you use squares of white cloth you can gather together the ends and tie them tightly with red thread. Or you can sew the edges of the cloth together. Leave one sachet bag on your altar. Carry the other with you, especially into the courtroom. "Feed" each bag daily with one drop of patchouli oil.

Break Bad Luck

Sometimes, the only way you can get ahead is to first change your luck. We often get into a bad luck pattern and don't realize that we can get out. This spell can break even the worst kind of bad luck.

Time: Waning or New Moon.

Ingredients: One lemon; whole cloves and short sewing pins with colored heads; a teaspoon of salt; jasmine oil; one tablespoon of ground patchouli; one-fourth cup of talcum powder; red yarn; a small dish to hold the lemon.

Mix the salt, patchouli, and talcum powder with four drops of jasmine oil, and put the combination in the bowl. Lay out the sewing pins, whole cloves, and lemon. If the lemon has a tough skin, use an ice pick or a darning needle to make holes in the skin so you can insert the cloves and pins. This part of the spell will take some time, so sit in a chair if you need to.

Stick pins and cloves into the lemon until the entire fruit is covered with them. As you do this, say: *A change is coming. It is now at my door.*

When you are finished, roll the lemon in the herb-salt mix. Leave the lemon in the dish, turning it each day to thoroughly coat the fruit. After a week, when the lemon is beginning to dry, wrap the red yarn around it a few times, leaving enough at one end of the yarn to hang up the decorated lemon. Each time you see it, think of your change of luck from bad to good.

Confusion to Enemies

This spell works on all enemies, especially anyone who is trying to control you and your life. It confuses them in such a manner that you soon are free of their interest. It will also break a hex.

Time: Waning Moon.

Ingredients: One black candle; a teaspoon each of verbena, lavender, patchouli, and galangal; one-fourth cup of talcum powder; a person figure cut out of white paper; a small nail for each poppet. A gingerbread man cookie cutter is an ideal size and shape for making poppets out of paper or cloth.

Oil the black candle with patchouli oil, moving from the candle base to the wick. Put it in a safe holder where you can leave it to burn out.

If you know for certain the person who is trying to exert control, write their name across the middle of the paper poppet. If this involves more than one person, make extra paper poppets and write one name on each. Draw in the facial features.

Mix the herbs together with the talcum powder while chanting:

> *As round and round this spoon does go,*
> *This mix with dragon energy grows.*
> *A fog builds thick so you cannot see,*
> *And blinds your mind to thoughts of me.*

Take the poppet or poppets, the nails, and the herbal powder with you as you go outside. If you are not placing the poppets in hidden places in your own yard, choose an out-of-the-way, slightly remote place for them. Don't put them all in the same place, although they can be placed within a reasonable distance of each other. Lay the poppet on the ground, and push (or pound) the nail through the paper, anchoring the poppet to the Earth. After you nail down the poppet, sprinkle some of the mixture over the complete body of the paper doll. Say:

> *Your desires of ill are buried here. I am set free of doubt or fear.*

As the weather or other forces destroy the poppet, so will the controlling person's desire and abilities be disintegrated.

If the weather is too bad at the time of the spell to go outside, put the poppets in a resealable plastic bag and put them into the freezer. The plastic bag prevents contamination of the freezer food and, while being in the freezer, freezes the offenders' actions. When you can nail them to the ground, that will permanently end their energy.

To make cloth poppets, cut out two figures from cheap cloth. Sew the two pieces together except for an opening on one side. Using a black pen, draw facial features on one side of the head. Stuff the body thinly with an herbal mixture and perhaps a little cotton filler. Sew the opening shut. You have a poppet you can use for protection or healing.

This is a very good spell to use when binding or tripping wrongdoers. Use this instead of a hex or curse so that the offenders find themselves unable to continue with crimes and are caught by their own actions.

Build an Invisible Wall

This little protection spell can be used whenever you need it, as often as you need it. It is stronger if you smudge every room of your house after doing this.

Time: Waning Moon.

Ingredients: One cup of salt; one-fourth teaspoon ground dragon's blood; one teaspoon ground rosemary needles.

Mix together the herbs and salt. Chant:

> *A wall I build so you can't see*
> *Whatever I do or wherever I be.*

Carry the mix outside, and sprinkle it thinly around the entire house. Visualize your house and property covered by an unbreakable bubble that reflects all incoming energies and spells.

LUCKY GAMBLER

Many people carry lucky charms, even when they play bingo. This is an enhanced version of a lucky charm.

Time: Waxing Moon.

Ingredients: A small lucky charm that appeals to you; a small drawstring bag; a vanilla bean; a bay leaf; and a small piece of galangal root.

Chant "Lucky charm, lucky me" while you put all the items into the bag and pull the strings tight. Reactivate the spell when you need it by touching the bag and silently repeating the chant.

LUCKY LODESTONE

Instead of carrying this lucky charm, you put a drop of the oil on a finger and then touch any money you have. Doing so helps attract more money.

Time: Waxing Moon.

Ingredients: A sterilized pint jar and lid; one lodestone with a pinch or two of iron filings; half a cup of almond oil; one teaspoon of lavender blossoms; a tablespoon of ground mint leaves.

Put the lodestone in the jar and sprinkle the iron filings on it. Pour the oil over the stone. Stir in the lavender blossoms and mint leaves while chanting:

> *Lucky lodestone, bring to me only opportunities,*
> *Fill my life with prosperity bold; rolls of money I can hold.*

BUSINESS LUCK

You can sprinkle this powder into your mailbox, your cash register, purse, or around the inside of your business and over the threshold of the main door. This is basically a quick-acting luck powder.

Time: Full Moon.

Ingredients: A half-cup of talcum powder; oils of frankincense, heliotrope, cinnamon, and sandalwood; a small packet of gold glitter (found in craft stores); a small piece of paper with the money rune drawn on it.

Put the talc and glitter together in a bowl. Add four drops of frankincense, two drops of heliotrope and sandalwood, and one drop of cinnamon oil. As you mix these together, chant:

> *Business luck comes through my door,*
> *And stays with me forever more.*

Tuck the paper with the money symbol into the powder container.

Remove Obstacles to Success

Begin this spell seven days before a Full Moon, counting the night of the Full Moon as the seventh day. Burn one candle each night in the order given. Try to repeat the spell each night at the same time.

This is a very detailed spell to open all roads to success and to remove and avoid any barriers and blocks.

Time: Waxing Moon.

Ingredients: One candle in each of the following colors: white, orange, blue, yellow, red, purple, and green; a metal holder. Seven sticks of frankincense incense. Oils: frankincense and honeysuckle. Stones in seven different colors, plus your personal crystal. A metal bowl and dragon statue or symbol. Also include any small statues or images of Otherworld creatures such as faeries, unicorns, and such. A small amount of blended herbs of success. Paper and pen. A small dish of water and one of salt.

Put *all* of the items needed for this spell near the sides of the altar, and cleanse them with your wand. Put the altar candle to the center back in a holder, the dragon statue on one side of it, and the incense holder on the other side. Set the water next to the incense and the salt next to the statue.

First night: Oil the white candle with frankincense from the wick to the bottom, then place it in the holder. Light the candle and incense. Write out in detail a letter of intent, stating what you desire, why, and what you plan to do when it manifests. Place the paper in the center of the altar. Spend a few moments visualizing success—not the form in which it will arrive, but simply success. Say this spell ending:

> *This intent, or something better, now comes to me through dragon aid. If the energy of this spell rebounds, it will be grounded at once in the Earth, that no harm comes to anyone. I await the manifestation.*

Let the candle burn out.

Second night: Dispose of remaining wax and incense ashes. Rub honeysuckle oil on the orange candle from the wick to the end; then put it in the holder and light it. Light a new incense stick. Read aloud your letter of intent. Make any changes in the wording if you feel it is necessary. Replace the paper, and say:

> *For change I call, and change must come.*
> *Success is mine. My quest is done.*

Say the spell ending and let the candle burn out.

Third night: Dispose of wax and ashes. Oil the blue candle with frankincense and put it in the holder. Light new incense. Again, read aloud the letter and put it back on the altar. Say:

> *My heart is set to reach this goal.*
> *I claim the prize. My life is whole.*

Close as before.

Fourth night: Begin as before. Rub the yellow candle with honeysuckle from the wick to the end and put it in the holder. Light it and the incense. Read the letter of intent and put it back on the altar. Say:

> *Ideas come like flashes of light,*
> *To help me plan and win this fight.*

Close as before.

Fifth night: Begin as before. Rub the red candle with frankincense oil from the wick to the end and put the candle in the holder. Light it and the incense. Read the letter and put it back on the altar. Say:

> *Honest action I will take. Intent I steady hold,*
> *Within my mind and in my heart. To win I must be bold.*

Close as before.

Sixth night: Begin as before. Rub honeysuckle oil on the purple candle and put it in the holder. Light it and the incense. Read the letter and put it back. Say:

> *A balanced life is what I seek. Happiness for all.*
> *Dragons wise and full of power, please aid me now, I call.*

Close as before.

Seventh night: Begin as before, making certain the altar is clean. Rub the green candle with frankincense oil from the wick to the end and put it in the holder. Light it and new incense. Place the seven stones in a circle around the candle. Put the metal bowl in front of the candle. Read your letter of intent and place it near the bowl. Sprinkle the herbs around the candle also. Set the Otherworld images near the dragon statue. Hold your personal crystal in one hand. While looking at the dragon, say:

> *Once more I call you, dragons wise,*
> *Of Fire and Earth, of seas and skies,*
> *To clear all paths that you can see,*
> *Between me now and victory.*

Indicate the Otherworld images and say:

> *Otherworld creatures who choose me to teach,*
> *I ask for full power that my goal I can reach.*

Look at your personal crystal. Say:

> *Precious one of power and might, I open to your wisdom this night.*

Close your eyes. Open to any thoughts that might come, thoughts to help you or to advise changing your goal. Lay the crystal on the altar. Point to the colored stones and herbs encircling the candle. Say:

Everything in the Multiverse is connected. All is part of the unknowable energy that created everything. I thank the dragons for helping me.

With your letter in hand, look at the dragon image again and say:

For seven nights I stood before you. Dragons, seven times you heard my desire.
You read my heart. You know the truth. You feel my secret intent's fire.
I ask that you send my spells on wings, to gather power to manifest,
So that success will make me sing, and will fulfill my needful quest.

Light the paper from the candle and drop it into the metal bowl to burn. Raise both of your arms high and say:

I call Earth to bind my spell, Air to speed its travel well.
Bright as Fire shall it glow, deep as tide of Water flow,
Count the elements fourfold, and in the fifth the spell shall hold.
So shall it be!

Close as before. When the wax and ashes are cool enough to dispose of, do so. Again thank the dragons and all helpers when the cleanup is finished. Say:

In no way shall this spell cause me or mine to suffer any negative effects. When the time of this spell's magick is finished, all unused energy will return harmless to the Cosmic Void.

After all, the last thing you want wandering uncontrolled around your environment, or life, is a ball of energy without a purpose.

True Love Come to Me

This powder can be used by both men and women. If you put this mixture into a small box with a powder puff, you can easily brush a little on you without looking as if you got hit by the kitchen flour.

Time: Waxing Moon.

Ingredients: Small box and puff; a half cup of unscented talcum powder; oils of jasmine, red rose, lavender, musk, and ylang ylang; one deep pink candle.

Carve the symbol rune for love on the candle and light it, saying:

This flame of love goes out to attract the best lover for me.

Put the talc into a bowl. Add three drops of jasmine, one drop of red rose, five drops of musk, and three drops of ylang ylang oil. As you mix, chant:

Lover, sweet lover, please look for me.

Love harmony waits for me and thee.

Pour the mix into the powder box. Use just a little of this powder whenever you plan to go out somewhere, even for groceries. You never know where you will find that special person.

DRAGON FRIENDSHIP

You can sprinkle this powder on your altar at any time, as a gift to the dragons who help you, or to attract dragons to enjoy your company.

Time: Full Moon.

Ingredients: A sterilized jar or container; half a cup of unscented talcum powder; a small piece of paper with the symbol of the dragon's eye drawn on it; oils of carnation, gardenia, lotus, and wisteria.

Put the talc into a bowl for mixing. Add four drops of carnation, four of lotus, three of gardenia, and seven of wisteria oil. As you blend together, chant:

> *I call to dragons, near and far, to join with me where'ere you are.*
> *I'll share with you a happy heart, when we meet and when we part.*

BINDING A PERSON

Sometimes it becomes necessary to bind a person's actions. Be very certain that the person in mind is the offender. Use this only on people willfully causing you trouble. If you use this spell on someone you just dislike, or consider a rival, it will rebound on you, bringing negative karma with it.

Time: Best done during the waning Moon.

Ingredients: Three pieces of thread, each a foot long, one each in red, black, and white.

The first knot ties one end of the three threads together. Continue to tie the threads together with each knot, and tie them in the numerical order shown below. After the last knot, burn the threads.

$$—X—X—X—X—X—X—X—$$
$$1 \quad 4 \quad 2 \quad 5 \quad 3 \quad 6 \quad 7$$

> *(Knot 1) In the name of the Great Lady, I bind you.*
> *(Knot 2) In the name of the powerful Lord, I bind you.*
> *(Knot 3) For the good to yourself, me, and mine, I bind you.*
> *(Knot 4) I bind your energy and intent that it isn't used against me.*
> *(Knot 5) I bind your harmful thoughts and wishes.*
> *(Knot 6) I bind your magick so it cannot find me.*
> *(Knot 7) Six knots I tied to justice find. The seventh knot makes victory mine.*

Burn the threads in a metal bowl. When cool, dispose of the ashes.

BINDING AN ACTION OR EVENT

Occasionally, you will find yourself caught in a negative action or event not of your making, uncertain who is causing the problem. Use a piece of black thread about a foot long. Although this is best done during a waning Moon, use it whenever there is a need. Call upon the dragons for extra power at this time.

As you tie each knot, concentrate on the purpose and visualize what is being bound. Tie the knots in the numerical order given, while saying:

—X—X—X—X—X—X—

2   4   1   6   5   3

Help me, dragons, old and wise, of Earth, Air, Fire, and skies.
Bind, bind, tie, and bind. Nothing moves but me and mine.
Static action is my will. These knots will now my wish fulfill.

Burn or bury the knotted thread.

There may be times when you need quick binding action as protection, and times when you don't have a thread or the time to do a spell. If you simply need to bind someone or something for a brief time—such as getting out of the area, away from their presence, or stopping an argument or possible incident until you are gone—silently tie a knot in whatever is available: shirt bottom, shoelace, hair ribbon, piece of grass, anything flexible enough to bend. Tie the knot right then, not when trouble jumps right on you.

STORING AND USING FULL MOON ENERGY

It is also useful to have Full Moon energy stored in a cord, ready to use during a waning Moon if a problem arrives. Do this knot spell on the Full Moon, using a white, silver, or gold thin cord about two feet long. Don't make the knots too tight, as you will want to untie them and use the energy at some time.

Nine is a magickal Moon number, so you will tie nine knots in the order given. Say the appropriate chant-line as you tie that knot.

—X—X—X—X—X—X—X—X—X—

1   2   3   4   5   6   7   8   9

Knot of one, this spell's begun.
Knot of two, my intent is true.
Knot of three, my will shall be.
Knot of four, power into this knot I pour.
Knot of five, the power I store is alive.
Knot of six, this power I fix.
Knot of seven, I add the leaven.
Knot of eight, to untie it waits.
Knot of nine, the threes are trine.

Full Moon energy lies in this cord,
Bound by the knots and my magickal word.
Full Moon strength is stored this night,
For later use by my spells so bright.

As a noun, the word *leaven* means "yeast," an ingredient that makes another ingredient start action to grow bigger.

If you need Full Moon energy during a waning Moon, simply untie each knot in the reverse order in which it was tied, saying:

I open the Moon Gate with my magickal key,
That I might reach the kind of power I need.
Full Moon magick fills my hands and eyes,
And the intent of my spell brings me the prize.

STORING AND USING NEW MOON ENERGY

Tie up waning Moon energy on the night of the New Moon, using a dark purple or black cord about two feet long. Thirteen is a strong magickal number, denoting the thirteen Moon months of each lunar year. Tie the knots in the order given as you chant. Keep chanting for as long as you tie knots. However, you don't have to repeat the chant for each knot.

$$—X—X—X—X—X—X—X—X—X—X—X—X—X—$$
$$1 \quad 2 \quad 3 \quad 4 \quad 5 \quad 6 \quad 7 \quad 8 \quad 9 \quad 10 \quad 11 \quad 12 \quad 13$$

I bind New Moon energy into each knot I make,
So there it grows stronger and safely waits.
When I release this energy in Full Moon time,
I will weave it into a spell to fulfill a wish of mine.

If you need New Moon energy during a waxing Moon, untie the knots in the reverse order in which they were tied, saying:

Dark Moon powers, strong and bright,
I unbind your energy here tonight.
Your hidden links to Air, Earth, Fire, and sea
Are mine to command. So will it be!

RED CORD OF FORTUNE AND DRAGON CHARM BAG

Dragons love the color red, especially the Eastern dragons. You can do this spell for yourself, or for someone else as a gift. You need a small red bag or Chinese purse that can be closed, and a thin red cord or piece of yarn about twelve inches long.

Time: During a waxing or Full Moon.

Tie four knots in the cord while saying:

> *One knot for luck. Two knots for wealth.*
> *Three knots for love. Four knots for health.*

Put the knotted cord into the red bag. If this is for you, place it on your altar or in a safe place. You can always add corresponding stones, herbs, and charms. You can draw symbols or planetary signs, and even put a drop or two of the correct oil on a cotton ball and place it in the bag with the cord.

For example, you can draw a Sun symbol, as shown in the Shaman stones, on a small paper. On the reverse side of the paper, draw the Jupiter sign. Hold the paper in your hands and chant:

> *Success and money from my work comes to me.*
> *Opportunities come. So will it be.*

Fold the paper over some small item that represents your job, then add it to the dragon charm bag.

Dissolve/Stop and Ground a Spell

Sometimes it becomes necessary to stop and dissolve a spell as well as ground its energy. Perhaps you didn't think through the spell's actions well, or you used a name when you shouldn't have. Or the spell is wildly flapping around the Multiverse and not manifesting. Or it appears to be manifesting in a way you didn't want. Remember: you are responsible for what you create.

Time: Any time, but is best done during the waning Moon or on the New Moon.

Ingredients: The same herbs you used in the original spell, but not talc powder if you used that. A black candle and a magenta candle. Use a Saturn oil of your choice for the black candle, and a Sun oil of your choice for the magenta candle. A small paper on which you write the name of the spell you do, along with a drawing of the dragon's eye symbol. A metal bowl or cauldron for burning objects.

Rub Saturn oil on the black candle from the bottom to the middle, then from the wick to the middle. Set it in a holder in the middle back of your altar. Rub the Sun oil on the magenta candle from the wick to the bottom. Set it in a holder next to the black candle.

Put the metal bowl in front of the candles, with the paper you've written on in the bottom. Sprinkle the herbs on top of the paper. You might want to have a long metal knife or wire available so you can lift the paper as it burns. This will help burn all of the paper.

Light the black candle and say:

> *This spell I sent returns to me. I stop its travel, three times three.*
> *Its power flows into the ground, that on me it won't rebound.*
> *Earth, Air, Water, Fire, dragons all, this is my desire.*
> *By Storm, be done!*

Light the magenta candle and say:

> *Faster than a dragon's thought, this spell's intent shall come to naught.*
> *Its desire and purpose I set free. This I do want. So must it be.*

By using the example spells I've given here, you can learn to write your own, if you so desire. The dragons are very good at helping with this, so ask for their aid.

Please consider that about 90 percent of suspected curses are misread intuitive feelings, simple ill-wishing by jealous people, or leftover energy balls that you forgot to ground. Even if the problem is a curse from another magician, you should protect yourself by binding, rather than sending a curse. If you are arrogant enough to play spell-tennis with a rival magician, you always run the risk that the tennis ball of energy will get out of control and explode. It invariably does. Then the negative karma lists for you both get any number of "bad" points added. The best revenge is to keep your home smudged with sage on a regular basis. This prevents any negative spells gaining entrance. The very best revenge of all is to live a good, happy, fulfilled life.

Crystals and Stones in Magick

The Enchanter will find many magickal uses for stones. Minerals, which are what stones are, hold magickal power and disperse it longer when placed around a candle, in a dragon box, or in a charm bag.

It is also very useful if you obtain a flat stone, at least as long as the width of your two palms, to use as a sink stone for your altar. You pour positive energy into this stone as often as you can. If you feel a resistance to your hands when held above the sink stone, you will know it is ready to use. Most stones used this way often take a little while at first to radiate energy. What you are doing with the stone is making it one of your personal magickal tools and recharging it. Depending upon the individual stone, you may have to cleanse it of negative vibrations or spend several weeks getting it powered up, or you may find it is ready to use at once. You also can power small stones as stone batteries for travel or add them to charm bags and dragon boxes.

You will find it easier to identify individual types of stones if you use a sectioned craft box. You can write the stone name on a small label for each section. This method of storage is helpful, too, if you decide to collect different stone pendulums to help in your work. Often two pieces of the same kind of stone will not look quite alike, or a stone's coloring may make you confused because it resembles a different type of stone.

You may use small tumbled chips of the following stones listed below. It is not imperative that you choose more than one stone for each Ring level. Choose a stone with a price that meets your financial resources and attracts you. If the stone doesn't feel right to you, however much you want it, don't take it, even if it is free. How a stone, or a tool, feels in your hand is the most important indication of your ability to work with the object.

Stones by Color

Black: General defense; binding; repelling negative thoughts or dark magick; reversing thoughtforms and spells into positive power. Ruled by Saturn. Dragons: Grael, Bullakasz. Elements: Earth, Storm.

Blue: Healing, harmony and understanding; journeys of the body or mind; calm emotions; restful sleep; purifying. Ruled by Neptune (greenish-blue), Jupiter (medium blue), Uranus (iridescent blue), the Moon (very pale blue). Dragons: Vunoket, Yanizar, Keetan, the Moon and Element dragons. Elements: Earth, Water, Air.

Brown: Amplifies all Earth element magick and psychic abilities; opens communication with all nature beings. Ruled by Earth. Dragon: Grael. Element: Earth.

Green: Fertility on all levels; money; marriage; good health; grounding and balancing; growth. Ruled by Venus. Dragons: Shemaleth, Naelyon. Element: Water.

Indigo or blue-green: Discovering past lives or karmic problems; balancing out karma; new and unique ideas. Ruled by Neptune, Saturn. Dragons: Bullakasz, Vunoket, Grael, Naelyon. Elements: Water, Earth.

Orange: Changing luck; protection by control of a situation; illumination; personal power; building self-worth; attracts luck and success. Ruled by the Sun, Mercury. Dragons: Salaquet, Talm, Fafnir, Sairys. Elements: Fire, Air.

Pink: Healing; true love; friendship; relaxation; smooths difficulties; peace; happiness. Ruled by Venus. Dragon: Naelyon. Element: Water.

Purple: Breaks bad luck; protection; success in long-range plans; spiritual growth. Ruled by Jupiter (pure purple), the Moon (pale lavender). Dragons: Memezah, Yanizar, Naelyon, Sairys. Elements: Water, Air.

Red: Energy; courage; defense; physical love and sexuality; strength; power; rebirth. Ruled by Mars (pure red), Pluto (deep reds, maroon). Dragons: Grael, Charoseia, Durankayta, Zeirahnak. Elements: Fire, Earth, Storm.

White: Spiritual guidance; Moon magick; visions and dreams; divination; carry to attract good luck and fortune. Ruled by the Moon. Dragons: Yen-Iamar, Memezah, Unteekah, and Jyn-Kuaan. Element: Water.

Yellow: Mind energy; mental creativity; sudden changes; communication skills; heightens visualization techniques; travel of any kind. Ruled by the Sun, Mercury. Dragons: Sairys, Salaquet. Elements: Fire, Air.

Additional Stones of Value by Name

If you work with stones, merely by color, not name, you should add the following list to make your spells more powerful.

Eye stones: The eye-shimmer in some stones, such as tiger's eye, cat's eye, or hawk's eye, is similar to the vertical slit in dragon eyes. Therefore, these stones represent all dragons. Cat's eye protects and increases wealth and gives protection and insight into problems. It also helps heal. Tiger's eye promotes energy, luck, and courage. It also protects and attracts money. Elements: Fire, Earth.

Fairy stone: Also called *staurolite*. Natural stones that have an equal-armed cross marking in the center. Protection; balance on all levels; money; good luck; good health. Element: Earth.

Fossil stones: One of the old names for these stones was "draconites." They are good for working with past lives, especially the ammonites. Also valuable for traveling in the Multiverse. Elements: All elements.

Holey, holed, or hag stones: Stones that have naturally formed holes through them. A symbol of the gateways through time and space that dragons and magicians use to move back and forth from the Otherworld and this planet. Element: Earth.

Lodestone: A naturally formed magnet and a representative of stars and meteorites. Attracts what you want; creates a drawing-power. Element: Earth.

Moonstone: Gaining occult power; rising above problems; divination. Planet: Moon; Element: Water. Attracts all dragons.

Pyrite: Sometimes called *fool's gold*. Intensifies good luck, money, prosperity, and total success. Planet: Sun; Elements: Fire, Earth. It especially attracts dragons of the Earth, mountains, and light.

Quartz crystal, clear: Amplifies magickal power; psychic work; scrying; pendulum divination. Attracts all dragons. Element: Storm.

The elements—Earth, Air, Fire, Water, and Storm—describe energy interactions. We often associate an element with a stone to describe the primary type of energy of that stone. Earth is dark green. Air is yellow. Fire, of course, is red, while Water is blue. Storm is a continuously shimmering vortex of violet, purple, and black.

The category "Storm" is a new term to describe an energy that lies between the usual four elements and Spirit. It is an elusive element, created when the other four elements' forces are working at one time. Storm is a very dynamic force that corrects imbalance, does massive cleaning, hastens spiritual awakening, and improves the vibrations. Don't confuse this element with the subclan of Storm-Bringers. It can interfere and redirect element powers if a far deeper balance becomes necessary.

The Storm element bursts into action when a massive cleansing is needed or when a rapid mental or spiritual awakening becomes vital. However, if you deliberately call upon the Storm element, take care you don't use it more than a moment or two. After the intervention of the Storm element, a person, planet, galaxy, or the Multiverse shows a marked vibrational change in its path and purpose. Since even the wisest magicians can't see the entire fate-picture of a person or the Multiverse, it is best to let the Storm element arise of its own volition. Storm tends to affect the user as well as a spell. Whenever Storm appears, radical shifts in life are certain to happen, for Storm builds a link or bridge to the Void of the Chaos dragons.

Although collecting the above listed stones by color, and the few by name, will help you do any spellworking you want, you may want to be more fine-tuned in magickal working. In this case, instead of choosing stones by color, use the following longer list of stones and collect them by use.

More Stones to Consider

Please remember, the following list of stones is for consideration. You do *not* have to buy any of them to finish the Five Inner Rings. I list them because they, and the elements attached to them, are of interest and can be useful.

When buying crystals and stones, go to a reputable shop and take lots of time before a purchase. Choose a shop that sells very few dyed stones and clearly tells you which ones are dyed. Howlite dyed blue may be listed as turquoise or lapis lazuli, but it will have no gold flecks in it. Plastic is sometimes passed off as amber. Real amber feels waxy and will float in a heavy saltwater solution.

If you buy by mail or online, try to go with a recommendation. For crystals, I suggest Montgomery Crystal Company online; they specialize in Arkansas quartz crystal and purchase directly from only certain miners. The owner is very knowledgeable in the field and sells only authentically described quartz crystals. The crystals are priced according to their rarity and grade and are not at all out of line in cost. The time you spend is well worth knowing you will get exquisite stones every time.

If you want to see and handle the stones in person, have a list beforehand of those stones you want to check out. The shop owner should let you take your time deciding. With me, a rushed sale means no sale. Nor do I avoid chipped, indented, or smaller stones. As humans, we live "chipped" lives. Imperfect stones have learned to strengthen their power to surpass their imperfections.

Choose stones that call to you. Hold them in your hand to check for tingling, warmth, pulses of energy, or fluttering "heartbeats." The best stone for you feels the strongest—provided it doesn't make you dizzy, uncomfortable in any way, and doesn't "bite," like the nibbling or stinging of static electricity. Take your time choosing. You may have to check stones in several shops to complete your list. Remember to listen to your gut feelings.

Regardless of where you purchase stones, you need to cleanse them, some more than others. And you will need to recleanse them after heavy use, and/or on a periodic basis. However, check carefully first to see if a stone can be washing in running water and soaked for three to five days in saltwater. This removes all negativity.

Some stones are either water-soluble or affected by water and should be cleansed with a Tibetan singing bowl or sage or frankincense smudging. A quick recleansing can be done by holding the stone and blowing on it softly. A few of these stones are selenite, lapis lazuli, malachite, turquoise, calcite, carnelian, labradorite, and most opals. Water changes their physical properties.

A few writers recommend that all stones, except crystal balls and a few others, be left in sunlight for two days to recharge. I don't recommend sunlight for any crystal-type stone. Not only can such a practice start a fire, but it can crack or discolor many stones. I believe moonlight is safer and gentler. Don't ever leave amethyst, aquamarine, aventurine, beryl, celestite, heat-treated citrine, fluorite, kunzite, lapis lazuli, malachite, opal, rose quartz, tourmaline, or turquoise in sunlight.

You can set stones on clear quartz, amethyst, or citrine clusters, or surround a stone with pieces of carnelian as a recharging method also. This is an excellent way to cleanse and recharge delicate crystals and stones. Citrine and kyanite are self-cleaning. Citrine in particular never holds negative energy, but changes it to positive and discharges the new vibrations into the surrounding space.

By frequently handling your stones, they become locked to your vibrations. If you want to tightly seal a stone, especially a crystal point, to you alone, there is a very strong method. Hold the crystal point-upward in your writing (power) hand. Touch the palm of your other hand to the point, then hold that hand about two inches above the crystal. Slowly begin turning the crystal clockwise with your power hand until you feel a slight resistance in the stone's turns. Breathe gently on the crystal to seal the binding. It's very unlikely after this that anyone else can use the sealed crystal. It is attuned to you.

I've tried to keep the following list to inexpensive stones that can easily be purchased without a prolonged search. If you need a particular type of stone-energy but don't like the feel of a certain stone, such as calcite, look up another stone with the same energy uses. However, if you choose merely one of the stones listed for each Ring, you do not need to buy any of these.

The dragon ruler of each stone can be determined according to the element.

Agate, fire: A very protective stone, it returns ill-wishing to the sender. It is also good for grounding excessive energy, raising personal vitality, and unleashing creativity. Element: Fire.

Agate, moss: Connects with nature spirits. Helps find spirit guides. Element: Earth.

Amazonite: Releases blockages; brings in good luck and career success. Is a link with nature spirits. Brings out truth and harmony. Element: Water.

Amber: Adds energy to spells. Creates a strong link with guides. Helps to remember past lives. Element: Earth.

Amethyst: Opens spiritual gateways and enables the development of psychic abilities. Guards against psychic attack; calms the mind; soothes the surroundings; helps make decisions; helps with meditation. Element: Wind.

Angelite: Aids in deflecting cruelty; connects to guardian angels; returns ill-wishes as compassion. Element: Wind.

Apophyllite: Helps you to tap into and read the Akashic Records, especially your own past lives. Relieves stress; removes blocks; excellent healer. Has strong links to the spiritual realms. Elements: Wind, Earth.

Aventurine, green: Heals the heart and mind. Helps with creativity and prosperity. Helps connect with nature spirits. Elements: Water, Earth.

Aventurine, red: Discernment, determination, creativity, find your higher path or purpose. Heightens mental alertness. Elements: Earth, Fire.

Bloodstone: Also called *heliotrope*. Reveals deceptions; gives self-confidence; can reveal past lives. Protects and cleanses the aura; use for weather and money magick. Element: Earth.

Calcite, black: Helps regain memories of the past that affect the present. Elements: Fire, Storm.

Calcite, honey: Gives insight for action; mental clarity; confidence. Connects to a source of spiritual guidance. Elements: Fire, Wind.

Carnelian: Drives away evil. Stimulates the memory and creativity. Helps link to past lives. Element: Fire.

Chalcedony, blue: Calms, balances, enhances telepathy. Shatters negative emotions and bad dreams. Use in weather magick. Element: Water.

Chrysocolla: Cleans all the chakras. Encourages creative thinking; overcomes phobias. Element: Water.

Chrysoprase: Reveals talents; fidelity in relations and business. Overcomes impulsive thought patterns. Element: Water.

Citrine: Energy, prosperity, opens intuition, magnifies power of manifestation. Element: Fire.

Fluorite: Grounds excess energy. Can cleanse the aura and reach nature spirits. Excellent to connect to the Akashic Records and past lives. Element: Wind.

Fossils: Most common ones used in magick are ammonites, sponges, and trilobites. Help with organization and long-lasting success. Excellent for focus on past lives, or for Atlantean and Lemurian meditations. Element: Earth.

Garnet, grossular: This group includes tsavorite and African green garnet. Attracts prosperity and good health. Represents wealth in all its positive meanings. Element: Earth.

Hematite: Grounds, clears confusion. Excellent for psychic defense and protection. Element: Earth.

Holey stone: Look through the hole at dawn or twilight to see faeries, elves, and visions. Protects from illness. One with three holes is very powerful. Element: Earth.

Jade, green: Helps with divination; teaches you to trust your psychic powers. Also gives abundance and protects. Elements: Water, Earth.

Jasper, leopardskin: A shaman's stone connected with wisdom and spiritual power. It brings what you need, not what you think you want. Use it in charm bags to amplify energy. Teaches telepathy with animals. Elements: Air, Earth.

Jasper, red: Excellent for weather magick. Stops psychic attacks and returns negativity. Element: Earth.

Kyanite: High-frequency energy, it connects to spirit guides. Removes blockages and illusions. Element: Storm.

Labradorite: Very mystical and protective stone; a bringer of light. Awakens natural magickal powers. Relieves stress; recalls past lives; accesses the Akashic Records. Element: Wind.

Lapis lazuli: Increases mental clarity; enhances psychic vision and past lives. Helps communicate with your higher guides. Element: Wind.

Magnetite: Also called *lodestone*. Element: Earth.

Malachite: Repels evil. Removes subconscious blocks. Manifests desires. Element: Fire.

Moonstone, black: Its real name is *black diopside*; it has either a cat's eye line or a four-rayed star. Good for divination; to uncover hidden knowledge and learn a new language. Element: Earth.

Moonstone, rainbow: Deflects negativities; releases emotional trauma; enhances the psychic. Element: Air.

Moonstone, white: Unmasks secret enemies. Removes illusions; reveals the truth. Element: Air.

Obsidian, black: Protects, grounds, and absorbs negativity. Aids in spiritual and dragon communication. Element: Earth.

Obsidian, snowflake: Links to Otherworld guidance; helps recall past lives; protects; brings good luck. Element: Earth.

Onyx, black: Deflects negative energy sent by others. Inner strength, willpower, discipline, protection. Link with Otherworld guidance. Element: Earth.

Pietersite: Also called the *Tempest stone.* Use to read the Akashic Records; go on a vision quest; removes blocks; dispels spiritual illusions. Can create sudden transformations in the user's path. Element: Storm.

Pyrite, iron: Also called *fool's gold.* Deflects danger; overcomes inertia; improves memory. Element: Earth.

Quartz, aqua aura: A clear quartz crystal coated with a microscopic layer of permanent gold. Protects from psychological attack; shields from negative people; calms and relaxes. Otherworld communications. Element: Water.

Quartz, rose: Emotional healing; attracts love; releases stress. Cleanses the entire aura. Element: Water.

Quartz, rutilated: Clear or smoky quartz containing gold, silver, or copper-colored hairlike strands. The stories of the East say the quartz with gold strands belongs to the dragons. Accelerates action; grounds to manifest a spell; gives insight into problems. Element: Storm.

Quartz, smoky: Grounds, organizes on the mental level. Aids to manifest one's desires and dreams. Guards against bad luck. Helps with concentration. Element: Earth.

Quartz, tourmalined: Storm.

Rhodochrosite: Attracts love; strengthens love ties. Recover lost memories; emotional healing. Elements: Fire, Water.

Staurolite: Also called *fairy cross.* Attracts faeries and good luck. Very good to remember distant past lives. Element: Earth.

Tektite: Helps to connect with past lives. Element: Storm.

Tiger's eye, golden: Grounds and centers the wearer. Gives clear insight and good luck. It will reveal the truth about karmic ties with others. Elements: Fire, Earth.

Tourmaline, black: Helps with astral travel and to process past lives. Element: Earth.

Tourmaline, green: Realigns the astral bodies after a trauma. Element: Earth.

Tourmaline, pink: Releases deeply buried issues tied to the emotions. Element: Water.

Tourmaline, watermelon: Gain wisdom from nature spirits. Removes imbalances and confusion. Teaches you to accept the past and move on. Element: Water.

Turquoise: Builds a spiritual bridge between this world and the Otherworld. Strengthens psychic powers. Element: Storm.

Zoisite (with ruby): Heals; strengthens the life force in preparation for a transformation. Helps to reach an altered state of consciousness. A very powerful stone to attract, communicate with, and work with dragons. Element: Storm.

Metals

Metals are all governed by the dragons in the Cloud Master clan. The Cloud Masters are the ultimate blacksmiths of the Multiverse. They taught the secret magick of blacksmithing, of working with metals, to beings on every planet and level of the Multiverse. You will learn more about the categories of dragon clans in the Dragon Warrior section.

A Full Ritual for Spells

The four-quartered circle is central in most formal rituals. It becomes a portal between worlds, a means of connecting better with dragons, deities, spirits, elemental powers, and other creatures of realms beyond this one. It is like a vortex, a sacred space, a gateway, a sanctuary within which we can focus our psychic powers. The area where you mark out your sacred circle becomes a place that is not a place, a time that is not a time, and a day that is not a day. These magickal actions will open a Gate between the worlds, creating a direct pipeline to Multiversal energies and your own mentally constructed astral temple.

The Enchanter casts a circle by pointing her or his wand at the floor or ground, visualizing a stream of brilliant light coming from the wand. Moving clockwise, she or he "draws" a circle nine feet in diameter (if that large is possible); be sure to overlap the ends. While drawing this circle, say:

> *By dragon power, this circle is sealed.*

Stand in the center of your now-sacred space and say:

> *Dragons of Spirit, highest of dragons and most powerful,*
> *Bless this space with your Otherworld fire.*
> *Let us be one in magick, O dragons great and wise.*

This makes a sealed space in which to work, build up the intended power, and then, when the spell is finished, release the magickal power all at once by mentally directing it to go accomplish your intent. When you open the circle by a backward sweep of your wand over the line, envision all excess energy soaking into the Earth. This grounds you, bringing you back to everyday life.

The four quarters of the circle correspond to the compass directions and the four elements. The Enchanter calls upon the four dragons of the elements to participate in the work or asks them to protect. If you ask for protection, be aware that the dragons will not be helping or watching; they will face outward in a protection mode. If you ask for their help, don't ask them to protect at the same time. Instead, call upon other dragons for that duty. See the chapter on categories of dragons in the Dragon Warrior division to aid you in selecting such help.

To ask for Element dragons to be within your circle, you need to face the appropriate direction for each element and call upon them. Begin by facing the east and saying:

> *From Sairys, ruler of the Eastern dragons fair,*
> *Comes now the wondrous power of Air.*

Turn to the south and say:

> *From Fafnir, ruler of dragons of the south,*
> *Comes cleansing Fire from dragon mouth.*

Turn to the west and say:

> *From Naelyan, ruler of dragons of the west,*
> *Comes the power of Water, three times blest.*

Turn to the north and say:

> *From Grael, ruler of dragons of the north,*
> *The power of Earth does now come forth.*

Turn once more to the east before moving to the center, where you will do your spellwork or ritual. At the end of your spellwork, say:

> *If this spell is blocked, or rebounds, send its energy safely into the ground to be made neutral. Never shall it return to harm me or mine.*

When you are finished and ready to open (or sometimes called "cut") the circle, stand again in the center and say:

> *I thank you, dragons old and wise,*
> *Of Earth and Fire, Water, skies,*
> *For sharing wisdom here with me.*
> *As we do will, so shall it be.*

Now face east and say:

> *Go in peace, dragons of the east.*

To the south say:

> *Go in peace, dragons of the south.*

To the west say:

> *Go in peace, dragons of the west.*

To the north say:

> *Go in peace, dragons of the north.*

Just before opening the circle, say:

> *Farewell to you, O dragons fair,*
> *Fire, Water, Earth, and Air.*
> *Together we make magick well*
> *By power deep and dragon spell.*
> *In peace go now. Return once more*
> *To teach me magick and ancient lore.*
> *Draconis! Draconis! Draconis!*

Sweep your wand backward over the invisible circle, and the ritual is finished.

If you feel you need protection as well as help, call upon the protecting class of dragons you chose right after you finish the round of calling the Element dragons. Go to each direction and say:

> *I ask the* [name of the class] *dragons for protection. Protect me in the east.*

Turn clockwise, substituting the correct direction at each cardinal point, and repeat the call. Then move to the center of the circle where you do your spell.

◉   ◉   ◉

A ritual isn't for spectators. Leave your Earth business outside your circle. If others are participating, everyone should keep silent unless it is necessary to speak. Always move inside a circle in the direction in which the circle was cast. Most circles are cast sunwise or clockwise. Only for certain types of magick, performed under a waning Moon, is the circle cast counterclockwise, or widdershins.

Remember, magick isn't finished until you formally end the spell and open the circle. Of course, to be totally correct, that magick isn't finished until it manifests your desire.

Again, it isn't necessary for you to cast a circle and call the Element dragons unless you are doing a formal ritual. Candle and herb spells can be accomplished without the magickal circle, if you wish. However, the spell seems to be stronger when you stand within that circle and "feel" the four powerful Element dragons helping you. Try using full rituals when the manifestation you want is very important to you. The choice is yours.

Amulets and Talismans

Although amulets, charms, and talismans are today spoken of as being the same, they really aren't. An amulet is a natural object, not man-made, that comes imbued with magickal power for protection or luck, and it is carried by someone. Amulets are believed to be a protective device that can ward off illness, evil, or harm, and bring the owner good fortune.

A charm is entirely different from either an amulet or a talisman. Originally, the word *charm* meant a singing or chanting spell that brought good luck when combined with a gesture. Now the word is used to describe a bracelet from which the owner hangs metal tokens to symbolize memories. Since the modern interpretation of *charm* appears to fall between the other two categories, these tokens can be used as either.

A talisman is a special man-made object endowed with magickal powers to accomplish special purposes, such as protection shields, personalized ornaments, or sachet bags. They also can be certain stones or jewelry with special engraving. The talisman is meant to be stroked or touched for good luck or protection, or hung in certain places in a house where their powers might be needed most. Sometimes the talisman itself is placed in a mojo bag, medicine bag, or "charm" bag with other similar objects, and worn on a cord around the neck. Naturally, this bag is quite small.

A talisman can be made of paper, wood, metal (such as a can lid), or a thin piece of clay. The symbols can be drawn on the talisman, using an indelible marker, a wood-burner, a metal-etcher, a thin stick or instrument to etch into moist clay, or they can be painted onto dry clay. Talismans are meant to be worn or carried by the person for whom they're made. Besides symbols, you can use the dragon alphabet or the Nordic runes to write out your name. You may add a word or two describing your purpose for making the talisman, such as "Protect Starfire" or just "Protection."

Eastern objects work well with the Eastern dragons; those dragons have known the objects' meanings since they were hatched.

The following list shows examples of both amulets and talismans used through the centuries. Since most magicians, and other people, today don't distinguish between the two types of charms, I see no reason for separate lists. I haven't listed any seals used by ceremonial magicians. That is an entirely different field of magick.

Acorn: Protection from lightning and storms; also strength, good luck, and longevity.

Beads: The man-made blue bead is still worn by people and animals alike to ward off the evil eye. However, necklaces of certain stones bestow certain qualities on the wearer. For example, amber has great healing power. Aquamarine beads bring luck in love, while onyx inspires deep thoughts.

Coins: Old Chinese coins are used in feng shui (the art of placement); they are strung on a red ribbon and hung to attract the best of fortune. However, there are several other ways to use them. It is considered lucky to carry a coin of your birth year or a coin minted in a leap year. Luckiest of all is a coin that is bent or has a hole in it. If you are given pennies as change on a Monday, it will bring you luck all week. One method to keep luck flowing in is to keep a jar filled with pennies in your kitchen.

Conch shell: Protection against evil, possibly because the conch had a connection with powerful sea creatures and deities.

Crescent Moon: A symbol made in this shape is said to be the most powerful of lucky images.

Cricket: Known around the world as a bringer of good luck. Although people in the Far East keep actual crickets in little cages, an image or engraving of a cricket is more common in Europe. If you hear a chirping cricket, it is bringing you great good luck. Native Americans say that it shows disrespect to imitate a cricket's sound. Across Europe and in the Far East, they believe you will have horrible bad luck if you kill a cricket, even by accident. Cricket images are often placed near the kitchen stove, or on the hearth of a fireplace, to ward off the evil eye.

Dolphin: Carvings of this sea mammal bring good luck to seaport cities. The dolphin also brings good luck to artists and musicians.

Elephant: Carvings and paintings of the elephant-headed Hindu god Ganesha bring foresight and the removal of all obstacles. However, any elephant carving or painting must have the trunk upright.

Fish: Early Egyptians made the image of fish in silver and gold to bring luck to lovers. In the Far East, the fish charm is said to give luck, wealth, and happiness.

Four-leaf clover: A symbol of good fortune for centuries. One leaf means fame; the second, wealth; the third, good health; and the fourth, a faithful lover. The very best luck comes with a four-leaf clover you find by chance.

Frog: This image attracts true friends and long-lasting love. It also speeds recovery from illness. In Egypt and Greece, the frog symbolizes inspiration and fertility. The Romans believed the frog brought good luck to a household. If embroidered on clothes, the frog can still bring you good luck, as can small frog figurines or the clothing closure known as a frog.

Heart: This image has long been associated with luck in love. It has a strong influence over any black magick.

Holly: This is an ancient symbol for good luck, friendship, and good will.

Horseshoe: Good luck and protection from evil. There are two ways to hang the horseshoe in its relegated place—over the main door to your home. Most people hang the open end upward, so no luck falls out. However, in parts of Europe people say you should hang the open ends down so the devil doesn't get caught in it. Sailors used to nail horseshoes to the masts of boats to ensure lucky catches of fish. Or, like Admiral Nelson, for victory.

Key: Sometimes given as a gift between lovers as a symbol of unlocking the door to the heart. In ancient Greece and Rome, a silver key was called the Key of Life and had the power to let one's prayers reach the gods. Keys were worn as talismans to remember things in the past and foresee things to come. In Japan, three keys tied together are believed to make a powerful lucky charm that aids the wearer to unlock the doors to love, health, and wealth.

Knot: Knots have long been used as magickal spells. If you blow on knots while you tie them in a thread, and then throw the thread into water, you can send someone ill wishes. To work healing on someone, blow on each of seven knots as you tie them in a thread or cord. Untie one knot a day thereafter and dispose of the thread in running water while saying, "Out of the body and be carried far away."

Ladybug: An image of this little insect is very good luck. If a real one lands on you, money is coming your way.

Pyramids (triangles): These amplify and intensify the talisman's original energy, but only if the point is upward. The Star of David, or two interlaced triangles, represents a link of female and male energies. Triangles come in more than the ordinary shape. The intertwined Celtic shape looks like three loops, yet you can plainly see it is a triangle. The same applies to the second shape, which is similar to a three-leaf clover; it is called a *trefoil*.

Rabbit's hind foot: This idea is a fairly recent belief. It is said that to gain good luck, one should keep the foot near you or carry it in your left-hand pocket.

Seashells (in general): As a symbol of powerful ocean creatures and deities, carrying a small shell is said to give you a safe journey over water.

Scarab: This Egyptian image represents the Sun, longevity, creativity, and good luck. When given as a gift, it is a wish for good fortune and long life.

Star: All images of stars, regardless of the number of their rays, are good fortune. The five-pointed star, or pentagram, can trap evil forces. Star shapes are also important in the study of magickal shapes and symbols. The illustrations in the Dragon Warrior section show stars with a differing number of points, beginning with four and working up to twelve. They are all ancient and have slightly different meanings.

Three-leaf clover: The first leaf is good luck; the second, prosperity; and the third, love. To the ancient Egyptians, the three-leaf clover symbolized immortality, riches, and protection from evil.

Turtle: A symbol of longevity, the turtle also has power over all kinds of dark magick.

Wheel: An emblem of eternity, the wheel is also connected to the Wheel of Fortune, the cycles of luck rising and falling. However, the image is said to attract very good luck and help win court cases.

Wishbone: The modern tradition says that two people pull on opposite sides of the bone while making a wish. The winner is the person who gets the joint at the top. However, an older belief is that if you clean the wishbone carefully and hang it up by a red ribbon, all your wishes will be granted for a year. Since the wishbone resembles a horseshoe, or a crescent Moon, it has been very lucky for thousands of years.

Zircon: Nature-made zircon has rather mysterious powers because it comes in many colors and is called by several different names. However, all the colors have special magickal and lucky powers. Yellow will attract love while reducing depression and empowering business goals. Red zircon will increase wealth and protect you from injury. The color orange, however, may be the most useful. Put a piece in your home to stop thefts when going on vacation. Also carry a piece of orange zircon with you for protection and to assure a safe return.

Geometric shapes interact with the electromagnetic fields you encounter around you. The shape of the talisman, what is etched onto it, and the magickal purpose behind it determine what vibrations and variations it creates. You should consider a person's personality, as well as the reason for creating the talisman, when you choose a shape and what you put on it.

The most effective shape for a personalized talisman is the circle, the symbol of eternity, totality, the cycles of life, and rebirth. A square will give balance and grounding to a very emotional person, so the talisman's energy doesn't have to keep regrouping from emotions. A crescent Moon activates a person's center of higher creative potential. However, it shouldn't be used for emotional people, as it will connect them with the swing of emotions caused by the Moon. The Celtic equal-armed cross helps balance the element energies around and within someone.

Middleworld Meditation

Use the meditation opening on page 7.

> *Your co-magician dragon is waiting for you. The dragon takes you by one hand while it opens an invisible door before you. When you step through, you find yourself in the Middleworld. The colors are brilliant, and the light that shines isn't from*

a physical sun. There are many people, human and otherwise, walking purposefully along paths. You can see temples through the leafy boughs of trees. Glimpses of flower gardens are all around you.

"First, we will see the Great Dragon Mother, Tiamat," your dragon says, leading you along a path sheltered by trees and lined with flowers. You hear a giggle as you follow. Looking out from among a bed of daisies are several small faeries. They wave, and you wave back.

Ahead you see the huge mound of a dragon, curled up in sleep. Tiamat's golden-green scales spark in the light as she breathes. You tip back your head to see the thick spiny ridge of her back. When you look down again, you find yourself looking straight into her open eyes. You realize that Tiamat can see every truth, every illusion, within you. You can hide nothing.

"Welcome to the Sacred Well of Balance," Tiamat says softly.

You and your dragon return her greeting.

"Enjoy your visit," Tiamat says, as her eyes slowly shut again in sleep.

As you follow your co-magician in another direction, you look back to see that Tiamat is curled around an ancient well, and a huge boulder with a half-white, half-black door in it—the Gate of Balance that leads to the Lowerworld.

You shiver as you pass the dark Grove of Shadows and Twilight, the mossy trunks of the tall evergreens close together, and limbs hanging down to obscure all but the path entrances.

A unicorn suddenly runs out of the Grove and stops before you. You slowly reach out one hand to touch the silky hair. The unicorn's words of welcome jump into your mind. You find it easy to use telepathy to communicate. After a short conversation, the unicorn races down the path ahead of you and disappears from sight.

A rocky cliff looms in front of you, broken by a dark wooden gate decorated with iron hinges and scrollwork. "That leads to Dragon World," your co-magician says. "We will go there later."

The dragon turns down a side path that soon leads the two of you to an area filled with temples built in very different cultural styles. Although the names on the temples are all in different languages, you find that you can read them all. This is the holy area of the Temples of Ancient Ways. Every spiritual path that did, or still does, exist on Earth is represented here by a temple. Your dragon friend waits while you talk with the spiritual teachers waiting beside the temples.

You may want to ask questions about a particular temple, or you may want to ask general questions of several teachers. Your dragon waits while you listen and learn.

"It's time for one more stop," your co-magician dragon says as the two of you walk down a different path. "We are to be guests of the Faery Queen for a time."

A door opens in a large Earthen mound ahead, revealing three more doors inside. There are strange but different designs on each of the inner doors. Your dragon gestures for you to choose one of the doors. When you choose, that door swings open to reveal the fantasy world where the elves, Fae, and Small Folk live.

A flurry of Small Folk, or faeries, circle your head like butterflies, giggling and laughing as they touch your face and hair. The human-size elves and Fae smile as you and your dragon walk through the door toward an open meadow filled with colorful tents and awnings. You hear the music of the Faire and party with the background of laughing voices. Dancers dressed in fantastic clothing and colors twirl to the musical notes carried on the soft breeze.

You and your dragon join the festivities, sampling the food and drink, talking to the festival-goers, and finally are introduced to the Fairy Queen herself. She has chairs brought for you to sit beside her while you talk. You can ask any questions you wish.

After a time, you find yourself relaxing to the notes of a harp nearby. You turn to look for the harpist and see the column of bright light to return you home.

Use the ending on page 8.

Planetary Powers and Hours in Magick

Timing for spells can be everything, especially if the result is of vast importance. That is why a good astrological calendar is so important. Spells can be affected by the Moon, the times of the day or night, the days of the week, the seasons, the weather, and your personal mood. This is why it's so important to keep a record of what is happening all around you when you do a spell. Only in this manner can you find what works best for you and what works against you.

Each day is assigned to a planetary body: the Sun, the Moon, Mars, Mercury, Jupiter, Venus, and Saturn. This magickal system, as well as astrology, is centuries old, and very likely came down to us from the Chaldeans of the Middle East. We know that the Greeks borrowed the Chaldean astrology system. Although there have been small changes and reinterpretations down through the years, the systems remain basically the same. Even the ancient astrologers knew some of the outer planets existed, but for some reason they disregarded them. It was only much later that Uranus and Neptune were added. Pluto wasn't included until the early twentieth century. Now scientists and astronomers are trying to "un-include" it again.

To determine which planet rules which hour, check the first chart of primary planetary symbols. The second chart fits the remaining planets and asteroids into the magickal picture by placing them with some of the first-named planets. In this manner, every astrological body has an important place of its own, in which it influences certain energy flows.

The asteroid belt, which lies primarily between Mars and Jupiter, isn't the remains of a planet, but the pieces of one that should have coalesced. The powerful gravitational pull of Jupiter, which holds the parts in their orbit, is too strong to allow them to form a planet, and at the same time too strong for the asteroids to pull free. The four largest asteroids have been named Ceres, Pallas, Juno, and Vesta. These were the first four of thousands to be discovered; Ceres was found in 1801. Many astrologers now use these asteroids when they cast charts, and they find that their inclusion produces an accurate influence.

One asteroid that isn't in the belt orbit is Chiron, which is about the size of our Moon. This maverick has its irregular orbit ranging from Uranus at the farthest to within Saturn's orbit. This orbit takes about forty-nine years to complete. Chiron wasn't discovered until 1977 and is believed to be an interstellar visitor that got caught in our solar system during its journey. It also shows a definite influence when placed in astrology charts.

The Nodes of the Moon, the five main asteroids, and planets beyond Saturn are not listed in the planetary hours charts, as you will see on the next two pages. However, all of these bodies are considered to be higher aspects of other planets. You can therefore use the similar planet's hours to work with them.

Hours of the Day

	Monday	Tuesday	Wednesday	Thursday	Friday	Saturday	Sunday
1	☽	♂	☿	♃	♀	♄	☉
2	♄	☉	☽	♂	☿	♃	♀
3	♃	♀	♄	☉	☽	♂	☿
4	♂	☿	♃	♀	♄	☉	☽
5	☉	☽	♂	☿	♃	♀	♄
6	♀	♄	☉	☽	♂	☿	♃
7	☿	♃	♀	♄	☉	☽	♂
8	☽	♂	☿	♃	♀	♄	☉
9	♄	☉	☽	♂	☿	♃	♀
10	♃	♀	♄	☉	☽	♂	☿
11	♂	☿	♃	♀	♄	☉	☽
12	☉	☽	♂	☿	♃	♀	♄

Hours of the Night

	Monday	Tuesday	Wednesday	Thursday	Friday	Saturday	Sunday
1	♀	♄	☉	☾	♂	☿	♃
2	☿	♃	♀	♄	☉	☾	♂
3	☾	♂	☿	♃	♀	♄	☉
4	♄	☉	☾	♂	☿	♃	♀
5	♃	♀	♄	☉	☾	♂	☿
6	♂	☿	♃	♀	♄	☉	☾
7	☉	☾	♂	☿	♃	♀	♄
8	♀	♄	☉	☾	♂	☿	♃
9	☿	♃	♀	♄	☉	☾	♂
10	☾	♂	☿	♃	♀	♄	☉
11	♄	☉	☾	♂	☿	♃	♀
12	♃	♀	♄	☉	☾	♂	☿

The Nodes of the Moon, of course, are not actual physical planetary bodies, but simply calculated points that relate the Moon's orbit to the actual orbit of the Earth around the Sun. The ancient astrologers knew the Nodes as knots or complications that they used in charting the heavens. They knew the North Node as *Caput Draconis*, or head of the dragon. The South Node was called *Cauda Draconis*, or tail of the dragon.

Although the Nodes, asteroids, and farthest planets are not often used in magickal practices, they are of real value to the magician who is willing to take the time to learn about them and their influences.

The planetary hours charts are calculated to the Central Time Zone in the United States and the Northern Hemisphere. You will need to adjust the actual hours according to the time zone in which you live. Also remember to adjust for Daylight Savings Time, if your area observes that.

Using planetary hours and/or the day of a specific planet adds extra power and influence to the intent of a spell.

The outer planets and the Nodes of the Moon are all concerned with energies beyond the self and universal connections. They are transpersonal planets. Their energy and uses harmonize with the other planets, and are accessed through those days, elements, and hours.

When working with the Moon moving through the zodiac signs, it can be helpful to call upon the dragon rulers of that sign. Check the planetary list below.

Planets, Properties, Zodiac Signs, and Dragons

Sun		
Dragons	Salaquet, Fafnir	
Metal	Gold	
Colors	Gold, deep yellow, orange	
Day	Sunday	
Element	Fire	
Zodiac ruler over	Leo	
Magickal uses	Success, fame, luck, monetary gain, health, self-confidence, prosperity, personal fulfillment, life energy, favor, promotion. People in authority, employment.	

Moon		
Dragons	Memezah, Naelyon, Sairys	
Metal	Silver	
Colors	White, pearl light gray, cream	
Day	Monday	
Elements	Water, Air	
Zodiac ruler over	Cancer	
Magickal uses	Fertility, love, medicine, luck, receptivity, home, children, psychic powers, intuition, divination. Domestic issues, short trips, temporary plans, the past, memory, personal wishes.	

Mercury		
Dragons	Talm, Sairys	
Metals	Mercury, niobium	
Colors	Orange, multicolored, yellow-green	
Day	Wednesday	
Element	Air	
Zodiac ruler over	Virgo, Gemini	
Magickal Uses	Intellect, communication, business, awareness, messages, perception, memory, creativity, divination, speech, inspiration, mental healing, education, relatives, travel, deception.	

Venus		
Dragons	Shemaleth, Naelyon	
Metal	Copper	
Colors	Light pink, blue, green	
Day	Friday	
Element	Water	
Zodiac ruler over	Taurus, Libra	
Magickal uses	Friendship, love, marriage, sensuality, the arts, creativity, partnerships, music, romance, social events, negotiation, refinement.	

Mars		
Dragons	Durankayta, Fafnir	
Metals	Iron, steel	
Colors	All shades of red	
Day	Tuesday	
Element	Fire	
Zodiac ruler over	Aries, Scorpio	
Magickal uses	Courage, victory, energy, ambition, goals, upheaval, strife, arguments. Strength, conflicts, surgery, endurance. Self-assurance, aggression, action, sex, danger, police.	

Jupiter		
Dragons	Yanizar, Sairys	
Metal	Tin	
Colors	Royal blue, purple	
Day	Thursday	
Element	Air	
Zodiac ruler over	Sagittarius, Pisces	
Magickal uses	Health, love, expansion, success, money, business growth, fame, honor, riches, heart's desires, career or job, legal matters, laws and rules, higher education. Judges, courts, doctors, freedom, new undertakings.	

Saturn		
Dragons	Bullakasz, Grael, Charoesia	
Metal	Lead	
Colors	Black, very dark blues, very dark purples, dark brown	
Day	Saturday	
Elements	Earth, Storm	
Zodiac ruler over	Capricorn, Aquarius	
Magickal uses	Karmic debts and credits, magickal knowledge, sacred wisdom, self-discipline. Knowledge, animal allies, death, reincarnation, binding, overcoming, protection, duties, responsibilities, limitations, endurance, long-term gains and goals.	

Uranus		
Dragons	Keetan, Sairys	
Metals	Platinum, uranium	
Colors	Iridescent blues, ice blue	
Hours of	Mercury	
Element	Air	
Zodiac ruler over	Aquarius	
Magickal uses	Deep shamanic journeys, magick, mental expansion, electricity, occultism, metaphysics, upheaval, astrology, divine inspiration, insanity, freedom, chaos. Planet of the unexpected, it rules over revolution of ideas and inventions.	

Neptune		
Dragons	Vunoket, Naelyon	
Metal	Titanium	
Colors	Green-blue, sea-green	
Hours of	Venus	
Element	Water	
Zodiac ruler over	Pisces	
Magickal uses	Psychic communication, imagery, journeys into inner visions, illusions, deception, martyrdom, earthquakes, divine secrets, addictions, con men, imagination. This is the planet of dreams and hunches, the realm of the subconscious.	

Pluto		
Dragons	Zeirahnak, Grael, Charoseia	
Metals	Electrum, plutonium	
Colors	Deep reds, maroon, magenta	
Hours of	Mars	
Elements	Earth, Storm	
Zodiac ruler over	Scorpio	
Magickal uses	Sensuality, lust, deep karmic personal journeys, massive transformations, upheaval, research, radical transformations, riots, chaos, merging with a partner, intimidating. Builds pressure while making changes out of sight; sudden explosions from that pressure. This planet rules ultimate, inevitable change.	

Asteroids

The asteroids, for some reason, are just called "Lucifer" by some astrologers. The metals for all the asteroids are tektites and meteorites. The dragon over all the asteroids, except for Chiron, is Fylufor.

Chiron		
Dragon	Charoseia	
Metals	Tektites, meteorites	
Color	Pewter gray	
Days	Any day; use Pluto or Uranus hours	
Element	Storm	
Zodiac ruler over	Virgo	
Magickal uses	Blends the personal and transpersonal issues and energies. Contact with unicorns and other fantastic Otherworld creatures. A high warrior and healer energy; very useful for the Dragon Warrior. Clears out past-life traumas and connections. Dissolves past-life blocks in this life. Transmutational cycles and work. Bridges the brain's two hemispheres. Unlocks doors to lost knowledge. Teaches sacred Egyptian teachings. Closes old doors to open new opportunities.	
Ceres		
Metals	Tektites, meteorites	
Colors	Camouflage green and brown; gold with pumpkin orange	
Days	Monday, Friday, Saturday	
Elements	Storm, Earth, Water	
Zodiac ruler over	Cancer, Taurus, Scorpio	
Magickal uses	Transformation, rituals for death and rebirth, healing anger, letting go of old pain, family loss.	

Pallas		
Metals	Tektites, meteorites	
Colors	Gunmetal, gray with blue tint, dark gray	
Day	Monday	
Elements	Storm, Air	
Zodiac ruler over	Libra, Leo, Aquarius	
Magickal uses	Crafts, justice, political and social concerns, strategy, police, militia, shields and barriers, creative visualization. Female warriors.	

Juno		
Metals	Tektites, meteorites	
Colors	Silvery, bluish gray; very light gray	
Day	Friday	
Elements	Storm, Water	
Zodiac ruler over	Scorpio, Libra	
Magickal uses	Marriage and divorce, law-giver, judge, trust, shared resources, healing abuse, money magick. Cutting away from someone.	

Vesta		
Metals	Tektites, meteorites	
Color	Dark reddish-purple	
Day	Tuesday	
Elements	Storm, Fire	
Zodiac ruler over	Scorpio, Virgo	
Magickal uses	Childbirth, the home, commitment to a path, sacred rituals, dedication to a deity, psychic development, inner spiritual union. Changing a lifestyle.	

Nodes of the Moon

In Hindu astrology, the Nodes of the Moon are read and interpreted as if they are actual planets. In each culture that used astrology and magick, we find evidence of the belief in dragons. These astrologers knew of, and used, calculations of the North and South Nodes of the Moon. The Nodes are not planets or anything physical. They are "knots or complications" that relate the Moon's orbit to the actual orbit of the Earth around the Sun. The North, or Ascending, Node is shaped like a horseshoe with the open end down. The South, or Descending, Node is a horseshoe shape with the open end up.

When reading a natal or progressed astrological chart, the North Node of the Moon symbolizes the manner in which the individual takes in energy, events, and influences, and any present-life uses the person makes of that energy.

The South Node of the Moon points to the release of negative energies, memories, and/or habits. It also hints at past lives that still influence the present life.

If you have a natal chart on which the Nodes of the Moon are marked, you can mitigate any negative interpretations by using a candle color representing the zodiac sign in which the troublesome Node lies. Carve the corresponding Node sign (horseshoe up or down) on the side of the candle before you do the spell. Meditate on your life, looking and listening for needed changes, while the candle burns.

North Node (called Caput Draconis, *Head of the Dragon*)		
Dragon	Nadra Tho	
Metal	Silver	
Stones	Moonstone, seashells	
Color	Silver-blue moonstone	
Day	Monday	
Elements	Water, Storm	
Zodiac ruler over	None	
Magickal uses	It represents the tensions in your life; the comfort of the past versus the uncertain future. Also: karma, what you need to accomplish in this life, and what you need to learn to do.	

South Node (called Cauda Draconis, *Tail of the Dragon*)		
Dragon	Nadrica Thysa	
Metal	Silver	
Stones	Moonstone, seashells	
Colors	Black moonstone with a shimmer, or gold or silver sheen obsidian	
Day	Monday	
Elements	Water, Storm	
Zodiac ruler over	None	
Magickal uses	Karmic rewards that you earned. It represents your past lives and their influences on your present behavior and thinking. Using past-life talents. Rewards you can claim.	

Days of the Week	Colors	Planet	Dragon
Sunday	Yellow, gold	Sun	Salaquet
Monday	White, silver, light gray	Moon	Memezah
Tuesday	Red	Mars	Durankayta
Wednesday	Purple, yellow	Mercury	Talm
Thursday	Blue	Jupiter	Yanizar
Friday	Green	Venus	Shemaleth
Saturday	Black, Purple	Saturn	Bullakasz

Moons in Magick

The Moon affects everything sentient on Earth much more than we think it does. For those unbelievers, merely check the local police, fire, ambulance, and hospital logs. You will see a sharp increase in accidents, violence, mental instability, and severe illnesses on the Full Moon. During the New Moon influence, you will see that same increase, but not in the severity of that of the Full Moon. The Full Moon appears to influence negative actions toward others, while the New Moon projects that action inward, toward the self.

To improve your accuracy in spell manifestation, you should correlate the type of spell to the phases of the Moon as well as to the planetary hours.

Nothing is closer to the Otherworld realm than our intent thoughts and vivid dreams. Thoughts are a form of vibrational energy that can easily bridge the gap between this physical world and the Otherworld. Dreams are even closer to the Otherworld's vibrations, for when you dream so vividly, you are already in the astral airs and headed on a journey to the Otherworld.

The Moon, being the closest planetary body to Earth, has a great influence upon the inhabitants of this planet, as well as on the dreams we dream and the magick we do. The time to do spells to receive something should be timed from a day or two after a New Moon up to, and including, the Full Moon. The time for releasing, or moving people and events away from you, must be timed from a day or two after the Full Moon up to, and including, the next New Moon.

Actually, dividing the Moon's power influence in this way isn't exactly correct. The Moon has four phases or quarters. There are four Moon dragons, a number which reflects the multitude of Moon goddesses found in ancient pantheons. Moon dragons are usually female, and all are members of the Astra-Keepers clan.

The Moon powers of the first and second quarters can be stored together in the same cord by knotting, or projected into the same stone on your altar for later use. However, you will need a different cord and stone to save the energies of the third and fourth quarter powers together.

Yen-Iamar rules the Moon power of the first quarter of the Moon's cycle. She is a midnight-blue dragon with silver-edged scales and luminescent silvery eyes. An Eastern dragon, she has dawn-pink feathery antennae and dark blue claws on her four feet. Her powers are subtle but long-lasting. Spells associated with her include laying a foundation for a goal, help in deciding upon a goal or future goals, guidance in working with herbs and other natural spell ingredients, and general spells to attract love and good luck. This is excellent energy to pour into your "stone batteries," or what is called a sink stone, kept on your altar.

Memezah controls the energy of the Full Moon. She has the shape of a European dragon, with a heavy body covered with light blue-edged silver scales. Her great eyes are golden topaz, as are the claws on her four feet. The spine scales are glittering jet black. Memezah is regal in bearing as leader of the Moon dragons, but not from ego. She is an expert at weaving Moon energy into large masses for spells. Spells associated with her include increase, all positive success spells on every level of being, scrying, a job, new home, friends, prosperity in general, travel, good health, and finding the right companion. Full Moon energy can be stored in cord knots for later use, or added to the sink stone.

Eclipses occur during a Full Moon, and therefore fall under Memezah's rule. Any kind of magick worked during an eclipse will be greatly amplified. The more complete the eclipse, or the closer it is to you, the better. A total solar eclipse is a powerful event you can use. However, a total lunar eclipse is even more powerful in a different way.

Unteekah handles the power of the third quarter of the Moon. She is an Asian dragon with a flowing, featherlike mane. Actually, her beautiful mane is a thin, flexible, floaty membrane that changes through the rainbow colors as she moves. Her four short legs have red claws. Her snakelike body is a mixture of rainbow-colored scales. The antennae over her black eyes are golden topaz, which end in glittery black balls that have the texture of dandelion fluff. If you have long-term spells "cooking" on your altar, Unteekah's Moon energy is excellent to hurry them along. Spells associated with her include those for ending unproductive goals, projects, jobs, spells, or relationships. The third quarter of the Moon is a good time to work with poppets or charm bags, or to sprinkle herbal powders for influence over a goal. This energy also can be saved in a second sink stone or knotted into a different cord.

Jyn-Kuaan rules over the New Moon, or the fourth quarter's flow of power. A European dragon with a jet-black body, she has irregularly placed iridescent silver and rose-pink scales. Her light gray eyes, which match her claws, hold a fiery-red tint deep within. Her spinal scales are edged in blood-red. Jyn Kuaan is an expert at pulling together New Moon energy for sweeping aside all influences of those who are against you in some negative manner. Spells associated with her include setting up house watchers and guardians, banishing negative thoughtforms or incoming spells, protection, dissolving illnesses, removing barriers to goals, interpreting dreams, expanding psychic awareness, and changing one's luck. This Moon energy can be added to the cord knots or stone you used for Unteekah.

Dreamtime, the Dreaming, or Dream Land, is a psychic realm that exists between this world and the Otherworld, but is controlled by the Moon. However, it is very difficult to map Dream Land. It appears to be connected to both Dragon World and Faery Land, at the same time being a separate, distinct place. It is hard to find unless you are dreaming. There are three Dream Gates: life problems that your dreams and subconscious mind try to solve; total fantasy dreams for pure pleasure and adventure; and prophetic, or true, dreams. True dreams can be of past lives, future events, or simply messages/studies from the Otherworld sent to you while dreaming. However, deep daydreaming can also take you to Dream Land.

If you are troubled by nightmares, negative dreams, and restlessness during your sleep, hang a dream catcher over the head of your bed. Native Americans believe that the air around us is constantly full of good and bad influences. Their invention of the dream catcher sorts out and catches the negative vibrations. However, dream catchers must be shaken out periodically. Just be certain to shake out the negatives outside or over your altar so that they don't hang about in the house.

The Moon itself spends about two to two and a half days in each zodiac sign as it moves through a month. Frequently, it stays between signs for hours or even a day; this is called "void of course." In a void of course time, or during a retrograde Mercury (explained later in this section), it is better not to do spells unless absolutely necessary. The Moon primarily affects the emotional side of any issue. To take full advantage of lunar energies added to zodiac energies, check the meanings of the Moon through the zodiac list that follows. If possible, try to coordinate the dragon of the exact quarter, plus the dragon that rules the zodiac sign.

Occasionally, there are two Full Moons in a month. The second one is called the Blue Moon. The same thing happens with the New Moon. The second is called the Black Moon. Both of these "extra" Moons are considered to be very powerful.

Moon through the Zodiac

Moon in Aries: Makes people argumentative and aggressive. Also bold and impetuous. Good time to start projects or direct energy for change.

Moon in Taurus: People are usually less stressed unless pushed. Use this energy to hurry things or make changes that consolidate projects.

Moon in Gemini: Lives are often tuned to the social but are disorganized, with scattered thoughts and wild energy in this time. Use time to search for answers and possibilities.

Moon in Cancer: Emotions are close to the surface. Plans are centered around home and family. Misunderstandings and hot words are possible. Use for family welfare and the home.

Moon in Leo: Incidents tend to get dramatic and blown out of proportion. Use to improve your self-esteem or remove any arrogance.

Moon in Virgo: Good time for detailed work and odd jobs left undone, as people are more helpful now. Use this energy to work closely on detailed projects and future planning and to solve everyday events.

Moon in Libra: Although this sign has scales for a symbol, during this Moon time people can dither on the idea of balance so much that nothing gets done. Use time to reach balance in life, friendships, and relationships.

Moon in Scorpio: Moodiness and brooding are common now. People can get extreme over imagined slights. A very good time for meditations and magick related to understanding deep spiritual ideas and mysteries.

Moon in Sagittarius: Prompts people to overdo or waste energy in a pursuit of fun times. This makes them scattered in energy and life itself. Use for studying divination and magick.

Moon in Capricorn: People get overly cautious and pessimistic about careers, the present, and future life when the Moon is in this sign. A good time to use magick on major life goals or strengthening your job position.

Moon in Aquarius: This is a sign connected with quiet rebellion and stubbornness. Often, people will unexpectedly reverse decisions. Use to create something new in your life—perhaps an entirely new direction and/or goals.

Moon in Pisces: This energy throws a veil of illusion over everything, which creates fuzzy thoughts that can block reality. Use for becoming more spiritual and compassionate. An excellent time to contact your personal dragons in meditation.

The Effects of Retrograde Mercury on Life and Spells

If you have heard of nothing else in astrology other than your zodiac sign, you have likely heard about retrograde Mercury, the mayhem dispenser of Murphy's Law. Three to four times a year, for about three to four weeks at a time, the planet Mercury "appears" to move in reverse when compared to Earth. Other planets also go retrograde, but none of them produce the uncertainty and chaos that Mercury does.

Retrograde Mercury and I have a definite hate-hate relationship. It causes me so many problems that I now mark those weeks in red on my calendar. Little Mercury affects such vital life features as computers, telephones—indeed, any electronic or technological device. Messages, packages, mailed payments, and especially e-mails disappear into the Multiverse, never to be seen again. Files may vaporize in your computer, if the entire system doesn't crash, leaving you to reinstall everything. Communications are a quarter turn off with nearly everyone. Misunderstandings are rampant. It can easily be equated with the Huns riding into town without prior notice.

Are the dragons affected by this crazy energy? At least one clan of dragons is. It took me several years of sporadically seeing the beautiful Snow dragons, and asking other dragons about them, before I learned they are special messengers, like the Roman god Mercury. I think the others withheld the information about these dragons because of their association with Mercury and its retrograde features. I finally learned that the Snow dragons have a mercurial temperament that matches the planet Mercury in our solar system. Not only that, but there are planets equivalent to our Mercury in every solar system of the Multiverse! Each of these "Mercurys" reacts to certain cosmic energy shifts in cycles similar to the retrograde Mercury we know. Thanks to the Ultimate Cosmic Source, none of these planets turn retrograde at the same time, or for the same length of time.

Ordinarily, the Snow dragons are constantly busy carrying new ideas for inventions, the arts, and all types of activities throughout the Multiverse, seeding them on all planets everywhere. Also, they act as messengers from deities, guides, guardians, and angels to people.

When each "Mercury" in the Multiverse turns retrograde, Snow dragons also react to the cosmic winds and temporarily either react strangely or go into a type of hibernation for the duration of this cosmic phenomenon. There is nothing Snow dragons can do to stop the retrograde action without destroying the system in which the planet moves. The only recourse the Snow dragons have is to hibernate for the duration (the older ones do this), or act erratically in response to the change (the younger ones do this.) Accept the inevitable, or go against the cosmic flow, in which one never succeeds. Wisdom comes with age to dragons, as it hopefully does with humans.

Our retrograde Mercury affects all zodiac signs but especially the signs through which it moves. However, it affects each zodiac sign differently, as you can see by the following list.

Aries: (Mars) You are easily distracted by new ideas, lack patience, are slightly out of sync with life, convey views and words that make others uncomfortable, and are misunderstood on any major issue.

Taurus: (Venus, Ceres) You are apt to make many small mistakes that eat great amounts of time when you try to make them right. You question your own values and resources, and fixate on certain ideas (such as security and money).

Gemini: (Mercury) You are very indecisive and struggle to reach any conclusions. You are prone to using extra-sharp words with others. Double-check any reports, for they will be full of errors.

Cancer: (Moon, Ceres) Thoughts of all your past problems arise and control your complete attention for long periods of time. After overextending yourself for others and having small memory lapses, you are likely to retreat into a shell.

Leo: (Sun, Pallas) You tend to exaggerate, boast, and get pushy and controlling. You will be resistant to any changes. Double-check all appointments.

Virgo: (Mercury, Chiron, Vesta) You will have little tolerance for disorder, even though your own space may have become a temporary mess. You might even become dictatorial with others, while you subject yourself and other people to constant analysis.

Libra: (Venus, Pallas, Juno) You make quick judgments that are probably wrong, as you totally lack discrimination. Being indecisive during this period, you misplace important documents and are too quick to sign contracts without reading them thoroughly.

Scorpio: (Mars, Pluto, Ceres, Juno, Vesta) You are very critical of others, mentally obsessed with negative thoughts, unsatisfied with anyone's explanations, suspicious, and hard to talk to.

Sagittarius: (Jupiter) You are more restless than usual, with scattered thoughts and lots of impatience. If you travel, you are likely to experience all types of misadventures and delays.

Capricorn: (Saturn) You are apt to be caught in bottlenecks in commutes and travel. Your depression and pessimism contribute to mistakes made by unclear thinking. Check all plans for solid foundations before you act on them.

Aquarius: (Saturn, Pallas) You will be cranky, eccentric, and have low energy. Plans tend to backfire. Any planned travel will be cancelled or delayed.

Pisces: (Jupiter, Neptune) You feel like you are in a fog, lack self-confidence, and are very sensitive. You have difficulty getting any ideas across to others because your communication skills seem to have temporarily vanished.

◎　　◎　　◎

Keep your spell magick to a bare minimum during this time. If a spell's energy can yield a changeling result, this is the time it will happen, especially to new or careless magicians. Call upon all the dragons you can for help, and be very precise in your intent during a retrograde Mercury. Any misfires should be immediately recalled and grounded.

The following list of probable daily woes is by no means complete, but it gives a general idea what to do or not do when Mercury is retrograde. If you look at an astrological calendar, you will see an RX, like a prescription sign, on the day Mercury starts its retrograde. You will see a D, weeks later, when it turns direct again.

Retrograde Mercury Problems

- Don't sign contracts. These papers won't be to your advantage.
- Back up all electronic files. You probably should make two backups, just in case.
- Expect trouble with telephones, fax machines, computers, e-mail, and all travel plans.
- Write down all messages, plans, and communications. It is inevitable they will be misunderstood, either by you or the other party.
- Take great care when communicating anything. The other person will not hear quite the same thing as you say.
- Don't make, or sign for, any major purchases, if you can avoid it. The purchase is likely to be a lemon in one manner or another. You will also have later problems trying to get it fixed.
- Don't make major changes in your life. Your thinking will be as fuzzy as everyone else's.
- Be tolerant of others and try not to criticize. You can count on making the next big error yourself.
- Expect the unexpected. It will happen however careful you are.
- Double-check appointment times or you will arrive on the wrong day or at the wrong time.
- Reconcile with people with whom you have immediate problems. But take care you don't make matters worse. Most times, reconciliation is easier for all under a retro Mercury.
- Rest and recharge your energy. Keep a low profile and avoid social events where libations could well cause ill feelings.
- Privately, review your opinions and routines. But don't make radical changes until you review them again when Mercury goes direct.
- Keep your spellwork to the kind that repairs past misdeeds, helps others, or removes problems (without your getting emotionally involved). Don't use any magick if you have negative feelings. You will invariably put the wrong intent in the spell and get slapped back by those emotions.

However, all this said, a retrograde Mercury is a good time to remedy past mistakes, review your goals in life, or branch off in a different direction. Just wait until Mercury goes direct to put any new goals into action.

The Lowerworld Meditation

As you explored part of the Middleworld earlier in this section, you should now prepare yourself for experiences in the Lowerworld. You will not visit the dark Underworld until you have advanced to Dragon Warrior.

Use the meditation beginning on page 7.

Your co-magician transports you immediately to stand before the huge Tiamat and request that you be allowed to visit the Lowerworld.

Tiamat looks deep into your eyes, then nods. The black and white door in the boulder opens, revealing only a dark interior. Your dragon friend takes your hand as you both step across the threshold of the Gate of Balance. Your next step takes you out again into the light, as if you pushed aside a curtain.

The atmosphere on this level feels heavier than it did in Middleworld. You sense no evil close to you. The only uneasiness you feel comes from the distance, where you can see an impenetrable black wall.

"That is the separation between the Lowerworld and the Underworld," your dragon tells you. "We are safe here. The Underworld is always heavily guarded."

You ask if the inhabitants behind that wall are allowed to reincarnate.

"Yes," the dragon says. "No one can be denied that privilege, for all have free will. The Council tries to dissuade them until they make changes, but the Council cannot stop the reincarnation."

You shiver as you think about the repercussions of the reincarnation of such people as Jack the Ripper, Hitler, or Attila the Hun. Yet you realize that the laws of the Multiverse must not have exceptions. The laws must apply to all for there to be fairness and spiritual balance. Even the karmic debts we get are by our decisions, our free will choices.

Your dragon leads you toward an onion-domed building in the midst of a fabulous garden laid out in geometric designs. The dragon explains that this building is called the Shrine of the Ancestors. You see a group of people waiting for you on the building's steps. Some of them you may recognize as deceased loved ones. Others are dressed in a wide variety of ancient clothing.

"Here are your ancestors, family, and friends," your dragon tells you. "If you don't want to talk to one of them because of past difficulties, simply tell them so. Then they will leave."

Your dragon curls up on the grass as you go forward to learn about your family's long history, meet ancestors, and reunite briefly with loved ones.

When you have talked to many of the people waiting there, you turn back toward your dragon and follow it on a path leading away from the Shrine. Soon, through the dark, hanging tree branches, you see a cave opening in a rocky hillside. You squeeze through the narrow opening to find yourself in a cavern completely lined with glowing rubies. Along one wall are several ledges wide enough to lie on.

"The energies in this room will balance your body," your co-magician tells you. "Lie on one of the beds so that your aura, your body's electromagnetic field, can be readjusted."

You lie down and immediately feel the air around you compressing, then expanding. This continues until you feel physically refreshed. You follow your friend into an adjoining cave, this one lined with blue sapphires. Again, there are ledges along one wall.

As you lie on a ledge, your friend tells you that the sapphires will rebalance your mental energies and remove any blockages that may be impeding your progress. You feel the same expanding and contracting as before, only this time within your mind. When the action stops, you rise and go into the next chamber, lined with glorious emeralds.

"This is your choice, or not, to undergo the rebalancing of your spiritual ideas," the dragon says.

You lie down on a ledge and immediately feel a stirring in the center of your abdomen. The feeling seems to rise above your body, yet still be attached. At first it is uncomfortable, but as it circles tighter and faster like a vortex, you relax. You feel as if you are almost floating on air by the time the movement stops.

When you stand, your dragon is gone. Alongside one wall, you see the column of light, ready for your return.

Use meditation ending from page 8.

(End of the meditation)

Dragon Enchanter Initiation

You have worked hard to reach this point in your studies. Now is the time to present yourself for the Enchanter/Enchantress initiation, so you can move on to the Third Ring, that of the Dragon Shaman.

Needed supplies: Altar cloth; small bowls, one containing sea salt and the other containing water; your altar stones. Lay your new red ribbon on the altar.

Preferable day: Full Moon.

Use the ceremony opening on page 52.

(Beginning of the initiation)

Close your eyes and relax your body. Visualize yourself standing in the long, narrow stone wall of the Enchanter Section. Before you is a small, plain altar decorated with a silver tray holding bunches of cut herbs. Curious to see if you recognize any of the herbs, you smell several bunches and find out that you do know the names.

"Very good," says a deep dragon voice behind you. "Now, tell me, what are the reasons for performing magickal spells?"

"To help others and myself live a balanced, fulfilled life," you answer. You continue with any other explanations you want to voice.

"I can give you control over anyone you want," the dragon says, as he watches you carefully with half-open eyes.

"Then give me power over myself" is your answer.

"Yes," the dragon says softly. "Only a tyrant wants to control others, when he cannot even control his own life." He hangs a red ribbon over your shoulders and fastens one end to your shirt with an upright triangular pin made from a piece of sandalwood. You smell the soft fragrance of the pin rise about you.

"Well done, Enchanter. You are now eligible to enter the Third Ring as a Dragon Shaman." He points to an open door down the hall.

You thank the wise initiator and go through the door to the next Ring.

Use the closing ceremony on page 54.

(End of the initiation)

THREE

The Way of the Dragon Shaman

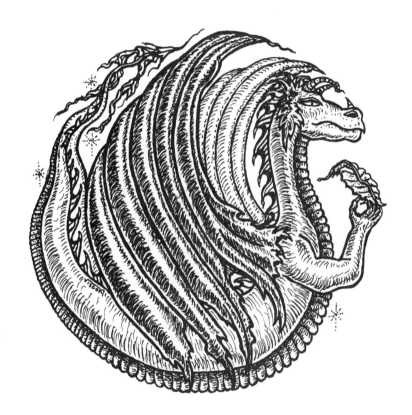

The Dragon Shaman's studies are not as detailed as the Enchanter's, but they will increase in difficulty. The Shaman works more with the Otherworld and human spiritual aspects than the Apprentice and Enchanter did. She or he must learn to concentrate harder on intent and visualize in detail and color, using all five senses. This means the Shaman will spend more time traveling to, and exploring in, the Otherworld than she or he has done thus far.

Now that you will learn many more details about the dragons and the Otherworld, I hope you are still recording in your private journal. Expect exciting adventures to happen, for they will.

Code, Color, and Other Items of the Shaman

The color of the Dragon Shaman Ring is a pure, bright red. This is the color of blood, of human life on this planet. However, few Shamans will want to wear red clothing. They are more likely to show their place in the Rings training by decorating their clothing or healing bags. Red is also the color of action, efforts, and power healing, such as the aura, chakras, and the shattered soul.

You will need to purchase two feet of half-inch red ribbon. As does the Apprentice, you will drape this ribbon across your shoulders while working or meditating, and you will use it to mark a section of the Dragon Hoard. I hope you are working on your ritual book, the Dragon Hoard, and writing each day in your journal, the Dragon Secrets.

The Shaman's role is to work with the healing Enchanters, or alone, as a life-energy and soul healer. The code of the Shaman is "To benefit all, I must travel and learn in the Multiverse. I am a Walker Between Worlds."

A symbol that can better designate the Shaman than a red patch is a green leaf pin, or a pin or pendant that represents the World Tree.

In this section, you will learn more about the elements, particularly the elusive element Storm. You will be introduced to the many dragon clans and subclans, their names and colors, and what energies they reflect. The Shaman also learns to make personal divination stones using dragon script and the shaman symbols, and to interpret the correct reading.

Since this section of the Rings is more intensely in-depth and full of new information, the Shaman will work harder mentally and journey-wise. By initiation time, the Shaman will realize what great strides she or he has taken in the studies.

Shaman Ritual Tools

You will need three very special stones for the work in this section. When not in use, these three stones should be wrapped separately in soft cloth and placed in a special box or bag until needed. The first is a piece of black onyx or obsidian that is tumble-polished, at least. A smooth surface makes the stone more comfortable to use. Obsidian especially can have sharp edges in the rough state. This black stone will be your cleaner stone that can vacuum up and destroy astral debris, parasites, and cording that you find in a person's aura.

The second stone is sometimes called River Rock crystal. These chunks of quartz crystal are found in Alaskan rivers only in the spring. They have been tumbled and carried down the rivers for miles, leaving them with a frosty, slightly rough exterior. The people who gather these stones slice a thin piece off one side or end to reveal the nearly clear interior. Not only are these crystals valuable as Retriever Stones for shamans, but they can also be used for scrying. When the Shaman is searching through the Otherworld for pieces of a shattered soul, she or he puts the pieces into this stone for return to the proper person.

The third stone is a simple piece of snow quartz, either a pointed or polished chunk. This is an inexpensive stone that is opaque quartz crystal, meaning it is so full of white "clouds" that you can't see through it. However, it is great for healing imperfections and damages in the chakras and auras.

It is also helpful to obtain small pieces of several other stones if you haven't already collected them: carnelian (aids astral travel), smoky quartz (grounds and stops psychic attacks), snowflake obsidian (clears away illusion), and amber (serves as a gateway to other realms). Amber was called petrified dragon's blood centuries ago. Any stone bearing fossils is excellent to recall past lives; it also has a unique energy that helps focus on ancient Atlantis and Lemuria in meditations.

Geodes have always been known as the ultimate shaman's stone. Their cavelike interior projects a strange energy field, similar to that in a vortex, and aids people in quickly reaching an altered state of consciousness.

The small black tektites, which are a type of meteorite, have a strange link to the Pleiades, one of the star groups mentioned in a later chapter on dragon history. Tektites are used in channeling and healing, but are also excellent for all star magick.

Having reached the Shaman level of the dragon training, you should be able to know by touch if a certain stone will work for you or not. Perhaps you have also detected an unusual presence in some stones. Many stones contain spirits or guardians who will work with humans. Some quartz crystals may even contain their own angel or nature spirit.

All stones appear to have the ability to share experiences with other stones of the same vibrations. Since there are stones that fall in between categories and vibrations, it isn't long before the same information is stored within all stones of the Earth. In a way, this creates a library of records, which corresponds to certain types of quartz crystals. However, this information is much harder to retrieve than in the crystals—and they can be difficult enough.

You will also need to make four dragon energy element shields. How to make these is explained later. This is a very simple project and doesn't require artistic ability.

Experience the Elements Meditation

Most magicians are aware of the usual four elements that are required to perform magick and make it work properly. Traditionally, these are Earth, Air, Fire, and Water. In dragon magick, these elements correspond, and are under the direction of, specific dragons, as you learned in *Dancing with Dragons*.

The Air element is ruled by the dragon Sairys, is pure yellow, and is associated with the eastern direction. It works with any type of air movement as well as any project dealing with the mental realm.

Fire is ruled by Fafnir, is pure red, and is associated with the south. Besides physical fire, this element affects all physical action, changes, and willpower. It also can be used when working on spiritual action, such as self-changes within.

Water is ruled by the dragon Naelyon, is blue, and is associated with the west. It works with the emotional realm as well as all water from tiny ponds to the oceans.

Earth is a solid element ruled by Grael. It is dark green, represents the north, and is the realm of physical matter, including the body.

The planet Earth has an electromagnetic energy field (an aura), just as humans do. This field is composed of various strengths of elemental energy in both positive and negative flows. When all four elements are empowered at one time and balanced with each other, this energy transforms into a dynamic balancing force called Storm.

The Storm element, guarded by the Storm-Bringers clan, is far stronger than the four elements plus Spirit. If you work with stones associated with Storm, they create massive transformations and cleansing, radical shifts in life. Use these stones for only short periods of time and only when you are ready for such massive changes in your internal and external worlds.

However, this is an element it is best not to form artificially, but rather to allow to coalesce by itself. Storm element is a link or bridge to the Void of the Chaos dragons. The Chaos dragons both destroy and create or, in this case, re-create part of an energy pattern.

Storm comes into action when a being's life-path or the direction of a planet or galaxy's future goes off course. With humans, this usually happens when the person goes through what is called a Dark Night of the Soul. She or he knows drastic changes are vital, but sees no solutions. The Storm-Bringers step in, taking decisions out of the person's hands and control. But when the clouds lift and the lightning stops, those who go through a Dark Night of the Soul find themselves and their direction in life changed in a manner they never expected. Changed only if they accept the cleansing. The Storm element works on one rule: be changed and work with the change, or be destroyed by it. Accept the transformation and become stronger.

The entire Multiverse works on the principle that no being, world, or situation can become static and still continue to exist. We see this in nature all the time. If a species of any kind can't adapt to changes in the environment, it becomes extinct and something else takes its place. Only the adaptable with strong wills survive. The Supreme Creative Force is unemotional when it becomes necessary to remove unproductive existences. But its projection of the Goddess as its female half reveals a love for all creation. All things are therefore given an opportunity to choose to change before stronger measures are enforced.

The only way to grasp the essentials of the working of elements is to experience each one through a deep visual meditation. This type of meditation engages all the senses, which you still have and use when traveling in the Otherworld. Your senses on this level will be stronger, brighter, and sharper than those of this physical plane.

Element Meditation

Use the meditation opening on page 7.

You are standing on a hilltop next to your co-magician dragon. A crisp breeze blows around you, sweeping down into the small valley just beyond. You slowly become aware that the breeze is blowing through you as well as around you. You hear soft voices and sounds, many of them carried from the other side of the Earth. Any noise made anywhere around the globe remains in the jet stream until it finally fades away. You see the individual air molecules bump together as they speed past. You can taste the sharp ozone of an approaching storm as those molecules rasp against your skin. Your dragon leaps into the breeze, riding the currents leisurely.

You release the idea that you can't fly and let the breeze carry you far above the hilltop. You swoop down toward the valley with your dragon, moving just above the trees, savoring the freedom this event gives you. Your mind opens to the freshness of ideas, letting the cobwebs blow away.

You look down to find you have quickly moved out over the ocean. Foam-capped waves roll toward the sandy beach, leaving behind driftwood and shells as they withdraw. Your dragon reassures you that being underwater will not harm you, as she or he dives deep into the ocean below. You follow and find the dragon spoke the truth. You allow yourself to spread out through the water, tasting the salt, smelling the fish that swirl around you as you pass, feeling the delicate but rough touch of a fin against your arm. As when in the air, you discover that sounds carry a long way through the water. The chatter of dolphins gets closer until several of them are swimming alongside, their funny smiles drawing your smile in return. Your emotional realm feels calm and washed clean. As the dolphins leap above the ocean surface in their lively dance, you too surface and see the red of hot lava and the wall of steam just ahead, where an active volcano joins the ocean.

"Don't be afraid," your dragon says. "You can't be harmed." The dragon soars straight toward the volcano and lands close beside the glowing lava stream.

As soon as your feet touch the ground beside your dragon, you become aware of many sensations you haven't experienced before. You see small firedrakes moving freely in and out of the lava. You reach in and one climbs into your hand. The two of you look at each other for a few moments before the small dragon leaps back into the hot lava. You realize you felt only a slight warmth and the prickle of tiny claws when you held the firedrake. The lava hisses and crackles where it meets the cold of the water, sending a burning smell into the air. The energy of Fire begins to course through your astral body, filling you to overflowing with a desire to move, to be active.

As you and your dragon fly away from the volcano toward a lush tropical forest, you realize you need the grounding of the element of Earth. Your astral body has absorbed an imbalance of Air, Fire, and Water. You dive straight down at the ground, entering the Earth without a sound and without a sign left behind of your entrance. You flip over to lie on your back, your arms spread wide in the soft soil. You hear small noises made by creatures who inhabit the ground, but none come near you. Each intake of breath fills your senses with a rich odor of dirt and the scent of flowers. You relax and take in needed Earth energy to balance you. You hear your dragon sigh with pleasure as she or he also soaks up Earth power. Your astral body comes back into balance.

You pop out of the ground to stand beside your co-magician dragon. You see a small double vortex hanging in the air above the tropical forest. Your dragon explains that you are seeing an example of the Storm element, an energy field that moves both clockwise and counterclockwise at the same time and the element used to create massive changes in all things. At any future time, when you feel this type of change is necessary, you can enter the Storm element.

Use the closing meditation on page 8.

(End of meditation)

I didn't take you into the Storm element because entering that is a very personal decision and really does create transformation. Only each Dragon Shaman can decide when she or he is ready for that experience. If you delay this decision, knowing that it is important, the Chaos dragons will introduce you to the Storm element. I've discovered that their insight into my experiencing Storm is better than mine, so I wait. It will come, more than once in your life.

Dragon Seasons

The dragons, to whom time has no meaning, have a firm grasp of planetary energy on every level of the Multiverse, and the spiritual vibrations behind it all. They don't recognize such things as time—certainly not in terms of hours, days, weeks, or months. Time is an abstract division created by humans and exists only in our minds. However, the dragons do seem to acknowledge the four seasons. These seasons, or similar ones, appear in one form or another on every planet in the Multiverse. Most seasonal changes on planets are quite noticeable, while others on different planets require close observation to detect.

Because dragons work with seasons and "time" as a flexible unit able to be molded to whatever is needed, they can easily and quickly adjust to the power-flow rhythm of any planet on any level of the Multiverse.

In Dragon World, we find four seasons reflecting the four important aspects of a dragon's life: Hatchling, Adolescent, Adult, and Elder. Of course, since dragons live extremely long lives, we can relate to their "seasons" only on a superficial level. However, comparing the dragons' names for bodily "seasons" to Earth's yearly seasons helps human magicians understand how to adjust mental images, which gives them better control of magickal energies that deal with "time" but are actually timeless.

According to the dragons, seasonal divisions reveal important information and lessons to be learned. These correspond to the first four Rings of human and dragon studies: Apprentice, Enchanter, Shaman, and Warrior. The fifth Ring of Mystic deals with esoteric subjects and cannot correspond to the regular four elements as the regular seasons do. The Ring of Mystic fits better with the elusive element of Storm, which is such a transformative energy that it lies between our world and the Otherworld, able to create changes in both. The Mystic also works between worlds and outside of time.

The dates given for the beginning of the Earth seasons is approximate, as the actual dates can vary by a day or two. Check the calendar. To use seasonal energy for long-term spells, consider that the Spring Equinox runs from March 21 until the beginning of Summer Solstice on June 21.

Spring Equinox: March 21

This dragon Eiglis is yellow-green. Works with the Air element and the dragon Sairys. Color: Yellow. Good for things pertaining to the mental realm. This season is useful for beginning new ideas or cycles that will require longer periods of time to complete. This is a good time for self-improvement efforts, creating motivation, changes in career or housing, improving material status, setting future goals, and strengthening yourself spiritually. A period of gentle but persistent flow of renewing energy.

Summer Solstice: June 21

The dragon Suuriy glows a garnet red. Works with the Fire element and the dragon Fafnir. Color: Red. Best for anything involving the action realm. The energy flow cycles become longer and faster now. This is a good season, as is Spring, to store vibrational energy in a red cord for use when Earth tides become low. Faeries, elves, and other nature spirits are quite active and willing to communicate. Continue to work on long-term spells and goals. Plant an herb garden, or grow herbs in pots, to better communicate with the nature spirits. Spend time outside in nature for firsthand instructions from the faeries.

Autumn Equinox: September 21

The dragon Shadalyn appears smoky brown. Works with the Water element and the dragon Naelyon. Is most useful for the emotional realm. The tides of Earth energy begin to slow down now in preparation for nature's rest period. From the beginning of this season until the end of October, you can still store energy, but this time by means of knots in a blue cord. This time period is for harvest of any completed seasonal spells. For spells that will need more months, perhaps another year, to ripen, you need to do extra visualization and meditation, as their growth period will be slower at this time.

Winter Solstice: December 21

The dragon Aettall is a very watery blue. Works with the Earth element and the dragon Grael. Good for things in the physical realm. Earth's energy tides are in semi-hibernation in this season. This is a good time for practicing divination, physically and spiritually cleaning your sacred place, doing an inventory on your magickal and spiritual progress, and setting goals for the next year. Do short-term spells that will be ready to manifest close to the next Spring Equinox. Work on your long-term spells to keep them strong and also to see if they show signs of manifesting early.

Seasons are similar to the rise and fall of ocean tides in energy. They are a visual, psychic-sense barometer of energy tides of this planet. Long-term spells benefit most when using seasonal energies.

Divination with the Dragon Script and Shaman Symbols

It is easy to make divination stones. Purchase bags of small or medium-sized oval stones that are used in vases to hold flowers upright. Choose a different color of stone for each set: dragon script, shaman symbols, and planets. Rinse and dry the stones. When completely dry, use black acrylic paint and a brush to mark the symbols on only one side of each stone. Use the following charts for the correct designs: planetary symbols, dragon script, and shaman symbols.

To make it easier yet, the Shaman can use the diagram as a model for making her or his own divination cloth. A piece of dark-colored hemmed cloth, one foot by one foot square, can be marked using a tube of black fabric paint. You can use the appropriate Shaman symbols in the correct places or designate that space with the symbol instead. The following descriptions will help you understand what each section represents.

Storm	Massive transformations coming.
North	Prosperity, success, stability in all life areas.
Chaos	End of a cycle and beginning of a new one. Time of turmoil.
West	Time of emotional changes; love and friendship.
Rainbow	Balance adjustments needed. New situations arise.
South	Hard work ahead.
Savage Heart	Don't say everything you think.
East	Visible movement. Be flexible with new ideas.

For a reading, reach into each stone bag and blindly choose three or four stones. Drop each group randomly across the divination cloth. Using the cloth divisions and the stones' meanings, you can get a thorough answer to your questions. It just takes practice, but it's fun. Read only the stones that have the marking visible and are on the cloth. If a stone is upside down, don't read it; the meaning doesn't apply to the question.

You also can carve the symbols in candles or write them on paper to add to charm bags; this puts more specific energy into a spell.

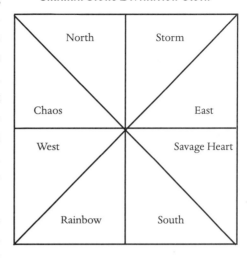

Shaman Stone Divination Cloth

The following lists will give you short answers to the appearance of any stone in a reading.

Dragon Script

A	Movement; important journeys. A new cycle of events in life. Progress after a period of inactivity. Use: To start things moving.	
B	The truth is revealed. Events happen that help you understand something you wondered about. Clearly seeing which decisions to take and which to sidestep. Use: Truth is revealed.	
C, K	Rough road ahead; fighting an uphill battle. Possible harmful gossip or lies. Beware of enemies you thought were friends. Use: To block enemies.	
D	A time of prosperity is near; a monetary gift or opportunity. Use: To attract prosperity.	
E	Changes are coming that you don't want. Your life is temporarily disrupted. Someone close to you is determined to control your life; you need to sever the connection. Use: To rebound any ill-wishing on the sender.	

F	*You are caught between two choices, neither of which benefits you. Your life is troubled because of recent choices. Use: To bring new opportunities.*	
G	*A dating or social opportunity comes your way. Someone strongly attracts you. Use: Love spells.*	
H	*Don't take chances with your money. Someone asks for a loan they won't repay. Use: General protection.*	
I, J	*Happy news comes from a distance. You see evidence that you can get out of a bad life cycle. An unexpected event brings celebration. Use: To change your luck.*	
L	*A busy schedule keeps you on the go. Work stress and heavy load. Use: To protect from stress and turmoil.*	
M	*A new person enters your life and becomes close. Possible addition to the family through birth or marriage. Use: To become creative in your life.*	
N	*A time of inaction in your affairs. A very stagnant period. Use: To gain peace and calm in your life.*	
O, Q	*You are close to reaching a goal. Something happens that makes you set new goals. Use: To reach a goal or gain a desire.*	
P	*Possible move to another city, state, home, or job. Sudden opportunity arises that leaves you no time to delay a choice. Use: To find a new home or job.*	

R	After a period of isolation, you are ready to mingle socially again. Use: To meet new friends.	
S	Psychic happenings signal you to work on spiritual growth. Use: To develop psychic abilities.	
T	Past karma steps in and demands payment in some form. Use: To regain good health.	
U, V	A cycle of roller-coaster events catches you off guard. Use: To reconcile with your family, friend, or lover after a disagreement.	
W	You meet someone who expresses an attraction for you. Uses: If single, to attract a soul mate. If in a relationship, to make it stronger.	
X	Opposition rises from a rival who doesn't want you to succeed. Progress is suddenly halted. Use: To remove barriers to success.	
Y	Sudden separation in a friendship, love relationship, or marriage. A family disagreement builds and explodes. Uses: To escape safely from an unpleasant relationship. Protection from harassment.	
Z	A sudden, unexpected opportunity to rent an apartment or buy a house. A move that benefits you. A life change that gives you stable roots. Use: To improve prosperity.	
End of sentence mark	A peaceful end of one cycle in preparation for something new. Uses: To open doors to new beginnings and opportunities. To erect a barrier between you and an old way of life.	

Shaman Symbols

Sun	☉	*Positive events are coming to you. If near Storm, upsets or illness.*
Moon	☾	*A relationship needs clear reviewing. If near Storm, beware of lies.*
Spiral	◎	*End of one cycle and beginning of another. Making job choices.*
Year Wheel	⊕	*Period of time necessary before events are finished.*
Storm		*Trouble, upsets, arguments.*
Movement		*Blockages removed and movement seen.*
Horns		*Prosperity and success are close.*
Cauldron		*In need of practical guidance in something. Learning from past lives.*
Shooting Star		*Your life events are temporarily out of control.*
Wind		*Movement choices arise, such as home or job.*
Shamrock		*Change of luck; period of good fortune.*
Double Axe		*Bad choices could put you in need of protection.*
Heart	♡	*Love, friendship, family gathering.*

Mountains	⌒⌒⌒	Barriers prevent you moving forward.
Doorway	🁢	Things are opening up.
Water	〰〰	Travel to distant places; several short journeys.
Eye	◎	Something hidden is now revealed.
Star	☆	Spiritual experiences or studies help you look to the future.
Knot	⸙	Unexpected complications interfere with plans.
Rainbow	🌈	All kinds of positive events are headed your way.

Planets' Meanings

Sun: Success; people in authority.

Moon: Intuition; temporary plans; love; the home.

Mercury: Business; communication.

Venus: Love; marriage; creativity; social events.

Mars: Courage; action; conflicts.

Jupiter: Positive time of good events; legal courts; doctors.

Saturn: Protection; need to overcome obstacles.

Uranus: Upheavals; unexpected happenings.

Neptune: Secrets; addictions; illusions.

Pluto: Massive transformation; changes.

Chiron: Events from your past cause present problems.

Ceres: Letting go of old pain.

Pallas: A need to take care and erect shields of protection.

Juno: Marriage or divorce; ending stale relationships.

Vesta: A change of lifestyle becomes necessary.

North Node of Moon: Tensions and stress fill your life.

South Node of Moon: Rewards arrive for past good deeds and work.

Example of a reading: Vesta, B, W, and Mars fall upright in the West section of cloth. North Node, Mountains, and Storm are in Storm section, while A, Heart, and N don't fall on the divination cloth at all. The question is "Will Randy and I have a good romantic relationship?"

Although Lily is searching for her soul mate, Randy doesn't appear to be the one. Something he has not told her will soon be revealed, and the revelation will cause a period of emotional upsets and conflicts. Lily is likely to suddenly end the relationship. With Storm doubled in this reading (the symbol plus the stones in that section), Randy won't want to let go of Lily (Mountains), but the tensions, arguments, and upsets will never stop if they continue to see each other. There will always be a trust and control issue with Randy.

Categories of Dragons

It was surprising to learn there are actually two distinct groupings of the dragon species. They work so well together that one would never expect clan distinctions. The only differences I saw for years was the distribution of work; Mesoamerican, European, Asian, or Middle East shapes; and coloring. I have no idea why the first dragons I met were of the Star-Born clan. Usually, one meets the Star-Moon clan first, because they relate to, and work with, humans much better. As a child, I didn't consider meeting Star-Borns any special privilege, and I still don't. Rather, meeting and working with any dragon is a privilege.

All members of the Star-Born group have five claws on their feet, if they have two or four legs. If there are no legs, they have three upper-front fangs. The Star-Born rarely have subclans. They also interact the least with humans. The Star-Born are primarily unusual colors and shades of colors, with indistinct spots, stripes, or patches. They wear the Great Seal of the Dragon pendant.

The Star-Moon dragons all have four claws on their feet, if they have two or four legs. If not, they have long, featherlike manes. This group has many subclans that make up a major clan. Also, they work with humans and other beings all the time. They distinguish themselves from the Star-Born by wearing a simple five-pointed star pendant.

One would think that the Star-Born clans were a managerial-level type of dragon. However, this isn't true. The major differences seem to be that they work less closely, if at all, with humans, and the fact that they have five claws on each foot, while the Star-Moon clan has only four. Perhaps the always curious humans are wearing on their nerves.

Female dragons often hold leadership positions. Some of the young females (past adolescent stage) and elders dedicate their lives to the clan, not as leaders but as spiritual High Priestesses. The dragons wouldn't give me the exact title, but it seems to be the equivalent in human history to very special Priestesses. These are very powerful dragons.

Sometimes, these Priestesses are asked by their clans to bear young because of the need to continue a specific trait, ability, or DNA structure. These young dragons are reared within the circle of Priestesses until they reach the adolescent stage. Then the little dragons are sent to the mother's clan to live a normal dragon life and be trained.

The following lists of clans, groups, dragon names, and colorings should help you identify the dragons you meet while on an Otherworld journey or while you are working magick. Using these lists will also prepare you for exploring their separate areas in the Otherworld.

Star-Born Dragon Clans

Chaos: Most of them work full-time within the Void; a few of them work full-time with the Light and Dark dragons. Leader: Ziri Kaar. Their colors are very dark, such as black, gray, magenta, purple, and green. They are the largest dragons except for the Savage Heart clan of warriors.

Cloud Masters: Also known as the Metal Masters. Leader: Hahdatai. This dragon clan taught all blacksmiths on all worlds and all levels how to work with the metals on their planet. They are hues of the metallic substances with which they work.

Fire-Heart: Historians for all dragons, concerning their Multiversal work. Leader: Meshlam. Aldram, Keeper of the Book, is from this clan. They are also responsible for keeping records on when, where, and how the dragons find the Annihilator, with the hope that a pattern will show that will allow the dragons to destroy this sentient evil. They are the general Star-Born colors, but have a pulsating red glow in their chests just behind their Great Seal pendant.

Mystic Star: Spiritual teachers of the four Mystery Schools. The Four Hidden Dragons guard the school gates to prevent entry by those not ready. The Mystic Stars do the actual teaching. Leader: Kyrzis. These are colored frosty lavender or a medium misty purple.

Rainbow: They balance the Multiverse energy flows that affect the dragon eggs and young ones in Dragon World. In other words, it is their duty to provide the best atmosphere so that their species might survive. Leader: Beh-Raph-Bo. Their brilliant coloring fluctuates according to the energy flows that brush against them.

Savage Heart: Warriors and Gate guardians to all Gates to areas of the Otherworld and throughout the Multiverse. Leader: Arallu. Like the Fire-Heart clan, these are the usual Star-Born hues. However, they have a distinct mark of two overlapping hearts on their foreheads. When calm, this mark wavers between blue and green. When they are working with other warriors and guarding Gates, this mark changes between yellow and orange. When they attend a Dragon Warrior's initiation, the mark glows softly with all shades of lavender, purple, gold, and silver. When a Savage Heart is engaged in fighting negative energy, this mark flashes streams of blood-red light.

Snow: A subclan of the Rainbow clan, they are messengers and creative helpers throughout the Multiverse. Leader: Eeza. They are colored like brilliant golden sunlight overlaid with sparkling crystalline snow.

White Dragon Breath: Also known as the *Gem Masters*, this clan carefully watches the stones on all planets for changes. Such changes predict the health of the planets. Leader: Uurnos. These dragons have the chameleon-like quality of blending in with their surroundings.

Star-Moon Dragon Clans

Astra-Keepers: They work with the energies of the planets, days, zodiac, the Nodes of the Moon—in other words, astrology in general. There are dragons of these individual energy flows, but they have no major Leader. They have midnight-blue wings, with this color spreading faintly onto their white body at the chest area. The subgroups working with the planets and such have individual and different coloring.

Storm-Bringers: This clan works with the elusive but powerful Storm element. They also work with certain Chaos Dragons. Leader of Storm: Charoseia. Leader of Chaos group: Ziri Kaar. The Storm-Bringers are a smoky black with slashes of lightning-white on their backs.

Time-Flight: These work with the elements and Seasons, helping to blend energies into a repeating, logical year. They have Leaders of individual groups, but no major Leader. They appear in all true bright colors.

Web Weavers: They work with Seers of the Merkabah, Seers of All Time, co-magicians, and Ring Initiators. Leader: Aia Cardys. There are also separate leaders for each smaller clan. This clan is a mixture of glittery and somber colors, marked with mystical symbols. The scales of some look like a mask around the eyes, a silver cap over the head, or head ornaments hanging on the forehead.

STAR-MOON SUBGROUPS

Four Hidden Dragons in the Rings Center: 1. Durka. 2. Hun-Tun. 3. Im-Miris. 4. Gark-Yin. See the Dragon Apprentice section for the coloring of these dragons.

Moon Quarters: 1. Yen-Iamar of the First Quarter. Color: Very pale pearlescent blue. 2. Memezah of the Full Moon. Color: Iridescent white. 3. Unteekah of the Third Quarter. Color: Very pale pearlescent lavender. 4. Jyn-Kuaan of the New Moon. Color: Iridescent black.

North Node of the Moon: Nadra Tho. As part of the Astra-Keepers, she is a silver-blue moonstone shade with a royal blue head. Forehead Ascending Node mark in black.

South Node of the Moon: Nadrica Thysa. Also part of the Astra-Keepers, her body is a multicolored shimmer in black moonstone with a royal blue head. Forehead Descending Node mark in black.

Sun: Salaquet. Colors: Yellow and gold.

Moon: Memezah. Colors: Intermingling, changing pale colors of lavender, silver, blue, and pearl white.

Mercury: Talm. Colors: Multiple shades of orange.

Venus: Shemaleth. Colors: Soft pinks and greens.

Mars: Durankayta. Color: Red.

Jupiter: Yanizar. Colors: Medium blue and purple.

Saturn: Bulla Kasz. Colors: Black and indigo.

Uranus: Keetan. Color: Iridescent blues.

Neptune: Vunoket. Color: Sea-green.

Pluto: Zeirahnak. Colors: Deep reds and maroon.

Asteroid belt: Fylufor. This dragon has been called *Lucifer* by some and belongs to the Astra-Keepers. Fylufor has the unique ability to change colors from sky blue with irregular spots of glowing white moonstone scales to sunrise pink with glowing pearlescent scales. However, his usual color of pewter gray always shows somewhere on his body. His actions sometimes appear to affect planetary events in an unpredictable manner. However, all his orders for activities come directly from the Great Goddess and the God, which is the same as saying from the Source. His influence covers not only the asteroid belt but such smaller globes as Ceres and others.

Spring Equinox: Eiglis is yellow-green and works with the Air element.

Summer Solstice: Suuriy glows a garnet red and works with the Fire element.

Autumn Equinox: Shadalyn appears smoky brown and works with the Water element.

Winter Solstice: Aettall is a very watery blue and works with the Earth element.

Earth element: Grael. Color: Dark green.

Air element: Sairys. Color: Yellow.

Fire element: Fafnir. Color: Red.

Water element: Naelyon. Color: Blue.

Storm element: Charoseia. Color: Stormy gray.

Light dragons: Llan Vys. White and very pale shades such as ivory, orchid, lilac, and so forth.

Dark dragons: Nalm Kor. Degrees of dark purple to almost black. Sometimes they have silver sprinkles across their scales, like stars.

Dragon Names in This Book

Aettall	Grael	Na-Gina
Aia Cardys	Hahdatai	Naelyon
Ajyt	Hecate	Nalm Kor
Aldram	Hun-Tun	Nangra
Amu	Hydria	Sairys
Arallu	Iliuyanka	Salaquet
Beh-Raph-Bo	Im-Miris	Shadalyn
Bullakasz	Juuja	Shemaleth
Charoseia	Kaudra	Soma
Dohdonta	Keetan	Suuriy
Durankayta	Kirki	Talm
Durga	Kyrzis	Tefnoot
Durka	Llan Vys	Tiamat
Eepepha	Medusa	Uurnos
Eeza	Memezah	Visn-Isp
Eiglis	Meshlam	Vunoket
Fafnir	Mirraglas	Yanizar
Fylufor	Nadra Tho	Zeirahnak
Gark-Yin	Nadrica Thysa	Ziri Kaar

Dragon Council Meeting Meditation

The Dragon Council is held in a place between the worlds (this world and the Other-world) and in a time outside of time. Representatives of all dragon clans meet in the "bubble" in space that appears near a secured part of Dragon World at certain star-times—the only way dragons bother to measure time, except by seasons. There is a question whether the dragon Elders create this space bubble as needed, or whether it appears on its own at measurable star-times. Or whether it can be called upon to appear as needed. The attending chosen dragons all hold high positions of responsibility and authority.

When inside this "bubble," you are surrounded by the blackness of space and the cold glitter of distant suns and planets. To dragons, seeming to hang in space with nothing to support them or to indicate what is up or down is nothing new or strange, but to a human this can be disconcerting at first. One thing is certain: you can't enter this Council meeting without being invited and accompanied by one of the participating dragons. This isn't a "drop in as you please" meeting.

It is not uncommon for these meetings to reconvene at the Gate to the Highest realm, near the cavern of the crystal-scaled dragon Kaudra. This second meeting is a special spiritual ritual of sacred communication with the Supreme Creative Force and the archangels. At the end of this meeting, the dragons are given advice and information about possible future events that will affect either certain worlds, certain levels, or the entire Multiverse.

The dragons rarely discuss what happens in the space bubble except with other responsible dragons. However, anyone can listen in on the second meeting. Just don't expect to be able to hear all of this telepathic communication. If dragons don't want you to know something, you won't be able to hear it, or won't be told.

Since most Ring students aren't quite ready to be invited into the space bubble yet, this meditation will be held at the Highest Gate in the Upperworld.

At some of these secondary meetings, you may see dragon emotions that are startling, depending upon the subject of discussion. Most students are aware that all dragons breathe out a type of energy we humans call fire. Dragons are naturally attracted by physical fire, which produces a form of energy. Candle rituals and spells that burn paper appeal to dragons, although they like to participate in positive rituals of all types, especially spiritual ones. What the student may not realize is that this fire-breathing from the nose and mouth can be used as a warning, a protective device, or an expression of anger. If you attend a secondary meeting, it is best to stand off to the side or in the back. Dragons will not deliberately harm you, but if you are in the line of fire from dragon anger, you will likely have a bad headache and skin that feels scraped raw for a few days.

As a Dragon Shaman, you can invoke more travel energy by mentally walking a spiral path to invoke Dragon Breath energy in the Earth's astral body. Each circling spiral lifts you higher into the astral and the special place where the Dragon Council will meet. Physically walking a spiral or labyrinth, tracing the lines of a hand-held model, or mentally walking the spiral changes your brain waves and creates an altered state of consciousness. If you mentally walk the spiral path just prior to entering a meditation, your journey between worlds will be faster and your senses sharper when you arrive.

Use meditation opening on page 7.

You find yourself part of a small crowd of beings standing a short distance from the gold Gate to the Highest. Directly in front of the Gate are several large, older dragons, who are communicating with the Goddess, the God, and the old dragon (She Who Dwells Within the Greatest) just beyond the Gate. Nothing said makes any sense to you even though you can hear the voices. It seems to be a routine discussion on various happenings throughout the Multiverse and the fact that the cloud-entity known as the Annihilator hasn't appeared for some time.

Suddenly, you feel the gaze of the oldest dragon beyond the Gate. You look straight into her eyes and know nothing in your life is hidden from her. You feel an urge to go to Kaudra at the crystal cave and ask if she will let you enter. Your co-magician dragon appears at your side and nods agreement. The two of you walk toward Kaudra, who uncurls and yawns widely. You feel her warm greetings within your mind.

"You must enter alone," your dragon tells you. "If you ask for advice, you will be told what you need, not what you want. If you are not open to such truth yet, sit a while in one of the shrine areas and think upon your life and goals. Return here when finished. I will escort you to a dragon healing session."

You enter the shadowy cave entrance to find yourself inside a huge geode lined with crystals of every kind and color. Straight ahead is the crystal bubble of the Dream Chamber. You bypass this and wander down a hall, looking into side chambers that contain meditation seats, ledge-beds, counselor benches, thrones with smaller seats, and small shrines. You enter one throne chamber and find that the God or the Goddess is sitting on a throne, waiting to talk to you. Angels stand beside the throne. You sit on the smaller seat and listen to the spiritual messages given to you.

The deity finishes and disappears. You walk back outside and follow your dragon to the Temple of All-Healing. This Temple sits within the Garden of Wisdom and Solitude, where a high hedge encloses an endless garden of all Earth's cultures and some from other galaxies. This Garden is filled with a multitude of shrines, temples, gazebos, and flower-covered shelters. The flower-lined paths lead you past small streams, waterfalls, fountains, ponds, and over short bridges.

The Temple of All-Healing is a massive white marble building with room after room of tables covered with richly embroidered blankets. Dragons and angels are working over many people already on the healing tables. Your dragon leads you to an empty table where a dragon patiently waits.

You lie down on the table, close your eyes, and relax. You hear beautiful music and smell the flowers from the garden outside. As the healer moves her hands slowly over you, touching and adjusting a place here and there, you relax even more under the current of warm, loving energy as it flows through you on its healing mission.

When the healer finishes, you thank her and go with your dragon back out into the great Garden.

Use meditation ending on page 8.

(End of the meditation)

Healing Auric Wounds

You will be introduced to the human auras and chakras first in this chapter before moving on to the more difficult technique of retrieving pieces of a shattered soul.

For this part of the Shaman's training, you will definitely need a polished piece of black onyx or obsidian to vacuum up astral parasites and other debris, as well as a snow quartz for sealing psychic wounds and the River Rock crystal called the Soul Retriever. The onyx is a trap and cleanser stone because it traps any negative energy and grounds it in the Earth.

The piece of black onyx should be a size that you can hold comfortably in one hand. If you choose obsidian, be certain that it has no rough edges, as obsidian is volcanic glass and can cut you. Snow quartz is a very cloudy, opaque piece of crystal. It is easier to find it in chunks than points, and is a little cheaper also.

River Rock quartz is a very interesting, and useful, piece of quartz crystal. These rounded or oval chunks of crystal are found and harvested just once a year from certain rivers in Alaska. They begin their journey by water far inland and are rough, nature-tumbled pieces with an exterior like bonded sand by the time the stones reach the harvest area. However, when the miners cut a thin slice off one side or end, they reveal a beautiful interior. Sometimes the inside view is completely clear, while other times it has fractures, veils, and inclusions that are breathtaking.

Placing the new stones in a Tibetan "singing" bowl and causing the vessel to ring by rubbing the rim with the wooden mallet is a beautiful way to cleanse stones. Singing bowls can be purchased in either metal or crystal. Crystal bowls are exorbitant in price—out of my financial reach, and I assume out of yours, too. The metal bowls, in my opinion, are far more reliable (unbreakable) and beautiful. Many of them are made by exiled Tibetans and hand-painted with special symbols such as Wind Horse.

The size of the bowl determines the note it sings. Some are quite elaborate, made of thick metal, and come in a special box with a cushion. However, these thicker bowls with no decoration do not seem to have the uplifting tones of the less expensive ones. I have had the best results with the slightly thinner, painted bowls—those with no fancy box or cushion.

You can use the harmonic tones of a Tibetan singing bowl to cleanse an area, a house, or a person's aura. The reverberating sound is a perfect balance of positive and negative energies. Using the small wooden mallet, tap the bowl three times to begin. Then gently rub the mallet around the outside lip of the bowl. This produces a beautiful humming sound. Carry the bowl on the palm of your hand, or a cushion, while you direct the tone where you need it to go.

You can also put small objects or stones inside the bowl while making it sing. However, I don't recommend you do this with delicate crystal points, as they might be damaged. The wonderful thing about a good Tibetan bowl is that it improves with age, becoming more powerful with frequent use.

The Ohm tuning fork will similarly cleanse an aura. A set of tuning forks, through an octave of sound, will also work, but that takes more learning time. The Ohm tone is a Multiversal sound. When the fork is lightly struck against your knee and moved about in a person's aura, or around an object, it attunes and rebalances both the physical aura and the spiritual body. It can open all energy blocks in whatever level they are. It loosens tense, knotted muscles with little discomfort.

If you do not have tuning forks or singing bowls, you can use special vocalized sounds as a cleansing instrument. Choose one of the appropriate sounds and chant it slowly while moving your crystal all around the patient. The sound "doom" is chanted for protection; "hreem" to call in guardians and teachers; "mmm" vibrates to build balance; "aahh" helps heal the body and mind; and "eeee" (as in "feel") increases energy. The sound "pah," which is a short, hard sound, is used by both Shaman and Warrior. Combined with a quick outward thrust of an arm, palm forward, this is a powerful defense against psychic attack or incoming negative energy, especially when traveling in the Otherworld.

The Dragon Shaman usually does not concern herself or himself with hands-on physical healing, since the Shaman's responsibility is healing on the spiritual level, which then works down to the physical body. However, she or he needs to know a few basics concerning the nonphysical parts of a human, such as the chakras and the auras. These vital astral "organs" can become imbalanced, nonfunctioning, blocked, or attacked, either by others or through the actions of the sick person. These imbalances may well contribute to the condition called the shattered soul, but they can exist on their own also.

It is important that the Shaman learn how to diagnose the body-mind-spirit imbalances of a person. That can mean finding the true source of a physical disease or a remedy for lack of prosperity. Often, a physical disease is tightly connected to an unfulfilled need in another area. For example, stress and lack of daily security can trigger many diseases, from insomnia and depression to heart problems. Science revealed recently that stress, particularly long-term stress, automatically releases a caustic chemical into the bloodstream. This chemical is quickly carried throughout the entire body, causing malfunctions in delicate cells and organs. The release of this chemical is a built-in function. The Dragon Shaman, and all magicians, must learn how to undo any damage, whether caused by this chemical, or by injury, disease, or magickally inflicted.

Energy can be changed and/or exchanged between opposites. The predominant energy will prevail. Intent, directed energy is capable of moving and changing anything, because, at the basic level, everything is vibrating energy. You simply need to find the fulcrum point, where deliberately applying energy will produce the result you want. However, all that said, we are not the powerful dragons, and we often can't accomplish what we desire to. That is why magickal studies with the dragons is an accumulative effort that builds the magician's power over a long period of time.

The body of every human (and other beings) is surrounded by an invisible electromagnetic field called the aura. In fact, every animate and inanimate object has an aura.

Some psychics visually see the aura as layers of colored lights, while others see it only as a pale white light. Still others "see" the aura and the colors with their inner eyes in their mind. There is no right or wrong way to view the aura, but it does take a little practice. When you try this, let your eyes go slightly out of focus and look just beyond the person you are viewing. The dragons say that this method is the easiest for humans. If in doubt, always silently ask your dragons for help, especially with interpretation of off-colors, flares out from the body, indentations, or dark places.

We generally speak as if a person has one aura, although we all have several layers of aura. Each layer extends further from the physical body than the layer before it. The first five layers are concerned with six of the lower chakras, as well as what the person thinks, feels, and is experiencing in her or his life. The Shaman needs to consider only the outer layers, which are important to the astral and spiritual aspects. Writers differ on the number of aura layers, as they do the number of chakras. I will discuss aura layers six through eleven, which is more than enough to work with. See the diagram.

The sixth aura layer links with the brow chakra in the center of the forehead. This is the area known as the third eye. This aura helps with cross-time travel, Otherworld journeys, finding parallel universes, and expanding the use of the psychic.

The seventh layer links a person with the past, present, and future. It attaches to the crown chakra. If a past life or lives are directly influencing and affecting the present life, the Shaman will find evidence of that in this aura layer.

The eighth layer looks like an iridescent egg shape around the human body, often as thick as four feet. It has energy waves rippling through it at all times. It connects with the transpersonal chakra that lies above the crown of the head. This is like a "tattletale" aura, as it contains evidence of all our experiences. If the Shaman suspects the patient's behavior is more to blame than outside influence, this is the aura to check.

The ninth layer is sometimes called the *ketheric aura*, and it is the only layer that doesn't surround the body. It exists as a small, whirling, flat vortex spinning above the head. Its objective is to connect all the aura layers with spiritual energy and the Otherworld. It is the body-place that contains the contents of the person's soul, or at least the door to that soul.

The tenth aura, often named the *integrative*, is simply a pathway between the physical world and the Otherworld. Its stage of development determines how difficult the person finds it to astral travel.

Layers of auras

The transmutational layer, or eleventh aura, sees that the complete person, on all levels of existence, is constantly nourished with energy from the very depths of the Earth.

Chakra is a Sanskrit word roughly translated as "Wheel of Fire." Hindu teachings describe seven major chakras that run from the base of the spine to the crown of the head. However, there are also many minor chakras, some of which are of greater importance than others. As you can see in the diagram, the seven major chakras are seated in the astral body (and connected to the spinal column) in such a manner that they regulate or affect every body part and each corresponding area of life. Each chakra has a specific color and function and attaches to special endocrine glands. Metaphysical healers use these chakras in healing work.

However, the Shaman needs to go beyond the physical into the more esoteric areas of the eighth and ninth chakras for spiritual work. The eighth chakra, or transpersonal chakra, isn't connected to the physical body but lies about eighteen inches above the crown of the head. It is actually the mediation center between the physical and spiritual planes for the intake of Multiversal energy. Although all chakras draw in this energy, the transpersonal chakra refines the intake to energy that feeds the spiritual level of each person. Blockage here can affect connections with the Otherworld, the dragons, and any guides and teachers. The block may be caused by the person because of lack of spiritual activity or interest. However, it may be imbalanced by others who disagree with that person's spiritual path choice, or any number of other malicious reasons.

In this case, the Shaman must learn to look all over the body, but especially at the eighth and ninth chakras, for what is called "cording." Discovering cording requires careful inspection in many cases. The cording will appear as a thin line leading away from the patient toward whomever is responsible. Don't let the cord's color confuse you. White does not mean "good" or "nice." Cording, of whatever color, indicates an attack, manipulation, a siphoning of energy, conveying illness and harm. Most people aren't aware they do this and would be horrified to be accused. However, others, such as psychic vampires and dark magicians, attach cords deliberately and with intent. A determined wave of your onyx cleansing stone will sever any cording, sucking up the debris, but the chakra must then be sealed with energy projected with your snow crystal. If the cording is resistant to cutting in this manner, use the sound of a tuning fork or a Tibetan singing bowl to sever the cord and quickly seal the chakra.

The ninth chakra is the universal chakra. It lies about six inches above the transpersonal chakra, and is completely disconnected from any remote attachment to the physical level. This chakra is a direct connection between the pure spiritual part of a human—the spirit and soul—and the Supreme Creative Force.

Two sets of minor chakra can be used by the Shaman as part of teaching the patient to help herself or himself. A minor chakra lies in the palm of each hand. These

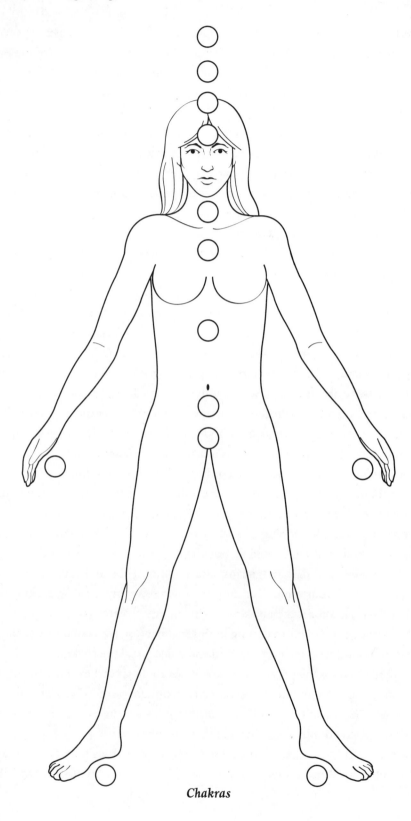

Chakras

can send, receive, or direct cosmic energy. If the patient holds a quartz crystal, amethyst, or piece of amber in each hand, she or he will quickly absorb the stones' energies. These will naturally blend with, and amplify, positive energy sent by the Shaman and the dragons.

The other set of minor chakra is the one in the sole of each foot. They provide a steady link with Earth energy. If they become clogged, however, it is useful to walk barefoot on the ground itself. They are of great use to all dragon students and magicians, as excess magickal energy can be sent through these areas to be grounded and neutralized in the Earth. If stone energy is needed for healing, place clear or smoky quartz near the sole of each foot.

Magickal diagnosis is also done physically by searching the aura and the area of each chakra for hot spots, cold spots, or other irregularities. The Shaman opens her or his intuitive senses while slowly moving her or his hands about six inches away from the patient's body. Move the hands in the air, primarily around the head and upper torso, without touching the person. As with viewing the aura, there is no one right way to "feel" the condition of an aura. You simply must practice and decide for yourself whether you see, feel, or see within your mind any irregularities and what your intuition tells you they mean.

It is wise to call upon your dragons for help whenever you do spellwork. The dragons see deeply into the karmic and present background of every human. This helps them in recommending any necessary changes or ingredients in a spell. They may even tell you if the imbalance comes from a past life. In this case, you would work to cut the link between that or those lives and the present one. However, if the disease is connected with a shattered soul and pieces are missing, you need to refer the patient to someone on the Shaman level for soul retrieval until you have learned how to retrieve yourself.

There are a few patients you will not be able to help regardless of what you do. Either they haven't learned the karmic lesson from their past or they have no desire to release the disease they have. It may give them the control and attention they desire. They may even be subconsciously sabotaging the spells because they don't believe in magick or your magickal abilities.

In terminal cases, non-working spells frequently mean that the patient's life cycle is ending as it should. All your spells would do is to temporarily extend the discomfort of the person involved. I realize that if the person in question is someone for whom you care deeply, you will do the spells anyway. That is, until your mind and spirit accept the inevitable. Then you will work spells for peaceful release of this life.

It is difficult for any Shaman to admit defeat. However, sometimes it simply isn't meant for you to interfere in an area. If you have prepared the spell ingredients correctly and held a deep intent and concentration while doing the spell, and in a month nothing has improved, try a different spell or reword the one you used. If in another month there is no positive result, then you are wasting energy if you continue. Sometimes you must simply accept that you aren't meant to make changes. The failure could be connected to any of the reasons given before. In such cases, consult with your co-worker dragon for advice. The co-worker is unlikely to stop you before you attempt any spells, for you need to learn to discern the vibrations that point to a failure of spells. Besides, you never know unless you try if the patient needs just a small nudge to make the necessary changes. Even the dragons cannot predict 100 percent accurately on some cases.

Healing the Shattered Soul

Every shamanic culture teaches the value of what is called soul retrieval. This expression has nothing to do with "losing" your soul by playing with psychic boards, attending séances, being possessed, or meditating. Instead, the soul-part shattered loose and went into hiding in the Otherworld. The term applies to people who have experienced traumas, personal tragedies, illnesses, and crises of such depth that a part of that person could not endure the inner pain. A soul also can become shattered from accidents, falls, head trauma, emotionally traumatic experiences, abuse of any kind, or heavy and prolonged stress.

The Shaman usually finds these soul pieces in the Underworld or in the dark forest of the Middleworld, called the Grove of Shadows and Twilight. She or he should never threaten or force any pieces of a shattered soul to return. If they are coerced into returning, they will seek the first opportunity to leave again. The environment and living conditions of the person to whom they belong must change to make the soul want to be whole.

Actually, everyone has at least a small piece of soul off wandering. As soon as we rebalance our lives, usually emotionally, the piece returns to us at once. The most difficult task all Ring students must do is find, talk to, forgive, and become at peace with what is known as the Shadow Self.

Some of your journeys may not go as you planned. Your exploration or patrolling can turn into an exploration of your Shadow Self, which is the hidden side we each have and all the beliefs, behaviors, and tendencies we dislike or repress in our personalities. The more you criticize this part of yourself, the more control it has over you. So, when you suddenly find yourself face to face with your Shadow Self—and you will—treat that Self with respect and kindness. That part can help you to recover pieces of your own shattered soul. It is necessary to slowly merge both sides for better personal balance.

The Shadow Self is a nebulous form—a part of every human's personality, mind, and being. It *is* a Shadow, just as a physical body creates a shadow in sunlight. It contains all the characteristics and habits that we keep hidden from society. We hide these negatives to avoid criticism, ostracism, and unfavorable remarks from family, friends, and social acquaintances. The Shadow Self isn't evil, nor should you deny its existence. You never attack it. You seek it out in the Otherworld and talk with it. Firmly, but politely, tell it that it can't control your life. However, as part of yourself, you need it to cooperate and work with you. Together you make a stronger, wiser being. Blended with the Shadow Self, you can easily track down and retrieve pieces of a shattered soul.

When you find your journey detouring to the Shadow Self, the Light and Dark dragons have taken over. Light dragons are just as likely as are Dark ones to take you firmly in hand to reshape your life. However, Light dragons are a bit gentler. Working with Dark dragons is usually a rough ride, but the results their methods bring are effective and lasting.

Shadow Self work is like a rite of passage. First, you learn to separate yourself from your old way of thinking and reacting. A transition of feeling in between states, or in a kind of limbo, follows. Slowly, you move into your new way of life and find you have changed.

You can meet your Shadow Self anywhere in the Otherworld, but the final confrontation is most likely to take place in the dark, rather spooky Grove of Shadows and Twilight, which is in the Middleworld. This is a sacred grove of tall evergreen trees with long branches that sweep the ground while others intertwine above. This produces a weak pattern of patchy sunlight on the wandering paths inside the Grove. You may meet the earthy, darker deities in this Grove, such as the Horned God or the Dark Mother, perhaps even the Hunter and Huntress. These deities are *not* the devil or demons of any type. As with the Light and Dark dragons, or you and your Shadow Self, they are merely a different kind of necessary balancing energy. These earthy deities frequently have valuable insight into your life and can help you contact your Shadow Self.

Prepare for this Otherworld journey by holding your Retriever crystal in your lap or placing it near you.

Use the meditation opening on page 7.

You find yourself in the bright light of Middleworld. Your co-magician dragon is with you for support only. She or he will not help you in retrieving soul pieces or talking to your Shadow Self. You are holding the Retriever crystal in your power hand.

As you look around at the cloud of butterflies and dragonflies attracted by your dragon friend, you become aware of a tingling within the crystal. The stone twitches slightly. When you look in that direction, you see a hesitant movement of something within a nearby flower bed. A rainbow shimmer reveals itself, then ducks into hiding again. You realize this is the soul piece you've been missing and want back.

You send out a mental call, coaxing, welcoming, a sense of "Hurry home, please." The rainbow shimmer shows itself again. You hold out the crystal in invitation. The rainbow piece hesitantly moves toward you, then darts into the crystal in your hand. You touch the Retriever to the crown of your head. A sense of comforting warmth flows down through your body as the soul-piece returns to its place. Before you can remove the Retriever, two more small pieces sweep through the crystal to join the first.

Instinctively, you realize the process won't always be this easy. These pieces of your shattered soul were ready to return because of the changes you made since becoming a student of the Inner Rings. If in the past you had any major traumas in your life, and the soul-pieces haven't returned, you will have to seek them out and coax them back. This may require several journeys.

"That is for another journey," your dragon friend tells you when she or he senses your desire to find any other lost pieces of your soul. "Now is the time to look for your Shadow Self. If you can have open talks with this Self, it will make your other work easier."

You follow your friend along a winding path until you see the deep shadows of the sacred Grove just ahead. You feel prickles on your skin as you try to see inside the thick mass of trees. Except for the narrow path that enters these trees, the Grove conceals whatever is within it. Your dragon walks with you as far as the edge of the path where it enters the Grove.

"This you must do alone," the dragon tells you. "I will be here if you should have a great need for me. If that happens, center your thoughts on me and you will instantly be with me."

You take a deep breath as you step into the shadows that cross the path ahead of you. You hear branches slide down behind you, covering the entrance. Determined, you walk deeper into the Grove, projecting waves of welcome ahead of you. The path wanders back and forth around the ancient trees, sometimes coming in a full circle, yet you never return to the same place. When you step between two tall monoliths, you see a quick movement in the shadows ahead and hear jeering laughter. You realize this must be your Shadow Self.

You move on, speaking out loud to this shadow of yourself, trying to convince it to talk to you. The annoying laughter continues as you walk along the path, deeper into the Grove.

"Are you afraid to speak to me?" you ask. "We are two parts of one being. We have become separated and confrontational only because we fear our differences. We should work together."

The laughter stops and an exact replica of you steps onto the path, hands on hips and a frown on her or his face. The Shadow Self tells you plainly what you said and did that created her or him. You hear a tone of shame when the Self mentions actions and words that were definitely wrong, and you knew it. You must take

*and admit responsibility. If you don't, this Self will be harder to talk to when you
meet the next time.*

*"Meet me again when I journey here," you tell the Self. "We should know each
other better. Maybe work together here in the Otherworld."*

The Shadow Self shrugs and disappears back into the darkness under the trees.

"It is a beginning," a deep voice says.

*You look to one side as the Horned God steps forward. He looks no different
than any man except for his dark and watchful eyes, a loincloth of skin, and the
pair of spreading antlers on his head. You clearly feel the powerful energy radiating
from this deity. There is no denying that the Horned God is real—and far stronger
in his magickal abilities than you guessed.*

*"Your Shadow heard and felt the true intent behind your words. Treat your
Shadow Self with love and compassion, for you created it." The Horned God points
toward the wall of trees. The branches lift to reveal the garden beyond. "Go now,
Child, and think deeply about this meeting."*

*You quickly exit the Grove of Shadows and Twilight. Your dragon is waiting. The
two of you discuss what happened inside the Grove, as you walk toward a splashing
fountain. There, for the first time in your Otherworld journeys, you cup your hands
and take a drink. The sparkling water seems to make things clearer to you.*

Use the meditation ending on page 8.

(End of the meditation)

Concentrated Intent and Visualization

Our belief that thought can be projected into the Multiverse and have an impact on
reality makes perfect sense. The energy of intent thoughts can actually be measured.
Since everything is a form of energy, and all is connected, then a concentrated thought
with deep intent will have an affect on the end result of that thought-desire. It will
attract to it all the similar energies it needs to manifest or make changes. This is the
entire foundation and basis of magick.

When we teach our brains how to slow to the alpha-wave rhythm, we have the
greatest results with magick and meditation, receive the most accurate new information from the Multiverse, function best on astral and Otherworld journeys, and are
better able to use our psychic abilities. Alpha is the relaxed state that registers seven to
fourteen cycles per second. You can most effectively create the alpha state by learning
deep meditation or training to use biofeedback equipment. But meditation is far more
fun and instructive.

During the alpha state, we easily step away from time and space (area) categories
into the timeless, endless Otherworld without a problem. While we are in this mind

cycle, our mind projects the energy of whatever thought or thoughts dominate. Since we have raised our conscious and subconscious minds above ordinary, distracting reality and entered the wide-open superconscious mind that contains the energies and actions of everything and every person who has ever lived on Earth, we create a direct pipeline between our intent and the manifested result we want.

However, what we little realize is that we make a daily impact on our own lives by the kinds of thoughts we constantly hold and dwell on. Like attracts like, remember? If you are consistently pessimistic, believe you are a pawn in life, don't think you deserve or never will have good luck and a changed and better future, then you certainly will get what your thoughts send out daily on the energy waves of the Multiverse.

It is actually much easier to influence matter than we suppose it to be. Dr. Masaru Emoto proved this by photographing the results of his experiments on water. The results of good words, good thoughts, and good feelings toward such a simple thing as a jar of water have profound, photographically visible effects on the droplets. When the concentrated thoughts are positive, the crystals formed by a drop of water are exceptionally beautiful. When the concentrated thoughts are negative, the droplets are deformed, drab, and ugly.

The average human body is 70 percent liquid (water). If we bombard our own minds and goals (again, a mental activity) with constant negative energy, through our lack of self-confidence, fear, or envy/hatred of someone else, we will receive only negative results. You must learn to visualize the positive result you want as an accomplished task. You must speak of it in the same manner. Don't say, "I want to find a soul mate." Rather, word it as a completed goal: "I thank you, dragons, for bringing my soul mate to me." Don't think about the in-between steps to this happening, or the exact scenario in which it will happen. Concentrate only upon your soul mate already waiting for you just outside the door for a date. Although it is best not to visualize facial features, you may well find that you instantly "know" she or he has dark hair, green eyes, or a lopsided smile that melts your heart. The same techniques apply, whatever your desire or the result you want from magick.

Practice monitoring your words for a week. You will be shocked at how you constantly surround yourself with negative energy, expectations, and talk. It is little wonder that manifestations often don't appear in the form we wish. They are warped and twisted into something else by the stream of negativity aimed at them—which is another good reason *not* to talk about your spellwork.

The next step to change this is to catch each negative word before it is uttered. Instead, rephrase the sentence in a positive manner. Of course, that still leaves the negative thought, which carries as much power as the spoken word. Rephrase the mental thought too, so that positive energy overtakes and erases the negative.

It is helpful to take a quiet time and write out on paper the positive manifestation that you are seeking. Don't be so detailed (such as demanding a job with a particular company) that you lose the opportunity for a better career elsewhere. Read the paper when finished. Close your eyes and visualize the manifestation as completed and waiting for you. Read the paper each day, even twice a day, and visualize the outcome. If you wish to add magickal energy to this, burn the paper after the visualization. Write out a new paper, visualize, and burn the paper each day. Doing so allows you to make small changes you might have overlooked when writing out the first paper. And yes, this does work. Perhaps not instantaneously, although that has occurred.

If you concentrate on the smallest detail in the manifestation, it may require more time for the energies to form this detail for you. But neither should you phrase your desire so broadly that there is little or no form for the magick to fill. Practice speaking and thinking in positive ways. Take time to write out and visualize each result you seek. If you don't take the time to learn these valuable techniques, you will not be able to change your future in the direction you want it to go. Use the written paper and visualization as part of a ritual or specific spell. Magick always concentrates and focuses energy. By learning how to think with intent and visualize the result you want, your success using magick will increase by leaps. True magick requires a lot of mental work.

Dragon Shaman Initiation

You have learned so much about yourself and about the Multiverse in which you live since you began your studies as a Dragon Apprentice. You are definitely not the same person you were.

The Otherworld experiences of a Dragon Shaman change everything and everyone they touch, directly or indirectly. The major changes happen in your personal mental and spiritual realms. This result keeps the Shaman from accepting a stagnant belief system or state of mind. All this study and changing were necessary in order for you to be able to advance to the last two Rings. Prepare for your Dragon Shaman initiation with confidence but also with humility, knowing that your work with the dragons and the Otherworld are a vital part of the continued dance of balance.

Ingredients: Altar cloth; small bowls of salt and water; your altar stones; incense. Place your new black ribbon on the altar.

Preferable day: New Moon, to symbolize the dramatic step you are taking to reach the Warrior Ring.

Use the ceremony opening on page 52.

(Beginning of the ceremony)

As you relax, knowing your co-magician dragon is beside you, you hear the approach of many dragons. They are chanting in their own language—the tones and countertones sounding like a vast orchestration, drums booming in the background. The chant vibrates through your body, wrapping you in the pleasure that you have worked hard to reach this initiation. Your heightened senses reveal that you are once more in the cavern where you signed your name in Aldram's book to become a dragon student.

You see the dragons surrounding you, and you recognize several Moosha warriors among them. The Moosha are the largest of the dragons and exude a seriousness that is often a little intimidating to sentient beings such as humans. Some of them bear faint scars from battles with the Annihilator and Rogue dragons.

As a Moosha stands before you, you realize that this great dragon will be your initiator this time. Although all dragons are ultra-sensitive to thoughts and the truth, the Moosha are even more so. Their survival depends upon their instinctive, automatic reactions in any confrontational situation. They are therefore the obvious choice to decide which students become Dragon Warriors and which ones aren't yet ready.

"Tell me the primary duties of the Star-Born and the Star-Moon Dragon clans," the Moosha says, looking down into your eyes and heart.

You answer the question with confidence. The Moosha nods solemnly.

"Do you deserve admittance to the Dragon Warrior Ring?" he asks.

You are startled by such a question. "Only you can decide that," you answer.

The Moosha nods again. He motions for certain dragons to come closer. You recognize the leaders of the elements, as each directs powerful, colored energy into your stones and tools on your altar. Then each dragon lays a small leafy branch on the altar.

"The Element dragons have found you worthy," says the Moosha, "as do I."

The great warrior hands two shiny bracelets to your co-magician. Your dragon solemnly puts a silver bracelet on the wrist of your power hand and a copper bracelet on the other wrist. Each bracelet is etched with dragon forms.

"These bracelets are full of Warrior power, yet they are also symbolic of the power you will give away in defense of the Multiverse."

The Moosha hands you a special wand. It is exactly the length of your arm from elbow to fingertips. One end holds a piece of black onyx while the other end has a snow crystal as a balance. The shaft is wrapped in the middle with gleaming copper wire.

"You will make a copy of this wand in the physical," the Moosha tells you. "It will become very important to you in certain of your magickal workings. You can also call its astral form to your hand whenever you have the need while traveling in the Otherworld."

You thank the Moosha as you run your hand over the wand, clearly feeling power radiating from both the stones and the copper wire. You know this will be a special *wand, one that you use only for certain rituals and spells, while you work with other wands for other things. All the wands will gather power from this Warrior's wand while it draws its power directly from the Multiverse and the Dragon World.*

The Moosha drapes the black ribbon across your shoulders as he chants. Another Moosha steps forward to chant with him. You realize the second dragon is a female warrior and remind yourself not to be caught in a static way of thinking.

As both warriors touch your shoulders, you find yourself facing the opening Gate to the Warrior Ring. Just inside the Gate is the bright light for your return to your body.

Use the closing ceremony on page 54.

(End of the initiation)

Now you need to prepare yourself to be a Dragon Warrior. The Dragon Warrior is the ultimate warrior of nonphysical violence, in this world or the Otherworld, and plays an important part in protecting both worlds.

FOUR

The Way of the Dragon Warrior

FOURTH OF THE INNER RINGS

The Dragon Warrior is one who defends the truth, neutralizes or binds harmful energy wherever found, and, if possible, returns all curses to the sender. Or grounds the curses harmlessly in the Earth. Dragon Warriors develop self-confidence that will carry them through anything, and they come out triumphant.

Be realistic as well as aware. Don't make trouble where there isn't any. Be open-minded, but not so open that your brains fall out. Use common sense.

Curse-breaking is also a duty of a Dragon Warrior. The harmful energy threads are identified and detached from the victim. If there are several cordings, tie the ends together so they can't reattach. After accomplishing this on the astral realm, the Warrior can use a mirror and the following chant to do a "return to sender" spell. This spell works to return any negative energy at any time, but is especially good for returning the detached cordings.

Hold any size and type of mirror in front of you with the reflective side facing outward. Mentally call upon your co-magician dragon to help. It will be that dragon's form seen in the mirror by the offender, not yours. Chant:

> In a mirror bright, not dark, an awesome figure reflects its form,
> Into a barrier, protective, fierce. I stand behind it safe from harm.
> No threats can reach me, here behind. No magick reaches to my heart.
> The mirror sends evil back to source. O evil powers, now depart!

Wash the reflective surface of the mirror thoroughly to remove any negative residue. Smudge the mirror with incense so its surface can't be used as a gateway by negative vibrations.

Many times while a Warrior is traveling with her or his dragon in the Otherworld, the dragon will send an energy cord to the crown of your head or the center of your forehead. This link connects the two of you so you don't get lost and are safer in uncertain conditions. To make a strong merger of power, you must be dedicated, responsible, and intent on what is happening. You will need to raise your vibrations as high as possible to match those of your dragon if you want to make a more secure connection through the transpersonal area above your head. Cooperate to let the dragon teach you how to change energy vibrations.

Code, Color, and Other Items of the Warrior

The Dragon Warrior lives by the code of her or his Ring: Live in and accept the Multiverse of many worlds. Be a warrior against evil wherever you find it.

The Dragon Warrior color is black, the color of the creative Void. The symbol is a circle, representative of eternity and wholeness. If the circle holds a five-pointed star in the center, it is even better because then this powerful magick is added to endless Multiversal energy.

Warrior Ritual Tools

If at all possible, now is the time for you to make your own personal Warrior wand, which you saw in the Shaman's initiation. This wand should be no longer than the distance from your elbow to your fingertips. Get a piece of small copper tubing, plastic, or glass of that length. Glue a polished piece of black onyx to one end of the tubing. If you wish, you can fill the interior with stone chips. Then glue a piece of snow quartz to the opposite end. This gives your wand a repelling end and an attracting end, or one end (onyx) to protect and destroy and one end (snow quartz) to fight with positive energy streams. The wand can quickly be twirled from one end to the other. Of course, you don't physically take this wand with you into the Otherworld, but you use its reflected energy-form as an Otherworld weapon.

The Warrior doesn't need any physical weapons, since her or his work all takes place in the Otherworld and/or in space itself. Anything you need in such travels can be molded by your mind out of Multiversal energy. However, you might be interested in looking over Tibetan metal finger claws. These are very popular at the moment among young adults in the Gothic movement. Such metal finger claws remind me of dragon claws; they are gentle when touching your cheek but are deadly against enemies. Their power, however, lies in their symbolic use during magick spells. They are not meant for physical fighting.

This chapter will explain how to protect and defend yourself while in the Otherworld, as well as how to attack a foe there and safely help to capture Rogue dragons and energies.

Since we are highly physical in everyday life, humans are more powerful in the Otherworld if we use mental powers and visualizations. In a Warrior, this becomes automatic reflex action on the mental level, using Shapeshifter and Berserker energies.

The following short meditation will help you understand better how to be a Dragon Warrior.

Use the meditation opening.

You find yourself drifting in the velvet blackness of outer space, distant stars glittering like sequins. Beside you is a Moosha, a Savage Heart Warrior. She uses telepathy to tell you that you will go on patrol with her and also practice some difficult astral movements.

The first exercise will be learning to speed-jump from a motionless stand to another place. You watch as she suddenly disappears, only to find her floating behind you.

"You do it with your mind," the Moosha tells you. "Visualization. Belief in yourself. Practice."

You do the leap but find she is there before you.

"Faster," the Moosha says. "You should be moving before your thought is finished, else the enemy will be warned."

You do several more leaps before she nods her approval. She gestures for you to go with her on the patrol of this sector of space. As the two of you move out, she instructs you to summon your Warrior's wand. As soon as you think clearly of the wand, you feel its shape and weight in your hand.

"Now," the Moosha says, smiling, "match each of my moves. Try to catch my strategy thoughts as they form, so you know where I will be next."

The first move finds you looking around for her and giving a startled jump when she tickles the back of your neck. The second move you overshoot your target and find yourself running straight into the huge Moosha. She shakes her head and sends a thin link from her forehead to the crown of your head. Now you easily hear her thoughts. The two of you dance in sync, matching and countering with each leap. Suddenly you realize she released the link a few jumps ago, but you are still in sync with her.

You both stop and listen with all your senses at the same time. The space around your body changes vibrations and sends a ripple of warning across your skin.

"Rogue!" The Moosha sends out a call for help as she moves to meet the danger. You move with her, staying far enough away to not hamper her moves.

An adult dragon appears in your path, its eyes glowing with hatred, a blast of fire burning toward you. Instinctively, you speed-jump out of the way, at the same time calling up your wand. You send bursts of protective energy from the onyx stone in the end of the wand. You have no time to mentally think through strategy, for the Rogue dragon is appearing, disappearing, attacking, seeming to retreat only to attack in another manner. The Moosha is attacking and moving so fast she is almost a blur.

Other Moosha Warriors blink into sight in a circle around the combatants. One of them tosses you one corner of a huge energy net. You quickly send back your wand as you catch the net and move into position with the others. The Moosha who instructed and flew with you leaps behind the nets as the other Warriors move forward. The Rogue dragon snarls and bellows in anger as the energy nets cling to him, trapping him completely.

As the Warriors drag the netted Rogue to the Underworld, the Moosha turns to you. You see several small cuts on her shoulders, oozing liquid. She ignores the wounds.

"You did well, Dragon Warrior," she says. "It was easy this time. There was only one Rogue. But you are welcome to fly patrol with me again."

You smile at her praise as you feel yourself drawn back to your physical body.

Use meditation ending.

(End of meditation)

Now you have a very good idea of what you can do while on patrol or in the Otherworld, as well as what is expected of a Dragon Warrior. You know what moves to practice during deep meditations, and you know evil firsthand by sensing the Rogue dragon.

The Long History of Dragons, Warriors, and the Multiverse

People have known about Atlantis for centuries because of Greek records. The Greeks and Egyptians placed Atlantis, a series of various-sized islands, in the Atlantic Ocean, past the Pillars of Hercules (the Straits of Gibraltar). The records are quite clear about this location, and about the fact that Atlantis sank.

The existence and destruction of Lemuria in the Pacific Ocean wasn't recognized until archaeologists learned to translate Aztec records in the New World, in about 1864 CE. Lemuria consisted of a series of islands, with the largest two reaching from off the coast of southern Alaska south to northern California. From there, much smaller islands trailed off to Southeast Asia.

I had never heard either Atlantis or Lemuria mentioned in connection with dragons until I started this book. I was aware of the Mexican and Central American pyramid ruins, the dragon images found there, and the Aztec records of "Mu." When the dragons told me of their long history with Earth, I was very surprised to hear how much the dragons have influenced the civilization and people of this planet.

In the very beginning of human life on this planet, the dragons of the Multiverse guided immigrant colonists from distant star systems to Earth. Several inhabitable planets in the areas of Arcturus, the Pleiades, and Sirius would be badly environmentally damaged in the near future. Only a few groups of people of each system heard and believed the warning the dragons brought. Some of those who believed decided to retreat to other safe planets in their star systems. Three thousand others listened to the dragons describe a budding planet in a distant galaxy. They knew that overcrowding any nearby planets would overburden resources, eventually leading to massive problems.

So, on the advice of the dragons, these space travelers built huge ships to transport them through time and space to a blue and white ball called Earth. Their space technology was very advanced and made it possible to make the journey in a year, by a series of space-time jumps, while the colonists slept in hibernation. Special flights of dragons escorted the silent ships until the vessels were in orbit around Earth.

The sleepers woke to news of disaster. The dragons had told them before the journey that the planet had two very primitive races of sentient beings who both showed early promise of great potential. The two races learned quickly and had developed a very crude but accurate system of elemental magick. They also had begun a spiritual awakening. Eventually, the two races would inbreed, and their complementary DNA structures would produce a stronger, survival-oriented, even more intelligent race. There was space for the immigrants, too.

However, what the dragons knew as the Annihilator—a negative, sentient cloud of deadly evil—had swept across this planet while the colonists were in flight hibernation. This evil caused serious physical illnesses among the two sentient races and the animals alike. It also triggered one natural disaster after another. These events threatened to leave the planet a barren, lifeless ball spinning through space. The damaged planet, too, showed signs of leaving its orbit, causing total disaster to its galaxy. The shock waves would reverberate throughout the Multiverse, leaving a domino effect of destruction in its wake, unless the dragons and the colonists intervened. The immigrants were desperately needed. There was no time for the dragons to follow the Annihilator.

The dragons woke the sleepers. The brightest, healthiest, and most likely to survive and produce children had dared the journey. These colonists knew that with their knowledge and skills, they had a chance of preventing the damage that this blue planet in a new galaxy could do to the Multiverse. These young people with skills in every field of knowledge began their exciting, challenging lives by settling in a spread-out colony on a series of islands surrounded by oceans. They called this settlement New Atlantis, after a large city in their history.

When the flights of dragons and the colonists in smaller-load ships landed on Earth, they instantly felt the primitive creative energy and communicated by telepathy with the survivors of the two races. They resolved to fight for the planet's life. And they won.

Within a short period of time, the settlers found it necessary to build a second large colony, plus several small stations around the planet. The second colony was named Lemuria. The survivors of the original races were widely scattered around the planet, making it impossible to contact them from just one colony. Space explorers established ports on Lemuria while settling their families in smaller ports on the continents.

The Atlanteans and Lemurians kept physical contact with the humans to a minimum, so they would grow and develop naturally. Only selected colonists were allowed to contact the humans, teaching them valuable skills in agriculture, medicine, and building. After two hundred years, the colonists were able to more freely circulate among the humans.

The belief, held for eons, that honored the Moon as a physical symbol of the Goddess came with those who reached Earth with the dragons. The Atlanteans based their year on the Moon, as they had on their home planets. A complete pass through the Moon phases here takes about 29.5 days—slightly different but recognizable.

The first year on Earth was one of observation of this new world. Since the anniversary of their arrival came on what we now call Halloween—what pagans know as Samhain—the star people, who called themselves *Atlanteans* and who named their Atlantic Ocean island settlements *Atlantis*, set the start of a year at that point.

Although the majority continued to honor the Moon and its effects on the body, mind, and spiritual energy flow, it wasn't long before most of the scientifically minded switched to using the Sun cycle to mark the year. This eventually caused a division between the scientists (most of whom were also priests) and the rest of the population. The exclusivity and special privileges of the scientists gave them the control and resources to do whatever experiments they wanted—the unethical, dangerous experiments that finally destroyed Atlantis.

During the same time, however, the colony scientists devolved in ethics and ideals, a change that eventually destroyed them.

At some point before Atlantis sank, the dragons warned all who would listen to retreat to the more stable continents to the east and the west. The dragons were helpless to stop the Atlantean scientists because of the law of free will and choice in the Multiverse. Some groups independent of scientific control—such as teachers, craftspeople, healers, and traders—chose to take the dragons' advice and moved to safer areas. Since the star people still had many small transportation aircraft at this time, some of them stole the vehicles and joined the explorers on Lemuria.

Every Earth culture that showed a remarkable explosion in the arts of civilization received accelerated learning from the fleeing Atlanteans, who settled among them. These cultures included those of Egypt, Tibet, India, China, and the Mesopotamian area. The transportation vehicles were destroyed, buried, or cleverly hidden—and never used again.

The large culture that stayed behind on Atlantis didn't believe the warnings of the scientists at first. They posed no opposition and, with time, merely settled into the new pattern of overlords governing them. As ordered, they turned away from the guidance of the dragons. Finally, the dragons withdrew themselves and withdrew any advice or support, retreating to other lands—some even into the Multiverse, where the rest would eventually go.

It was fifty to a hundred years after the last large group of star people fled that the scientists of Atlantis made the fatal mistake of misusing powerful crystal energy. They had already violated the mixing of human and animal DNA and had become abusive tyrants over the remaining people, alienating themselves from the dragons and the other fantastical beings they found on Earth. They changed the freewill spiritual ideas into shambles, forbidding private worship and using their "built" state religion to gain ownership and control over every means of trade left on the island. Privately, they denounced the spiritual ways as fraudulent. Then the scientists built fleets of warships, armed with deadly crystal weapons, and tried to conquer large sections of the continents on either side of Atlantis. Since they used a raid-and-destroy strategy and never felt a need to establish bases after the first few were annihilated, the wars never ended. It was during experiments on deadlier, more precise weapons that the scientists accidentally set off a chain of internal Earth reactions that destroyed their culture.

As a way to hide their actions, the scientists had from the beginning established their laboratories and experimental ranges deep inside dormant volcanoes. The ground around these places was either naturally bare of vegetation or was cleared of such, making it easy to patrol with armed guards. The volcanoes gave the scientists ample ground for their secretive business, since the tall, tunnel-ridden peaks dominated every island, large and small, throughout the Atlantis chain. All it took was one slight miscalculation and a misfire of a giant crystal weapon to set off a chain reaction of explosive volcanoes. The massive explosions created devastating earthquakes followed by enormous tidal waves. In a matter of a week, the glory of Atlantis was no more.

Unfortunately, this unimagined string of events also affected nearly every continent and culture on Earth. The Atlantean islands all sank deep into the Atlantic Ocean when the tectonic plates shifted and the tilt of the Earth's axis changed nearly three degrees. Some sections of coastline suddenly rose to become miles-high countries, while other land sank to seashore level. Other areas were subjected to great damage as huge, thick sections of the Earth's crust broke loose and skated across a continent to settle in a completely different country.

The air was filled with dust, ash, tiny pieces of vegetation, and once-dormant bacteria, all caught in the Earth's planet-circling winds we call the jet stream. New diseases, in addition to diseases once known only in select areas, spread around the globe. These diseases, along with enormous weather changes and weakened sunlight from the ash cloud, caused great hardship to all inhabitants, plants, and animals for many years afterward. It was only through the knowledge of the immigrant star people that any trace of civilization and humanity rose up from the ruined land.

The island chains of Lemuria in the Pacific Ocean escaped total annihilation, even though they too were volcano-created. Using the Atlantean mistakes as an example, the Lemurians moved even further away from technology and science, except for natural experiments uncovering plant medicines. Those people who feared government control, and wanted an even freer lifestyle, left for Tibet, Egypt, Central America, and other early remaining cultures. Some disappeared into the wilderness of the North American continent.

When first Atlantis, then Lemuria, sank into the seas in tragedies caused by the scientists, small airships bearing skilled people left secretly to live among the humans.

These colonists passed on a valuable personal craft to the humans. Many of the immigrants were a combination of Warrior/Healer, with skills needed to survive. Slowly at first, then more rapidly as the demise of Atlantis neared, the Warrior/Healers taught the needed skills in certain advanced Earth cultures. The Healer ideals gradually weakened through the centuries while the Warrior side strengthened. However, you can follow this thin thread down through history up to today.

Most of the original Warrior/Healers belonged to a special religious and mystical group. With the dispersion of people from Atlantis, and then Lemuria, the training behind this important group of people was lost. The Warrior/Healer rank devolved into such later groups as the Viking Berserkers who worshipped the god Odin or the Muslim Assassins of the Middle East. Instead of healing, these men and women became hardened killers who could shapeshift into raging animals with unending strength and no fear of death.

Modern equivalents of these toughened warriors would be the Navy SEALs, the Green Berets, the Army Rangers, and other very elite military groups. However, the healing (except for healing their companions), mystical, and spiritual aspects are no longer a part of these groups. A strange offshoot of these military groups are the new Warrior/Healers, each struggling alone to fulfill a personal spiritual destiny. Almost all of them have been in the military, primarily in the elite forces, and are now living as civilians. They practice alone and all are searching for, and individually building, new paths to spiritual understanding.

On the other hand, there have been many cults established only on religious or racial hatred that have also amassed weapons. These groups, such as the Ku Klux Klan, and Aum Shinrikyo in Japan, specialize in terror, violence, and secrecy.

According to the history of India, the Celtic clans came roaring out of the East. However, the Celts are not of Eastern origin, and no country north of southern China mentions the huge Celtic clans. Beyond China, there is only the Pacific Ocean, the legendary home of the islands of Lemuria. Celtic legends say their origins are in the four special isles, but nothing remains to tell us where they were. If those isles were Lemuria, then the Celts are descendants of the original people from space who first settled Atlantis. This doesn't mean their bloodlines are pure; they aren't. Neither are the bloodlines of any other culture.

The dragons say that the Celts were one group among those who fled the sinking of the Pacific islands. Like Atlantis, Lemuria consisted of more than one body of land. The sinking was a delayed reaction to the demise of Atlantis. Volcanic eruptions, earthquakes, tidal waves and weather changes eventually destroyed both groups.

When Lemuria began to show signs of approaching natural catastrophe, there was another migration of groups of people. It is quite probable that the wild Celtic clans were part of that migration. They took with them, and continued to use, many of the Atlantean/Lemurian ideas—such as the lunar year, Samhain as the beginning of the year, adeptness at certain crafts, and specific spiritual ideas.

As invaders crossing the Asian countries and then the Middle East to the Mediterranean, they developed a fighting technique that was second to none. Even the Greeks had a difficult time preventing a takeover. The Celts absorbed many ideas from the other cultures they encountered on their trek.

The Asian cultures, in varying degrees, also learned from the star people. Blending the original Warrior/Healer archetype with the spiritual, Asia produced several formidable sects of monks who were adept at healing, fighting, and dedicated to spiritual studies. These can be loosely traced down through history.

The Chinese general Sun Tzu, one of ancient history's greatest military minds, wrote *The Art of War* sometime between the sixth and fourth centuries BCE. This book, and a new sect of Buddhism called Shingon, had a profound influence on the later development of the ninja cult in Japan. The ninjas became cunning warriors and practitioners of magick. The skills and traditions of ninjutsu were cloaked in secrecy and mystery. Today the scope of the ninjas has diminished, and they only use the fighting arts.

Coinciding with the arrival of Shingon Buddhists was the influx of Chinese warrior-monks after the collapse of the Tang Dynasty. About 184 CE, in China, a mystic leader organized a cult called the Yellow Turbans—a religious military sect that used Taoist magick.

The Chinese Shao Lin warrior-monks were well versed in the arts of war, from strategy to the deadly T'ai Chi Ch'uan, known today as *kung fu*. The Ch'ing Manchu forces finally destroyed all but five of the monks.

The mystic warrior cult of Asia Minor, open to male soldiers only and based on the god Mithras, gained many sincere followers when it migrated with the Legions back to Rome. At one time Rome had forty-five temples of Mithras. Temples to him have been found around the entire Mediterranean area and as far away as Britain. Mithras was not a god of violence and killing but of soldiering in general. The ceremonies of this mystic warrior cult were very secret, and have remained so.

One theory states that a certain mark on a person's palms reveals that he or she led several past lives as an Atlantean and Lemurian. This mark resembles a large *M* but is stretched out with very sharp points to the top of the M. Usually this mark will appear only on one palm, but sometimes you will find it on both.

However one looks back at our unrecorded history, dragons and humans have been together a very long time. Because of certain restrictions that were placed on studying or keeping copies of very ancient knowledge, humans chose to break their valuable connection with the dragons. We paid a high price by believing the lies and allowing the liars to control our thinking. A tiny fraction of the ancient wisdom of dragons was kept alive by secret magickal groups, particularly in the eastern Mediterranean and Balkan areas. Secrecy and fear of religious retaliation made those groups highly reluctant to admit that they had this wisdom. No one can blame them. Avoiding death and persecution are built-in survival traits. Cultures in those parts of the world have suffered anyway, all in the name of religion, race, and cultural origins. We cannot ask them to sacrifice more. Instead, we all need to step forward and back their ancient truths with magickal solidarity and loud protestations against any kind of restrictions on free will and spirituality.

Laws should be based only on universal ethics and the brotherhood/sisterhood of all beings. Rules shouldn't be made to limit freewill decisions and thinking. If all humans concentrated on individual spiritual improvements and ignored the other religious paths that preach that "more members make us more right" and there is only one correct religion, the cultures on Earth could avoid almost all religious wars. And all wars, on one level or another, are religious wars.

We humans have studied magick and true spirituality a very long time, but we still have an unfathomably long way to go. Little steps eventually can be measured as big steps. This reveals our ability to consistently use true positive energy for the good of this galaxy and the Multiverse. As long as dragon studies of the Five Inner Rings have sincere students, the vibrations of the Multiverse will stay balanced and healthy.

The Dragon World Meditation

A visit to Dragon World will not only enlighten you about dragons—it is a fascinating place on its own. Your co-magician dragon will accompany you, since visitors are rarely allowed far beyond the Gate without a companion.

> Use the meditation opening.
> *You are standing just inside the Gate of Dragon World. Your dragon friend tells*
> *you that Dragon World, a separate side area of Middleworld, consists of several*

contrasting areas. Although all students and travelers are allowed to enter Dragon World, visitors are carefully monitored at all times unless accompanied by a co-magician dragon, and then are only allowed to visit the Stone Circles. You have permission to make short trips to each section.

A female dragon, on her way to the Hatching Grounds, decides to go with you and explain more about Dragon World.

"Every type of dragon has its living needs met in Dragon World," she tells you. "It is a secure area of the Otherworld for all nesting females—dragonettes just hatched and learning to care for themselves, as well as the gathering of family groups on what you humans would call social occasions and 'weekends at home.' Although duties may take certain dragons on long missions, we still are extremely family-oriented, and all dragons will fight to the death for the safety of any young and the survival of Dragon World. Dragons are among the few species that match for life."

"What do dragons really eat?" you ask. You've wanted to ask that question for some time but were afraid it would offend.

The female laughs. "Contrary to your old Earth fables, we don't eat fair maidens, cows, or anything else like that." She laughs again. "We exist on remaining magickal energy floating around, as well as Multiversal energy. Why would we want to eat such tough, bony things as maidens or cows?"

It isn't long before you see what appears to be an endless, quite hot desert. Heat waves rise from the surface as far as you can see. The female carefully walks around small hills of sand until she reaches the one she seeks.

"Watch where you step," she warns. "There are nests of hatchlings everywhere, for this is the Hatching Grounds." She carefully uncovers her eggs, rolls each one over, and croons to them all.

By this time, your feet feel as if they are in a fire from the heated sands. When you notice your co-magician is actually walking on air, about a foot above the desert, you mentally project yourself doing the same. You give a sigh of relief.

"The Hatching Ground is used by all dragon families," your dragon friend says. "These Grounds stretch all the way to the western oceans, where water dragons and their families spend time. Those dragons related to the Water clan also nest there. They have their nests among the shoreline ocean grasses and flowers, each nest carefully hollowed out of wet sand beyond the tide lines. Dragon World has vast oceans of living space for Water dragons."

"Am I really seeing an oasis over there?" You point to a wavering blur to your right.

"Yes, there are a few oases across the Hatching Grounds. They have drinking water. And sometimes you find a group of rocky outcroppings," your friend replies.

You look around you, but you only see the female dragon covering her eggs with sand. "What of those clans, besides the Water ones, who don't care for all this heat?"

"Dragons of the warmer types live and rest in the surrounding areas of the Hatching Grounds," your friend tells you. "Although all dragons know how to regulate their resistance to colder temperatures, a great many of us prefer the heat of this area. The landscape of the Hatching Grounds gradually changes at the edges. First there is a section of pre-desert shrubs in the rocky ground among the boulders. The vegetation and availability of water increases the farther you move from the hot sands."

"Excuse me," you say to the female dragon as she approaches. "How do you find your eggs? There are no visible markers that I can see."

"Each dragon mother knows precisely where her eggs are buried in the sand because she follows the vibrations of her young. Both dragon parents and their friends use telepathy to communicate with the unhatched dragonettes after they have been in the shell for an equivalent of six of your months. Full hatching time is equal to thirteen months." As if she reads your mind, she answers the unspoken question. "But all dragons mate in the dark depths of space that exists between levels of the Multiverse. That has always been our way."

You and your co-magician join hands as you jump to a far northern area of Dragon World. This cold area makes your teeth chatter when you arrive.

"This is a land of snow and great cold, a place for colder types of dragons. They need and use the heat of the Hatching Grounds for their eggs, but they prefer the normal arctic atmosphere for regular family life." Your friend makes mental adjustments to the temperature. You are partially successful in adjustment but still find the air too cold.

"Come. We will go to the great Stone Circles, where distant truths are found. It is the correct temperature for you there."

At your dragon's thought, you find yourself standing outside triple concentric rings of monolithic stones. They are rough to your touch and natural-looking on the outside. However, when you step inside the first ring of stones, you find that the inner sides are translucent. As soon as you look at a stone, something like a video plays across its "screen" side.

"These stones are very powerful," your co-magician says. "Each stone is capable of showing you a portion of ancient dragon history, some virtue or truth that could enlighten you, or doors of approaching opportunity that may help."

You discover you can't understand what you see and hear. Your co-magician dragon translates what is being shown. The stone is giving you peace, healing, and guidance for a positive path or goal with which you need help.

"The more you study and work with dragons, the more information you can gather from these stones." Your dragon friend puts a hand on your shoulder. *"But I think you have heard enough to think upon for this time."*

You nod in agreement. You feel yourself being returned to your body.

Use meditation ending.

Otherworld spirit guides and angels, who work cooperatively with the dragons, can also aid you. All positive beings of the Otherworld work with the same goal in mind: to help those who seek help to better themselves, and to guide as many of us who want to find the spiritual path that is best for each of us. The Otherworld doesn't recognize religions, just spirituality.

Star-Pattern Magick

There is a long history in Earth magick of using different shapes of stars to symbolize esoteric wisdom and Multiversal energies. You can carve these symbols onto candles, write them out on paper for spellwork, or trace their shapes with a finger to set certain dragon and Multiversal energies into motion. The Warrior projects these shapes in the Otherworld, thus using them as a kind of weapon.

Triangle

Some stars have more than one design, revealing the correct number of points but seen and defined differently by various cultures.

The three-pointed star, or triangle, represents the balance of the three main levels of the Otherworld. Three is a mystical number that can give luck, courage, and endurance. A long, jagged lightning bolt design represents a series of running pyramids or triangles.

The set of interlocking triple rings invokes the Fate goddesses, and their influences on body, mind, and spirit.

Interlocking triple rings

There is one very special three-pointed star called the *Eye of the Dragon*. When looking at this triangular shape, with its prominent point downward, you see a three-sided pyramid, a "three times three" power. This is an ancient design that was copied by gem cutters in medieval times. Traditionally, the Eye of the Dragon

Eye of the Dragon

Knot of Eternity

Pentagram

Hexagram

Elvenstar

cut of gems was said to be very magickal and sacred to the Nine Muses and the Nine Morgans.

The four-pointed star represents the four primary Elements of Earth, Air, Fire, and Water. The Greeks used it to invoke the four elements. Use it to create balance and completion, and to bring in stability.

Another four-pointed star, originally from China, is the *Knot of Eternity*. The four-leaf clover shape is for good luck. The strange Earth Diamond, also called the *Eye of Fire* in Nordic tradition, was associated with the dark side of the Goddess as Earth Mother and reincarnation.

The five-pointed star is also called a *pentagram*. It attracts elementals and angels if the fifth point is upward. If it is down, this star attracts distorted energy. The pentagram originated in Mesopotamia some four thousand years ago. It then became a Sumerian and Egyptian stellar sign. It is a symbol of harmony, health, and mystic powers; it will either trap or repel negative energy.

Another five-pointed image is found in the adjoining five circle-edges of the sacred rose of the Goddess, which represents hidden meanings.

The six-pointed star is a pattern of two overlapping triangles, called a *hexagram, Solomon's Seal*, or the *Star of David*. It is symbolic of perfectly joined positive and negative energies. In the Pythagorean systems, the six-pointed star represents change and luck. Use it for protection through balancing opposites.

A seven-pointed star is also called a *heptad, Mystic Star, elvenstar*, or *elf star*. It can be traced back to ancient Akkadia and the Akkadian belief that seven planetary spirits act as guardians to certain magicians. The number seven was also considered the most powerful and sacred of all numbers to the ancient Egyptians. It is excellent for contacting dragons and for indicating that you are ready to study with them. It activates healing energies. A protective symbol, the seven-pointed star can balance all the chakras.

This star symbol was associated with the Seven Sisters (the seven bright stars of the Pole-circling Ursa Major) and the Seven Sisters of the Pleiades, known to the Greeks. Legend says that seven Egyptian priestesses founded major oracle-shrines in the ancient world. In the Middle East, these priestesses were called the Seven Pillars of Wisdom. In Southeast Asia, they were known as the Seven Mothers of the World and "the seven beings who make decrees."

Octagon

The eight-pointed star, or *octagon*, is a design beneficial for attracting strength and growth after traumatic events. It switches the life path into a new cycle. It also can correct and balance karma. It represents the union of disparate principles. In ancient astrology, a black eight-pointed star indicated all the stars.

A nine-pointed star is the traditional symbol of a spiritual initiation. It is filled with great power because it is composed of three joined triangles. Use it to end one cycle and begin a new one. This is another star symbol connected with the Greek Nine Muses, the Celtic Nine Morgans of paradise, Nine Korrigans of the sacred isle, and the Nine Moon Maidens of Scandinavia. This nine-fold goddess symbol protects all who use it.

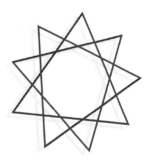

Nine-pointed star

The ten-pointed star symbolizes satisfactory completion. A similar design is called *Penelope's Web*, representing the Fate Goddess who cuts life's thread. It is very useful in magick that affects your career or a future job.

Ten-pointed star

The twelve-pointed star is a direct representation of the zodiac and astrology. Each point of this star signifies a zodiacal house of an astrological chart. Activate the energy of this star by tracing its lines in a clockwise direction; the astrological chart moves in a counterclockwise direction. By activating this energy during disturbing aspects of your life, you can minimize the negative effects. In the Middle Ages, the

Twelve-pointed star

twelve-spoke wheel changed its association from the goddess Fortuna to the roulette wheel, the gambling Lady Luck of today.

Star shapes can be used as weapons by the Dragon Warrior in Otherworld defense situations. Stars can be mentally thrown or projected as barriers, shields, or walls around an enemy. If an enemy is surrounded by star shapes, their energy goes inward and binds the enemy in electromagnetic bonds. If projected during magickal working, the stars can produce the same effect against attackers.

Discernment and the Levels of Evil

Magicians should be very careful about what they call "evil." Often, evil exists only in the eye and mind of the beholder. Most evils, or negatives, are recognized by all, however. Other people and events may be called "evil" only because of certain societal or religious restrictions. Be careful that what you label "evil" isn't actually only evil in the minds of certain religious leaders or dictatorial social leaders.

Small evils are the most prevalent, the hardest to detect, and the easiest to let slide. The Chinese knew this, so they used statues of dragons and Fu Dogs to destroy small evils. Evils are all small in the beginning. They grow by stirring up negative thoughts and deeds in others and then "eating" these thoughts to grow larger. That is one reason the dragons who supervised the writing of this book were so emphatic that students of the Five Inner Rings be taught discernment of the levels of evil. It is impossible to stop all the small seeds of evil released by such warped minds, even in captivity.

No being can stay positive all the time. With a nudge here and there, we fall into negative energy patterns. Students of the Five Inner Rings must therefore remain alert at all times for small evils and annihilate these energy forms whenever they are discovered. These evils, most of them created by the inmates of the Underworld, are like mindless robots with "destroy" buttons only. They, like their creators, have no compassion, sympathy, or desire to do anything good. The wisest dragons have long debated whether these evil thoughtforms are even alive, since they have yet to discover any with souls.

The Lowerworld has a gated section called the Underworld that shows up as an inky purple wall. Its only Gate is patrolled by the Savage Heart warriors, the Moosha. This section of the Otherworld holds the spirits of evil, violent, insane, and twisted beings to keep them away from all levels of the Multiverse. After you are escorted through this Underworld by dragons, you will better understand what true evil is. Granted, not every evil soul is locked in this place. A few manage to stay free.

Even these evil ones, from all over the Multiverse, have the freewill right to reincarnate at any time if they so wish. The Council of Justice must tell them, however, what karmic penalties they are likely to face in another life. For that reason, most prefer not to reincarnate, since their price for reincarnation can be very high.

There are a few truly Rogue dragons, as there are other rogue beings. Some choose to roam the Multiverse like time bombs that damage, threaten, or destroy all who cross their path simply for the evil of destruction and pain. Often, these Rogue dragons and similar sentient beings team up to terrorize entire galaxies—physically, mentally, and emotionally.

There are a few dragons who choose to disobey the laws, just as there are rebellious humans. These rebellious dragons quickly exile themselves to the space realm to avoid being locked in the Underworld. The Moosha warriors must constantly guard against free Rogue dragons getting their captured fellows out of the Underworld prison.

The Rogues are frequently responsible for aiding other negative beings in creating disasters on physical planets throughout the Multiverse. These unconscionable dragons are a threat to the balance of the Multiverse through their destructive behavior. Because of this, the other dragons call them the Annihilator's Offspring, a reference to the most deadly entity anywhere.

Most Rogues travel in groups or packs. A few very powerful ones are loners, skilled at attacks by stealth and magickal shapeshifting. Those in packs are less skilled in battle-training and magick. They depend upon forces of numbers to win battles. Both kinds of Rogue dragons are very dangerous.

When word is sent down from the Highest, Warrior dragons take great energy nets, with the ability to stun the Rogues into helplessness, before transporting them into the Underworld with the other dangerous creatures. Sometimes, the Rogues move out of the area before the Warriors arrive, or some of them manage to fight their way free and escape. Nearly all beings held in the Underworld are not open to changing their habits or ways of living. Terms and words such as *serial killers, torturers, abusers of other creatures*, and *all the evil one can imagine* don't begin to describe the Rogues' offenses. And these offenders come from all levels of the Multiverse.

So, it becomes clear to us that even the wisest of dragons have comparable problems to ours on Earth—that there is no perfection, except within the all-powerful Supreme Creative Force.

Dark Areas of the Underworld Meditation

The Underworld is the segregated area off the Lowerworld, a kind of Otherworld prison, where truly evil beings or energy pools are kept forever—that is, unless the sentient beings ask to be reincarnated. No one can be denied rebirth if they wish it, no matter their past or their present lack of change or remorse. All beings in the Multiverse have that freewill choice. Most choose not to reincarnate because of their fear of what karma would be involved in doing so.

There is only one Gate into and out of the Underworld—Prison Gate. Rogue dragons and half-sentient pools of negative evil remain forever unless they escape with outside help, such as that given by other Rogue dragons.

Use the meditation opening.

You, your co-magician dragon, and four huge Savage Heart Warriors are standing at the inky purple Prison Gate, set into an impenetrable wall. You can't see an end to the wall's length or any top when you look upward.

The Lowerworld behind you seems ordinary enough, although it isn't as bright as the Middleworld. However, the Underworld beyond Prison Gate projects an atmosphere of violence, evil, and despair.

The Moosha enter the Gate first, quickly stepping to surround you as you and your dragon enter. The Gate slams behind you with a boom that makes you shiver.

The Underworld, except for its forever-twilight tinge, looks ordinary. There are meadows, forests, a shallow winding river, and groups of rundown buildings scattered across the area that you can see. You hear the sounds of battle in the distance, yells and screams suddenly cut short. The clang of metal weapons moves closer. A gang of warriors races out of the forest toward you, only to suddenly stop when they see the Moosha warriors.

"Who are they?" you softly ask your dragon friend.

"Beings sentenced to the Underworld," your friend answers. "Those you now see are out of your planet's past. Humans with warped personalities and minds. They are unrepentant of their violence and desires for evil ways. There are other such beings here also."

You mentally reach out for the vibrations of the inhabitants and just as quickly withdraw your thoughts. Your slight touch revealed the presence of many Rogue dragons, including the one you helped capture. There are also many sentient beings from other parts of the Multiverse, as well as nonsentient pools of destructive negative energy.

"Are any of these allowed rebirth?" you ask one of the Mooshas as your group leaves the gang of fighters behind and makes its way toward a temple that sits near the river.

"No one can be denied," one of the Warriors says. "A few sentenced here do become repentant in time and face whatever karmic debts are given to them in their new life plan. A few but not many. We escort any unrepentants who want to reincarnate."

"What of the Rogue dragons and the other evils I feel here, the ones that you would not call sentient?" You look behind yourself to see that the gang of fighters

is following your group at a distance. They want to destroy, but the presence of the Warriors deters them.

"We must constantly guard the Underworld against their escape," *another Moosha says.* "Their sentence here has no end. Those are never released unless large bands of Rogue dragons break them free."

"The Annihilator's Offspring," *mumbles the first Moosha.* "A few times, undetected pools of negative energy have breached these walls, but not often."

"Any of the inhabitants of the Underworld can come to the Temple of Despair." *Your co-magician dragon points to the building close ahead.* "But only the truly repentant can enter the Inner Chamber of the Priestess, be soul-cleansed, and then be escorted to the Hall of Justice and Rebirth in the Lowerworld."

"How does the Priestess know who is sincere and who isn't?" *you ask.*

The members of your group pass between two huge stones at the doorway of the Temple. The stone on your left has the name Hammer and Anvil *carved into it, while the other stone reads* Fire of Truth. *When you pass between the stones, Fire of Truth makes a loud noise like a huge chorus of crystal bells. As you enter the Temple's door, you hear the other stone tolling like a deep bell. You look back to see one of the evil warriors retreating from the stones. Your question is answered.*

The Priestess is waiting on her throne when the Moosha lead you into her Inner Chamber. She is a tall, thin woman dressed in a long, plain, white gown. Her face and hair are completely covered with a gauzy veil that obscures her features. You realize that the Priestess could be from any level of the Multiverse, for there are no clues to her cultural or racial heritage. Her gown's long sleeves cover her arms and half her hands. Gloves made of silver chains and gems cover her visible fingers.

"Greetings, Dragon Warrior." *The Priestess communicates by telepathy only.*

You return the greeting and find that many questions are rolling around in your mind. She answers, without you having to form any questions into a coherent fashion.

"The wise judges in the Hall of Justice and Rebirth make all the final decisions on what a returning soul needs to accomplish or pay off in karma. The person can present a statement of their wishes, people to be with, lessons to learn. All this is considered. Dragons, teachers, guides, angels, and travelers like you can speak in defense or support of any soul, if you desire."

"What about new souls that arrive here?" *you ask.*

"The wise judges also meet with arriving souls. If new karmic debts or credits need to be added to the record, this is done before sending the soul to the Upperworld, where they will be assigned studies or duties. The returning evil ones are taken straight here, to the Underworld."

The Priestess sends a picture into your mind. You remember that the Upper-world is reached from the Lowerworld by the Glory Gate, with the dragon Kaudra at the other end.

"You must go now," the Priestess says, as the deep voice of Hammer and Anvil echoes through the Temple of Despair.

You turn to your dragon friend, but feel your physical body pulling you back.

Use the meditation closing.

Finding Your Animal Allies

The Celts used, in their language, the term *animal allies*. Other cultures may use the expression *power animals* or *animal spirit guides* instead.

We all need our own animal allies, and already have them whether we know it or not. These allies may be mammals, birds, aquatic creatures, reptiles, or insects. They can become guides, guardians, companions, and the bearers of omens and messages. Like special crystals, most of the animal allies choose you; you don't choose them.

The engraved stones help us by warding off evil, increasing our personal power and relieving stress. By providing a visual link, stones engraved with the image of an animal ally can help you make contact with that ally. These stones also increase your personal power by creating a link with the animal.

As Native American and other shamanic cultures have shown us, every person can have animal allies. You can use the next meditation to explore possibilities and reveal the allies now with you. Just by doing the meditation, you might find new ones choosing to work with you. Read the following shortened list of allies; it will make you more alert to creatures seen during the meditation.

The meditation itself will help you decide which of your animal allies is the strongest and most apt to appear, and which are your secondary allies—those that can appear if a different form is more useful. Become friends with your allies, even if they make you slightly uncomfortable. You never know when their talents may be needed. These listed talents are not all each creature can do.

Badger: Tenacity in self-defense.

Bear: Stamina; balance; transformation; fierce, unannounced defense.

Butterfly: Always prepared to move. Long life; joy; a new life cycle.

Cat, domestic: Knows when to fight and when to retreat. Self-assured. Search for hidden information.

Coyote: Cunning; illusion; ability to move silently and seize opportunities.

Crow: Cunning; skill at stealthily moving things; knowledge.

Deer, stag: Swiftness; grace; transformation; elusiveness in hiding. Guide to spiritual knowledge.

Dog: Alertness to danger; finding the truth; removes confusion and seeing through illusions.

Dolphin: Releases negative emotions; discovers ancient secrets. Joy in life.

Dragon: Protection without fear. Transformation through magickal teachings.

Dragonfly: Rapid movement; mystic messages; listening to intuition. Escaping through speed and elusiveness.

Eagle: Swiftness; strength; courage; hidden spiritual truths; wisdom.

Falcon: Sharp sight; using the psychic; magick; astral travel; soul healing.

Fox: Slyness; invisibility through illusions; ability to silently move away from aggressors.

Frog: Escaping by freezing movement and then rapidly getting away. Initiation.

Hawk: Decisiveness; boldness; fierce defense. Recalling past lives; messages from spirit.

Hedgehog or porcupine: Resistance to anyone's control by countering them immediately. Self-defense if threatened.

Horse: Endurance; speed; cooperation. Overcoming obstacles.

Hummingbird: Not being intimidated; swift movement. Happiness and relaxation.

Jaguar/Black panther: Ferocity; strength; direct attack. Change future events; learning hidden knowledge.

Leopard: Confidence; boldness; cunning; stealth.

Lion: Strength; courage; strong ties with family and friends.

Lizard: Facing fears; using illusion.

Mouse: Using stealth to become invisible; cunning; secrets. Beware of double-talk.

Otter: Wisdom; uncovering new talents.

Owl: Silent movement; finding hidden truths; unmasking deceivers.

Pegasus: Astral travel and poetic inspiration.

Raven: Slyness; boldness; transformations; messages from spirit or through divination.

Scorpion: Swiftness in defense. Ability to return dark magick to the sender.

Snake: Shedding negatives of any kind. Cunning, fast movements toward or away from attackers.

Spider: Weaving webs of illusion to trap enemies. Divine inspiration.

Squirrel: Being prepared for changes or discovery.

Swallow: Swiftness; success in journeys.

Tiger: Fearlessly takes action. Powerful energy to face unpleasant events.

Turtle: Patience to develop new ideas. Don't be rushed into action if it isn't to your benefit.

Unicorn: Strength of mind; personal power and confidence.

Whale: Using sounds to heal or create a diversion. Ancient magick.

Wolf: Intelligence; outwitting enemies; escaping aggressors; intuition. Dreams and magick.

◎   ◎   ◎

This meditation will allow you to use the sharp senses of two animals to familiarize yourself with their powers. You can repeat the meditation with any other creatures you wish. This practice will sharpen your own psychic senses for work in the Otherworld. Be alert for the appearance of any animals not mentioned in the meditation. If these creatures continue to appear in meditations, you know they are to be animal allies who can aid you during Otherworld travels. Their traits also can be of use to you on other occasions.

Use meditation opening.

You are standing at the edge of a forest, watching a Full Moon rise in the evening sky. You hear a crackle, the brush of one fir bough against another, and look down to see a large wolf standing by your side. As you stare into his golden eyes, you feel yourself falling into the wolf's spirit.

You are startled to see through the wolf's eyes. The place where you stood looks entirely different. You are seeing everything from a much lower level. But the wolf's sight misses nothing, including a moth flying from tree to tree. The wolf's nose identifies several woodland creatures you don't see, such as a foraging rabbit, a young stag across the clearing in the shadows, and the wolf's mate standing behind him. His ears go forward as the stag steps out into the moonlight, the tall grass brushing against his legs.

The wolf's head turns as an owl glides silently out across the meadow. As you stare at the owl, you feel yourself shooting into the owl's mind. Below you, the wolf goes back into the forest to join his mate.

The owl glides on, its sharp night sight sweeping over the meadow in search of mice. You feel the whisper of air through the wings as his feathers are slightly adjusted to the circle he is making—first one way, then the other. The scene below is in black and white, but with shades of darkness that make the meadow as bright as daylight. The owl hears a faint rustling noise in the grass below, and you marvel at the sharpness of such a tiny sound.

However, you have no wish to be involved in the owl's nightly mouse hunt. As the owl glides swiftly downward, you think of your body and leave the owl to its hunt.

Use meditation ending.

Mentally and psychologically adopting an animal ally's abilities for a short time can be quite useful on occasions. By projecting an air of invisibility and moving slowly but confidently like a fox, you should be able to move out of a crowded room without being noticed. Or sit as still as an owl on a branch while people near you forget your presence. It just takes practice. And as you discovered when patrolling with the Moosha, illusion and speed are valuable weapons in the Otherworld.

The Shapeshifter and Berserker

Most people use the words "Shapeshifter" and "Berserker" interchangeably, although these conditions have two different meanings. The Shapeshifter has learned to control this unusual ability, while the Berserker hasn't or doesn't want to. At times, the Shapeshifter will automatically change in reaction to danger but still maintains control over the basic process. The Berserker lets go as soon as she or he feels the inward shifting of emotions. No restraint is applied.

If either Shapeshifters or Berserkers find themselves in a dangerous situation, they will instinctively shift. The changes in their aura and attitude most often cause the attackers to withdraw. Pure animalistic energy surrounds them, their eyes may change visibly, and they may growl deeply. When they are forced to fight, they fight ferociously and by instinct, using supernatural strength and speed. They use no specific techniques, but depend upon pure instinct. They often do not even remember what they do, except that there has been a fight and they won. There are no countermoves to instinct.

Both Shapeshifters and Berserkers, after the danger is past, will recognize that their sight and hearing were sharper in every detail. Smells were more individual and intense. Their skin may turn whiter or gray-tinted. Even their eyes may shift in color and/or pupil shape. They may retain these super senses for a few hours after the shift.

It's not unusual for humans to be born with shapeshifting talent, and for that trait to lie dormant (but not always) until puberty. It can affect both men and women. Sometimes it appears to be almost a family trait, as generation after generation will produce one or more Shifters or Berserkers. Usually, though, the person with this trait is singular and becomes a kind of family outcast. A Shapeshifter's talents appear slowly to those around her or him, probably become of self-control. The signs of a Berserker shifting is more sudden, violent, and uncontrollable compared to a Shapeshifter.

We are most familiar with Berserkers through Viking history, although the Celts also knew of, and respected with uneasiness, a group of similar warriors called the *Riastarthae*. As part of Viking culture and the Vikings' formidable fighting techniques, the Berserkers had no desire to control their unpredictable shifts into mindless bodies expressing vicious animal tendencies. Their own culture was uneasy about Berserkers, requiring them to live near, but apart from, the other villagers and fighters.

The Celtic Riastarthae was a warrior cult that glorified its supernatural powers and the elite status this gave its members. Records say this group were touched by "warp frenzy," which turned them into cold-blooded, twisted, distorted monsters capable of superhuman feats. Like the Viking Berserkers, the Riastarthae were highly gifted warriors, capable of psyching themselves up into a state of mindless frenzy.

Such warriors reacted on instincts, using fighting techniques learned in past lives and in this one. In ancient times, shamans and priests had the teaching abilities and insight to help such a person learn to control this trait. But nearly all of them wanted to keep and exploit their abilities—it gave them a certain village status, however dubious that recognition.

Only rarely is such a person unable to learn to control the depth and strength of shifting, even today. The Shapeshifter changes by willpower or in an automatic reaction to threats and danger. They may have been Berserkers in past lives, but they learned how to gain and use control. As was discussed above, the Berserker enjoys the negative social status and has no desire to learn control.

There are many Shapeshifters and Berserkers in the world today. Both types have been the same in several past lives. All of us come into this life with at least one animal ally in our auras. Some of these allies are positive as a species but negative as individuals. These animal allies tend to remain concealed unless a person seeks them out. The Berserker's main ally also attaches to the aura at birth but often shows signs of ability when young and throughout life. Berserkers act out their violent anger and desires for actions. They tend to attract like-minded companions or join gangs. The abilities of both the Shapeshifter and Berserker readily become apparent if exposed directly to military service, gangs, frequent personal danger, or martial-arts training. Military service and the martial arts are very good, though, for they both teach self-control.

Dragons, especially the Savage Heart Warriors, shapeshift frequently. If you should be nearby when any dragon has to fight Rogue dragons or pools of evil, you will see very controlled Berserker talents on display. These appear in the lightning-fast movement, the instincts that ensure the Beserkers are where they need to be when they need to be there (being in sync with the action), their ability to disappear (become invisible) and reappear where least expected, and their ability to automatically counter any of their opponents' plans. These strategies are part of a true Warrior's instincts. So, having Berserker abilities isn't bad—having a lack of self-control is.

Dragon Warrior Initiation

Now is the time for you to be acknowledged in the Otherworld, through initiation, as a full Dragon Warrior. Many ancient Warrior/Healers, men and women who are now spending time in the Otherworld, will be attending this initiation. They are proud to have you join their ranks. As you know by your study of dragon history, not many humans have been initiated formally as Dragon Warriors for a very long time. So prepare your mind and spirit for the honor that is to be bestowed upon you.

Set up your altar as usual with the necessary items. It is best to perform this on a Full Moon.

Use the ceremony opening on page 52.

You find yourself once more in Dragon World near the Stone Circles of Distant Truths. A large group of humans and dragons awaits you there. You instinctively know that the human men and women have been Warrior/Healers in many historical eras of Earth's history. They all smile as they escort you into the center of the three stone circles. The female Moosha with whom you did a patrol stands ready to initiate you.

She leans down and says quietly, "Are you ready to be marked as a true Dragon Warrior?"

"I hope to be worthy," you say.

"Who will stand as surety for this Warrior's integrity, honor, and courage?" The Moosha looks at all in attendance.

"We will!" everyone answers.

You can feel their sincerity washing over you. You feel the intense pride of the Earth Warriors as they all step forward to stand by your side. The dragons tip back their heads as they sing in booming voices that are answered by other dragon voices from throughout Dragon World.

"What are the rules a Dragon Warrior must follow when going into the Otherworld?" the initiating Moosha asks you.

As you answer, the Moosha nods at each statement. When you are finished, she uses one claw to scratch a painless mark on the center of your forehead.

"This is only visible when you are in the Otherworld," she tells you. "It is the Warrior symbol of a dragon with its tail in its mouth. This symbol stands for enlightenment, eternity, and the Multiverse in general. It is not given out lightly."

One of the human Warriors hands you a long, strong walking staff. "This is both a weapon and balance when you journey," he says. His eyes are full of pride.

As you thank him and take the staff, you see a door open in the air before you. It is the portal to the Dragon Mystic section. You step through the door and see your co-magician dragon waiting there for you. You feel yourself being drawn back to your physical body.

Use the ceremony ending on page 54.

Now is the time to prepare yourself—mentally, emotionally, and spiritually—for the step into Dragon Mystic training. If you are taking the Inner Rings training seriously, this will be the most important decision you can make in perfecting magick.

FIVE

The Way of the Dragon Mystic

FIFTH OF THE INNER RINGS

A true Mystic is one who seeks the deep truth and knowledge, as well as the spiritual side of magick. The ongoing, lifelong journey of a Mystic is to develop her or his spiritual path (whatever that may be) and personal inner path of integrity and truth. The role of the Dragon Mystic is always to study, explore new ideas, and try to be worthy of stepping into the center of the Five Rings for higher, more in-depth knowledge.

The final stage of the Mystic's journey begins by discovering and developing communication with the very personal Hidden Dragon Heart within each of us. This Heart lies at the center of your being, deep within your subconscious mind. You can only discover the depth of the Dragon Heart's power, and learn to understand and use that power, by linking, or becoming one, with your primary dragon teacher. Only by frequently melding your mind and thoughts with this teacher can you hope to accomplish the high vibrational tasks that might fall in your path of destiny.

The Hidden Dragon Heart within you is deeply buried in your subconscious mind. If you step into your astral body, as during meditation, you will find the Dragon Heart behind your eyes, with connecting threads to your third eye and the crown chakra.

Code, Color, and Other Items of the Mystic

You will need a violet and/or silver-gray ribbon, of the proper length for your status as a Dragon Mystic. The code for this section is "We are all part of the Web of Life. All things, animate and inanimate, are connected." The Mystic's symbol is a shooting star or a nine-pointed star. This is not the same as a meteorite. The shooting star represents the Mystic's journey of surprises and sudden enlightenments, for that is exactly how the journey will always be.

If you desire, you can carry a walking staff and wear a hooded robe during any magickal spells or rituals. Wearing special magickal clothing aids in switching your thoughts and attention from everyday life to the magickal and spiritual. However, such robes and clothing are not required.

Mystic Ritual Tools

There are really no new tools that the Mystic needs, although you will probably add tools of your choosing as you find what attracts you. One object that Mystics invariably collect are quartz crystals. The information below on special crystals will therefore be of interest to you.

It is always wise to keep small stone "batteries" available for emergency use. The kind of stone doesn't matter as long they are small enough for you to easily carry in a small bag if you need to travel.

Take the stones in your hands, rub them gently, and visualize dragon power flowing through you into the stones. Say:

> *Dragons of the elements, Sun and Moon, and every star,*
> *Pour your power into these stones, be you near, or be you far.*
> *Fill each tight, from edge to edge, with your energy pure and bright.*
> *Flood these stones with Dragon Breath, the Multiverse's strongest Light.*

Put the empowered stones into a special bag. Then breathe gently into the bag to lock them to your vibrations. This prevents any other magician from using them.

You can use the energy from only one stone by holding it while chanting. Or you can call upon all the stones by holding your hands above them. When calling upon the stone "batteries" to release their stored power, say:

> *Stones, awaken. Answer my plea.*
> *Pour out your power. Work well for me.*

This is an excellent time to remind the Dragon Mystic that using the Charm of Making at the end of a spell is quite powerful.

> *By glow of Sun, the power's begun.*
> *By moonbeam's light, the spell is right,*
> *To create desire by Earth and Fire.*
> *Water, Air, make magick fair.*
> *Powerful Charm of Making, creative magickal undertaking.*
> *Storm, be formed!*

Study of Special Crystals

Quartz crystals as a whole are fascinating to most people, and doubly so to Dragon Mystics and other magicians. In fact, any person with budding or developed psychic abilities is drawn to such stones.

The following list of descriptions will help you identify various types of quartz crystals. If you look at each crystal carefully, you will find that each one contains more than one special marking within it, or in its shape. Put the crystal on a piece of dark velvet and use a good magnifying glass to see markings you might not otherwise see. The world of quartz crystals is fascinating. These features can appear in clear quartz, amethyst, citrine, smoky quartz, or rose quartz. The more opaque the crystal, the more difficult it is to find these markings.

This list will also make you aware of terms used by crystal merchants. The cost of a crystal rises steeply according to rarity, number of combined traits, and size. Take care when buying Lemurian seed crystals. These are frequently misrepresented. The only reliable source I personally know for any crystals is the Montgomery Crystal Company, found online at www.montgomerycrystalco.com. I'm sure there are other such sources, but I haven't dealt with them.

If you should get a crystal with a drop (or drops) of water in it, do *not* drink this water if the crystal breaks. At least two miners have died after doing just that.

Abundance: One large pointed crystal with at least seven other small points around the base in a vertical position.

Angel aura: Created by bonding clear quartz crystal with pure platinum and silver, which produces an iridescent display of delicate colored light. This is a permanent bond.

Aqua aura: Created by permanently bonding clear quartz crystal with pure gold. This produces a striking blue with enhanced opalescent shades of shimmering violet.

Atlantean: Record Keepers with equilateral triangles are said to have Atlantean records. Atlantis has been the marker, especially for Arkansas crystals, for a very long time.

Channeling: Sometimes called the "sage" of the crystal clan, this is a spiritual-growth crystal with seven sides. The seven edges are along the sides, which reach up to a triangular point that slopes backward.

Clusters: A formation consisting of a number of crystal points, all growing from a common base.

Cross: The form of an equal-armed cross may appear to be engraved on the crystal's surface, or into it.

Devic: Usually has many internal fractures and inclusions. Sometimes the crystals have no points or terminations. The crystal contains a great number of internal fractures and inclusions that often reveal the forms of elves, faeries, other nature spirits, or animals.

Diamond window: A four-sided vertical diamond shape appears as one of the six main faces. Or a vertical, diamond-shaped window is connected to a line that leads to the apex of the crystal. The side points connect with the angles of the adjoining faces. The bottom point may be attached to a line that runs to the base of the crystal. Sometimes this window is large enough to be called an extra crystal face.

Dolphin: See *Guide*.

Double diamond: Two diamond windows on one crystal. One may be above the other.

Double-Terminated: A crystal with a termination or point on both ends.

Dow: Three seven-edged channel faces of the same size on the pointed tip, with alternating three same-sized triangles.

Elestial: Also called *skeletal crystal*. The features on this kind of crystal are flat, to nearly flat points, with irregular cut-in triangular spaces. It usually looks burned; it isn't pretty. It may contain drops of encapsulated water and have strange cryptic markings.

Empathic: A self-healed crystal that has been damaged but grew the damaged areas back together. This crystal has had a very hard life, but it has beautiful internal rainbows caused by the fractures.

ET: A double-terminated crystal with multi-terminated small crystals on one end.

Etched: A crystal with natural geometric and/or hieroglyphic-looking marks.

Faden veil: A linear veil mostly found in tabular crystals. It looks like a thin fuzzy piece of white string that runs through the crystal.

Fairy frost: Inclusions of water, gases, air, and internal fractures. Beautiful interior veils.

Generator: All crystals are actually generators, even though this term is used to denote one type. At one time, this meant that the tip of a crystal's point was dead center, and each of the six faces was a triangular shape.

Golden healer: A natural, permanent iron coating on or under the surface of a crystal.

Growth crater: A four to six-sided indent left on a crystal by the base of a separated stone. There may be more than one crater.

Guide: Sometimes called a *dolphin*. It has a much smaller, perfectly formed crystal attached naturally to one of the sides.

Hera: Self-healing with beveled edges and a terry-cloth texture on a multipointed tail.

Herkimer diamond: Found around Herkimer, New York, they are small, stubby, double-terminated quartz crystals that are usually very clear. They can stimulate the third eye. Use them for dreams, visions, time travel, dimensional shifting, and to open dimensional doorways.

Hydrolite: The hydrolite crystals are sometimes called *enhydros*, meaning they contain drops of water. Never leave such a crystal in sunlight or in an overheated room.

Included: Crystals containing other minerals—such as silver, calcite, chlorite, manganese, shale, clay, or sand.

Isis face: The main face has five edges, like a triangle on top of a rectangle.

Key: Groups of several points (often tabular crystals), attached at the sides.

Laser: Long, thin, tapering crystal with at least one termination point. The girth decreases toward the tip. It has ribbed or stepped sides, and it looks frosty or greasy-clear.

Lemurian seed: Record Keepers with elongated or irregular triangles; they also must have horizontal steplike grooves or striations on the sides. They often have natural etchings that look like hieroglyphics. This is a fairly new identity of crystal, found in the Diamantina area of Brazil. They are said to be found individually, lying in beds of sand without attachment to any matrix. However, these are similar to the identification marks used to describe Atlantean crystals for years, so I'm not certain yet if this is actually a new crystal or a slightly different form of an older one. They are very clear. Users say they are coded, programmed, and filled with ancient Lemurian knowledge and wisdom. You can recover the information they contain by rubbing the grooves with your fingers while meditating. Besides being powerful libraries, they aid in reintegrating pieces of a shattered soul.

Library: A crystal with a strange irregular formation of flat, stubby crystals on its sides. These attachments are merely slight rises and don't have the usual crystalline shape.

Manifestation: Also called a *Creator*, a *baby within*, and a *mother with baby*, because it contains another perfectly formed crystal completely inside it. Many are quite tiny and require magnification to see clearly. For a crystal to qualify as a Manifestation, the inner crystal must be visible.

Master programmer: Also called a *master matrix* or a *root directory crystal*. It will have most if not all of the known geometric symbols naturally etched on its sides or inside.

Moon: See *Selene veil*.

Mystic fire: Created by bonding the underside of white topaz with an extremely thin layer of titanium, which produces a sparkling array of blues, greens, purples, reds, and browns.

Occluded: This crystal appears to be filled entirely with chlorite or sand. Sometimes the inner material cannot be identified.

Penetrated: A major crystal that is half-penetrated by a partially embedded, smaller crystal.

Phantom, black: Has small, black outline of a crystal point inside it.

Phantom, white: Has a small white outline of a crystal point inside it. Sometimes there is more than one phantom. You can use it to access the Akashic Records and past-life memories. It helps to connect people with spirit guides.

Quantum: Also called *triple quartz.* Three crystals with single terminations joined at the sides to make a row. These must not be broken out of another cluster.

Rainbow: A clear quartz crystal with inclusions of water or another mineral that reflects rainbow colors when turned in the light. Also called an *iris quartz.* Slightly different from the rainbows created by internal fractures. These can be very expensive

Record keeper: Has a geometric symbol (usually a triangle) naturally etched into the sides or interior. May have more than one such marking. Can be used to access ancient information as far back as Atlantis and Lemuria.

Rutilated quartz: Clear crystal containing thin strands of gold, titanium, asbestos, or actinolite inside it.

Scepter: An ordinary crystal point with a cap of new crystal overgrown on its pointed end. Can be any color or variety of crystal. Symbolic of the Goddess and the God.

Selene veil: Also called a *moon crystal.* It has an interior faden veil that resembles a Moon phase—such as a complete circle, a semi-circle, or a small rounded sliver.

Snow (milk): A cloudy, white form of quartz. Its appearance is caused by trapped inclusions of gasses, air, and water that make it opaque and snow-like. Comes in either points or chunks.

Soul mate: Usually single-terminated, these are two crystals growing naturally side by side, of equal length and size.

Spirit guardian: Two double-terminated crystals naturally attached at the side, of equal or nearly equal length. Very personal crystals for connecting you with spirit teachers, guides, and guardians. Can also help you find ancient, forgotten knowledge.

Stepped face: One or more very visible "steps" formed into one or more facets.

Tabular: A crystal with one pair of opposite sides being wider than the others. This gives the crystal a flat look. May be two or more tabbies naturally attached.

Teacher: Deep inside this crystal one can see the tiny form of an animal or human-like being. Sometimes there is more than one. These figures have been known to change into another form over time.

Time link: Has a parallelogram on one of its point faces. A parallelogram is a quadrilateral form with parallel and equal-length opposite sides. A time link is good for recalling past lives.

Time travel: Also called a *mythic crystal*. This is a double-terminated snow or milk quartz. It is opaque because of the large amount of trapped air, gasses, and water. It can have tiny clear spots.

Tourmaline quartz: Clear quartz with pieces of black tourmaline suspended inside. It is considered to have double the power of ordinary clear quartz.

Transmitter: Has a prominent triangular face. On each side of this face are two seven-sided faces with a smaller seven-edged channel face opposite.

Veil: Also called a *wall crystal*. It has an inner fracture or inclusion that completely divides the interior. This wall or veil may appear solid or gauzy. Sometimes these crystals also have rainbows.

Window: See *Diamond window*.

◎   ◎   ◎

I purposely waited until last to discuss the strange Merkabah crystal, a man-made, three-dimensional form of interlocking triangles. It is very possible that its name, shape, and uses migrated from Atlantis to Egypt before the islands sank. The Seers of the Merkabah study and regulate the mysterious power of this stone. If a student isn't responsible enough or ready to delve into deeper mysteries, the Seers will put a wall around a stone in such a manner that the student gets no information.

The name *Merkabah* comes from the highest of ancient Egyptian Mystery Schools and is found in many languages, including Egyptian, Hebrew, and Zulu. In ancient Egypt, *Mer* is a place of ascending, *ka* means the individual spirit, and *bah* is the "light vehicle," or physical body.

In Hebrew, Merkabah means both "Throne of God" and "chariot that carries the body and spirit from one place or dimension to another." Since there is a distinction made between individual spirit and physical body, it obviously refers to a time-dimensional movement, not death or dying.

This crystal produces two counter-rotating fields of energy spinning in the same place. In other words, one field spins clockwise while the other spins counterclockwise. This makes the Merkabah an interdimensional vehicle that can move one's reality from one dimension to another. It controls time-shifting and the interaction of light dimensions. It can open the conscious mind to other dimensions of the Multiverse. It also amplifies the power of thoughtforms and concentrated intent.

The Merkabah's energy field is activated by the expanded awareness of a student to the Multiverse, dragons, and infinite possibilities. If held during a meditation, the Merkabah helps with time travel and visiting other dimensions, and it enhances the part of you that astral travels and taps into universal energy for magick.

Learning to Scry

Magick mirrors and balls have been used for centuries by the magicians of this planet. The ancient Egyptians used polished copper mirrors with handles. This type of mirror was exported to places as far away as Europe. The Aztec priests made their mirrors from polished obsidian or pyrite. The Chinese used fairly small, circular mirrors with a handle and mystical symbols painted on the back side. Like the medieval Italian mirrors, Chinese mirrors were made of gold, silver, electrum (a mixture of gold and silver), or other precious metals.

These mirrors were used not only for divination but also for spirit communication, directing energy, banishing negative energy, and detecting/expelling negative beings. In some instances, the magickal mirror became a kind of cross between a bothersome spirit detector and a mousetrap. The only way to rid the mirror of the trapped entity is to call in the Savage Heart dragons. They can safely and permanently remove the entity to the Underworld. If you release the spirit from the mirror otherwise, you can count on an angry houseguest, intent on making life as miserable as possible. This is one reason no one should "play" at magick or with magickal devices.

Scrying balls and mirrors need to be periodically cleaned and reenergized. You can do this by rubbing them with mugwort leaves (fresh or dried) or by smudging them with sage. I find that actually washing the crystal, onyx, or obsidian ball or mirror with pure water and a little mild soap before smudging helps the most.

It also is practical to have a special oil to rub on any candles you burn during a time of divination. The following oil is very potent for that purpose.

Mystic Oil

Time to make: Waxing or Full Moon.

Ingredients: A teaspoon of almond oil and oils of clove, cinnamon, myrrh, and sandalwood.

Put the almond oil into a sterilized vial. Slowly add one drop each of cinnamon and clove oils. Add five to seven drops of sandalwood oil and five drops of myrrh oil. Close the vial with a tight lid.

With the change of each season, on the equinoxes and solstices, I like to expose all my divination tools to outdoor lunar energy. Since this isn't always possible, an alternative method is to set up a substitute system on my altar. I set the crystal balls, tarot decks, and any divination stones on the altar around a silver candle. Then I arrange three round mirrors (with the magnifying side toward the candle) in among the tools and anchor them with children's clay so they stay upright and reflect into each other. I hold the candle while imprinting it with the purpose I want done and oil the candle with mystic oil. I set the candle itself in a metal holder, which I put inside an iron cauldron. I light it, along with lotus or jasmine incense. I repeat this calling down the Moon spell for three nights: the first being the day before the Full Moon, the second on the Full Moon, and ending on the evening of the day after the Full Moon. The last night I smudge my entire house with sage or a stick of frankincense.

Scrying is a term usually associated with stone balls, particularly quartz crystal. I don't care for totally clear crystal balls; we have nothing to communicate to each other, it seems. I prefer ones that have fractures and inclusions. However, you may find that a highly polished ball or slab (mirror) of black onyx or obsidian works better for you. Remember, size has nothing to do with getting good results. The smallest balls are often the best. The ones rejected by others may be the very ones waiting for your arrival.

Some magicians prefer special handmade magickal mirrors. Making such mirrors is a long, tedious process that, for me at least, doesn't produce any results. If you want to try making your own mirror, there are many books available that give detailed instructions.

Images and impressions frequently appear first in your mind, not the ball or mirror. If you hold the tool, place a dark piece of cheap velvet under it as a background. Look deep into the ball by letting your eyes go slightly out of focus. Blink when you need to. The trick is to let your inner eyes see deep into the device. Sometimes a sideways glance is better than straight on. Try each method and type of device (if possible) to see what works best for you. Practice for just a few minutes at first. Don't strain your eyes, as doing so won't help.

One evening as I sat at my desk thinking about the new dragon magick I had learned, I idly glanced at the crystal ball that sits there. This ball is full of mist, fractures, and what looks like shiny walls. A single movement inside the ball caught my attention. As if I were looking through a window, I saw the colored figure of a magician against one of the "walls." Intrigued, I watched him for some time as he went about whatever magickal work he was doing. I have no idea if he was from the past, present, or future, or if he was somewhere else in the Multiverse. My husband broke the connection by speaking to me, and the magician disappeared. It must have been that the magician and I were on the same magickal dragon frequency at the same moment, rather like crossed telephone lines.

The reason I mention that story is to illustrate that you shouldn't expect a certain thing when scrying, but instead you should unhurriedly follow any idea or movement that appears. If you try too hard or have preconceived ideas of what you will see, you will rarely be successful. But you should have a definite question in mind when you scry, so that your results will at least hint at an answer.

When you do get results, they are similar to my watching the magician, or the answer you seek could come through symbols, which must then be interpreted by the seer. As with decoding dreams, there is not one list of symbol meanings that fits all situations. Symbols are personal, with different connotations for each person.

When I thought about the vision of the working magician, I realized he was doing one of the new dragon spells. This was confirmation that I was following proper instructions, and that I should probably be communicating more often with my dragon co-magicians.

Learning to Change Your Life

Don't wait to see what your future dumps on you. Create your future with deliberate, well-planned intent. Our probable futures are based on our current train of constant thoughts, our prolonged attention on any one subject. If your thought patterns shift in a significantly positive or negative way, so will your future. Shades of *The Secret*, but this "secret" was known by the star people before they came to Earth, and books on the subject were highly popular in the 1970s. We all need to develop self-control of negative and damaging thoughts. Know your own strengths and weaknesses, for this knowledge gives you greater control

Karma is a Sanskrit word for the cosmic law of cause and effect, action and reaction—in a word: balance. Remember, karma is both positive and negative. Learn to draw on your karmic credit, for the supply is endless.

Thought is a refined energy and easy to change. Even matter isn't solid but formed of lower vibrational energy. Everything is energy. Energy is magnetic in that it attracts other energies that match its quality and vibration. Thoughts and ideas are a type of energy blueprint. If you think about something (for example, fear) long enough and intently enough, it will manifest or happen. What we think about the most, we attract. Form always follows thoughts and intent.

To change your life and remain in control, you need to change your basic attitude toward life and your future. Creative visualization in a positive mode has to become a continuous awareness. You must realize that you are the constant creator of your future. Don't allow pessimism any room to grow in your mind. Like attracts like. The same applies to hate; revenge; the "I can't" syndrome; "fate" due to family, education or whatever; the "poor me"; jealousy; envy; and so on.

By using positive spellwork for your desires and future, you are rearranging energy patterns. You create change. Spells are catalysts for change; your intent determines whether that change is good or bad. Doubting yourself is self-sabotage. If you expect conflicts, roadblocks, challenges, or ridicule from family and friends, you will surely get just those things.

You already have everything within you and available to you to make your life just how you want it to be, to become what you wish to become. If you truly make yourself believe that something is possible, then it *is* possible. You make changes in your life by your thoughts, your will, your creative visualizations.

If you want to learn about your past lives so you can balance negative karma points, recall forgotten talents and skills, and determine why certain people and/or repetitious events are occurring, you need to journey to the Hall of Akashic Records in the Otherworld. In fact, it will take more than one such journey to even begin to learn all that you need to know. Since this is a personal journey, you should get there without a guided meditation this time. Besides, you already have lots of meditation experiences behind you now.

The Hall of Akashic Records is found in the side area of the Akasha Recorders clan, adjoining Middleworld. Their leader is Juuja. The Hall is a beautiful, white, marble building set in a serene landscape of ornamental pools, statues, fountains, trees, and flowers. Inside this Hall are the records of every life of every person who has ever lived. It is a giant library of books, scrolls, and tablets. If your dragon friend doesn't accompany you, you should ask the Door Keeper at the entrance for help. Otherwise, you will have trouble finding your personal records in the vast corridors of shelves and cabinets.

Some records will be in unknown languages or will read only as moving pictures without sound. You will need help to decipher these at first. The Door Keeper will find a reliable attendant to give you all the aid you need.

There really is no reason to visit this Hall unless you are prepared to see only the truth and learn from past mistakes. Your records can reveal why you don't care for, or why you have trouble with, certain people. Don't expect to find out you were a famous person. That is highly unlikely. Ordinary people outnumber the so-called famous and are most prepared spiritually to work on balancing karmic residue.

Don't waste time searching for your "life's purpose." Everyone's goal is the same: live as good a life as you can and grow spiritually. Be the best person you can be.

If you find you are repeating unhealthy habits and lifestyles, reprogram your mind with positive images of change. If you are choosing to be with the same or similar companions, and those relationships are repeating negative patterns, it is your responsibility to change your path.

Some of the first things you need to fully understand about karma are that any karmic challenges are opportunities to make changes, that people are in your life for a reason, and that you need to find a method that will truly release anger and resentment you have against yourself and others.

I learned something about karma, with which other writers don't agree. However, it has proven to be true in my experiences with karma-linked people in particular. And wherever karma affects you through others, it affects everything else in your life. As soon as you really learn the lessons from your past lives and stop repeating the mistakes, the karmic repayment stops. Karma is a learning system that balances errors and repays you for good you've done. It isn't a "hell" punishment nor a sentence to torture you forever. There is always a traceable thread of the positive—no matter how thin—running through the worst parts of life. Too often, we are too busy enduring our way through pain to notice. We see the positive in retrospect.

You create your future by changing negative polarities through constant reminders and by watching your actions, words, and deep thoughts. Learn to feel the power of the Supreme Creative Force in all energies.

The Upperworld Level Meditation

As part of changing your present and future, it is valuable to once more visit the Upperworld. Prepare for your meditation as usual. Have paper and pen ready to make notes at the end of this meditation. After such a exciting, informative experience, it is too easy to forget things if you don't write them down.

Use the meditation opening.

You are standing in an area of the Upperworld where there are hundreds of different styles of shrines. There is a shrine for each of ancient Earth's pantheons as well as deity shrines of other worlds in the Multiverse. However, the other worlds' shrines are not open to you at this time.

You decide which pantheon interests you, and you enter the open door of that shrine. You can ask to talk with any deity of that pantheon as well as any priest or priestess.

Ask the questions that you have and the answers are clear in your mind. Spend as much time as you wish here. You may also visit another shrine or go to the Gate to the Highest and talk to the Goddess and/or the God.

After a few more questions, you wander back toward the area of the shrines. You see several other human and humanoid beings also exploring this area as part of their Dragon Mystic studies. One being, then another, stops to talk with you. You quickly learn that telepathy is a Multiversal language that makes it possible to communicate with any being in the Otherworld.

As a group of students gathers around you to talk about dragon studies, you realize that you can make friends with these beings. You may even see them later in your Otherworld journeys, meditations, dreams, and magickal work.

All the co-magician dragons of these students, including yours, appear to lead their charges off on other explorations.

"I think you would be interested in visiting the Dome of Multiversal Stars," your dragon friend says. *"It lies in the area where you find the Time-Flight and Astra-Keeper clans."*

Your dragon leads you to that Gate and the Door Keeper allows both of you to enter. This is a very quiet area except for faint songs of birds. The gardens are very exact in layout and trimming. A huge octagon of connected domed buildings occupies the center of the gardens not far from the Gate. Your dragon and you go directly there.

When you enter one of the open doors, your co-magician says, "The Time-Flight and Astra-Keeper clans work with the birth charts of all reincarnating souls returning to all worlds of the Multiverse. By using judgments from the Hall of Justice in the Lowerworld, these dragon clans determine the exact birth time, place, and birth conditions for each soul. If you wish, you can talk to an Elder about your personal birth chart for this life."

You agree, as there may be information available to aid you in changing your present and future. Your barely think your agreement when an older dragon approaches. You realize this must be a wise Elder, and you greet the dragon with great respect.

You ask about your present life chart, what karmic lessons or choices you have, and why certain people or patterns are in your life. If you have more specific questions, you are free to ask those also.

After a time, the Elder bids you farewell and moves off to meet with other visitors who have entered the Dome. You discuss a few points of your experiences with your co-magician dragon. Then you feel the pull of your physical body.

Use the meditation ending.

Now is the time to make notes on everything you learned on this Otherworld journey. Write down even the things that didn't quite make sense to you, for they may enlighten you about your life at a later date.

Working with Light, Dark, and Chaos Dragons

Dragons are very fond of bright and shiny colors. They delight in pure shades in candle colors and in gold, silver, copper, brass, bronze, and electrum in metals. They take absolute delight in the black shimmers within the Void and deep space, as well as the rainbow flashes caused by bolts of positive energy and Light. Their perception range within the color spectrum is deeper and far more accurate than ours. In comparison, we are nearly blind to colors, deaf to the music of the heavenly stars and planets, and ignorant of the felt beauty of pure positive emotions.

In their vast variety, dragons have an endless supply of knowledge and wisdom to share, if only we would believe them. We need to open our minds to their quiet telepathic messages and put into practice what we are taught. Knowledge without positive action is wasted. Yet the dragons are patient if there remains the tiniest spark of hope. We are very fortunate to have the opportunity to have dragons as willing teachers.

The Void is a place where no being can go except for the Chaos and Star-Born dragons. The color black holds all colors within it. The color of the Void is black. All manifestation energy (positive mixed with negative) comes from the Void. It is the duty of the Chaos dragons to work in the Void of unformed matter.

There is a direct connection to the Chaos dragons in the Void from the Upperworld. Souls in the Lowerworld who want to reincarnate must receive the power to do so from the Void and the Chaos dragons. However, a legitimate journey to the Void can't happen until after the soul talks to the Council in the Lowerworld and a plan is laid out for the soul's new life. Then that soul goes to the Upperworld and waits at the Chaos Gate until the Chaos dragons come for her or him.

Once a plan is agreed upon by both the Council and the requesting soul, the new life can't be rejected. This plan is patterned to learn from karmic mistakes, pay off such debts, attempt to help certain people, and learn new things. All sentient beings of the Multiverse have the same karmic laws and must go through the same procedure before reincarnation.

If the soul requesting reincarnation is one from the Underworld, she or he will be directly taken to the Void to avoid exposing other beings in the Otherworld to their violence. These souls have no input into the next life. They are neither repentant nor cooperative. However, according to the freewill law of the Multiverse, they must be allowed to reincarnate if they wish to do so.

This Council, which meets at the Hall of Justice and Rebirth, is composed of compassionate beings who have reached a level of soul-balance equal to the angels'. However, these beings prefer to keep their personal identity and work with troubled souls who wish to reincarnate. There are also a certain number of dragons who work with the Council at all times.

Dragons live an extremely long time—no one is certain how long. At physical death they deliberately transfer themselves into the Lowerworld, where they must follow the same rules to be reborn. No species in the Multiverse is ever exempt from the cycles of living, dying, resting, learning, and being reborn with a life plan that is worked out for its benefit. A life plan that appears to be difficult and negative at first can become a very positive life through wise choices. Ways to avoid bad karma are always provided, if one thinks clearly.

There appears to be a link between the dragons and all sentient beings that arose so far in the past that even dragons don't remember this beginning. And dragons have the longest remembered correct history in the Multiverse. If it weren't for the wisdom of dragons and their sharing of that wisdom, sentient beings would be far less evolved than we are.

Dragon wisdom goes far beyond psychic areas, expansion in healing and technology, and lessons about our galaxy and beyond. Their wisdom includes the opening of our delicate spiritual senses to the Supreme Creative Force, or whatever name suits you. They teach us on a subconscious level to develop and open these inner senses, which are like a spiritual magnet. When these psychic senses work, the knowledge we gather attracts us to the path of spiritual growth that will help us the most.

The Void is a place where all elements are mixed in a homogenized mass—neither fluid nor solid, neither hot nor cold, a universal spot of no form. To many cultures, the Void represented the Great Mother of the Deep, the Dark Goddess who formed the Multiverse and all within it. The Void gives off scintillating streaks of black and white colors that no human has ever seen. There are no words to describe these tints and hues of color.

Three distinct clans of dragons work in or around the Void. Only the Chaos dragons actually go into the Void. However, large groups of Light and Dark dragons work close to the Void, dismantling incoming flows of mixed energy into individual particles of negative and positive that are similar to atoms and electrons. These particles are sent into the Void to be re-created into a new manifested, reenergized form. They also weave outgoing threads of manifestation energy.

When I speak of Light dragons, I mean that this type of dragon's energy radiates out through its skin and is composed of the entire spectrum of light as we know it, including X-rays, ultraviolet, infrared, and radar. However, there are spectrums of light not known yet to humans. This "entire light" causes Light dragons to ripple in and out of sight and often causes their coloring to shift quickly through all the color bands. They appear transparent, then solid, and then transparent again. This is especially true if they become excited or upset.

The Dark dragons tend to grow darker in color if they are upset. Their colors are already very dark: the deepest hues of purple, magenta, blue, and black. Yes, there is more than one tint or shade of black. Our eyes simply cannot register this color range.

Some of the Light and Dark dragons, when they are not actively working, spend time in individual no-time places near the Void instead of returning to Dragon World. There, separate swirling pools of light and dark energies have not yet been mixed and balanced. Light dragons hold their tails in their mouths while sleeping or resting, as do the Dark dragons.

The ancient Hindu writings recorded information about the Chaos dragons. They called them *tad ekam*, or "That One," which referred to unformed matter. The Chaos dragons are very dark colors such as black, deep gray, pewter, purple, magenta—colors so dark they all appear black at first sight. They are the largest of the dragons, with huge, heavy bodies and enormous wings. Their serpentine tails are either barbed or have a spiked knob on the end.

As their clan name implies, the Chaos dragons' results are "chaotic" to us. They make changes in a big way by going beyond our limited view of events, straight to the heart of a problem. Be certain you can tolerate their help before asking for it. Their job is to separate and remix energies, leaving opportunities for complete transformation and rebirth. In short, they are the Storm element personified in dragon flesh and shape.

You need to learn to use your psychic senses to detect the ribbons or streams of energies coming from the Void. To correctly use these energies, the Mystic has to discern whether these energies are positive or negative. Then she or he must learn how to weave several strands together and add Elements for balance while visualizing with intent to produce a manifestation. In other words, you go to the source of the Multiversal energies to create the most powerful magick.

A Visit with the High Elders Meditation

This Otherworld journey is a very important part of the Dragon Mystic's studies, for the Mystic needs to understand the seriousness of the duties of certain Otherworld groups who try to protect all the planets of the Multiverse. With such knowledge, you will be more appreciative of the role of Dragon Mystics.

Use the meditation opening.

You are in Kaudra's crystal-lined cave in the Upperworld. Your co-magician dragon is with you. You have been granted permission to attend a meeting of the Duaar, composed of High Elders from all worlds on all levels of the Multiverse.

As all the gathered beings move into the cave and into the transparent crystal bubble there, you see sentient Elders from all over the Multiverse. There also are mythical beings—including elves, faeries, and angels—and some you don't recognize.

"This is called the Dream Chamber," your dragon whispers as the two of you enter behind the Elders and sit in an unobtrusive place.

"How do the members of the Duaar get chosen?" you whisper back.

"They are chosen because of their wisdom and the fact that none of them have ever been government or religious leaders. All follow freewill spiritual paths. They each work with a small group of people on their original world, trying to lead them to the Truth. They hope, in this way, to influence positive changes."

The Duaar discuss the growth pains affecting planets, including Earth, throughout the Multiverse: war, physical violence, prejudice, religious clashes, disease, declining ethics, hunger, and poverty, as well as the gradual loss of personal freedoms. Some member speak sadly of the conflict of living in balance with a planet and its environment. Similar troubles affect all the represented worlds.

A few planets in the Multiverse are sliding backward into chaotic social conditions, which threatens all levels of growth for sentient beings, particularly their continued existence. Others, such as Earth, are in a critical cycle but with many options yet to correct the situation. None of the Council knows yet what the final outcome will be.

The first step is freedom of spiritual paths without organized religious organizations trying to impose each of their views on everyone else. It is almost a unanimous decision with the Duaar that a control-attitude by religious organizations and governments is responsible for both the chaotic and lackadaisical responses of a world's inhabitants.

Energies should be attuned more to population control and making changes for a happy, positive life. Each culture, race, country, and planet should care for itself and ask for help from others only when disaster hits. Invasions and war must end. No culture, race, country, or planet is as it was in the beginning, due to the movement of groups, natural disasters, and many poor choices made by religious and national leaders. It is therefore time to forget what happened in the past (except for the lessons learned) and go forward from this point. There never was, isn't now, and never will be "one path for everyone," whether one is speaking of government, spirituality, ways of thinking, or how anyone thinks about any particular subject.

"All on Earth are part of an automatic diversity, as it should be," says the Earth representative. "That fact should be realized as truth and accepted. This also applies to all planets on all levels of the Multiverse. The successful planets all accepted and applied these ideas by mutual consent, after experiencing thousands of years of violet history similar to that of Earth. In doing this, most of these planets pulled their planet's very existence back from the brink of total disintegration."

Everyone nods in agreement, knowing this is the truth but realizing that they dare not impose this truth by force.

You feel the dragon Kaudra as she projects the image of strands of all possible futures onto the ceiling of the Dream Chamber.

"There are very few events that cannot be changed." Kaudra's telepathic voice is heard by all. "You can only try."

You watch the Duaar as they send positive energy currents from the tips of their fingers to influence mergers of strands, and as they try to weave strands with their hands and minds.

Quietly, so you don't disturb their concentration, you leave the meeting. However, you do have renewed hope for Earth and a greater understanding of the heavy duties of members of the Duaar.

Use the meditation ending.

Dragon Mystic Initiation

You have now reached the hard-won Mystic initiation. Prepare yourself mentally, emotionally, and spiritually for this important ceremony. It takes place in the private, special meeting place for dragons—the one that is between the worlds and beyond time, a time outside of time.

Set up your altar as usual, with your Mystic ribbons and other necessary items. It is best to do this initiation on a New Moon, as this ceremony marks the end of the Teachings of the Five Inner Rings and the beginning of private studies should you decide to seek out the ancient wisdom of one or more of the Higher Mystery Schools.

Use the ritual ceremony opening on page 52.

You are floating in the transparent bubble in space, the one used by the dragons for their private meetings. The space all around you is a black color with the pinpoint glow of distant stars. However, all the dragons within the bubble are brightly lit by starlight. Aldram is there with his ancient book. The leader of the Initiator clan, Visn-Isp, is there himself to perform your initiation. This is a great honor.

Visn-Isp reaches out and touches your Mystic ribbon with one claw. "Have you noticed how the color of each ribbon corresponds to the studies required in each Section the Inner Rings?" he asks. "By the time you reach this Mystic ceremony, you have a rainbow selection of colors to use in magick. Colors are magickal in themselves."

He hangs an electrum medallion, strung on a violet ribbon, around your neck. The medallion is engraved with a circle containing a five-pointed star clutched by a dragon. Light from the stars, and from the dragons themselves, glistens off the medallion.

"This sacred medallion, plus this astral Mystic ring, symbolize to all those who see you journeying in the Otherworld that you had the endurance, patience, and willpower to reach the rank of Dragon Mystic." Visn-Isp slips an electrum with a faceted black stone on a finger of your power hand. You notice that the black stone sends out sparks of every imaginable color.

"I am honored that the dragons have allowed me to take this journey through the Rings to greater knowledge and inner growth," you say.

The image of a portal appears to one side of your group. Aldram stands beside the door, his ancient book and quill in hand. Between you and the door and between you and the dragon Aldram, strange-colored flames leap high. There is no way to avoid the flames if you wish to sign the book and enter the Gate to the Center of the Five Rings.

"Here is the key to the Center Gate," the Initiator says, handing you a brass key. "To become a true Mystic, you have to walk slowly through the flames to reach that Gate and to sign Aldram's book again."

"Thank you all," you say as you take the key.

You straighten your shoulders, visualize the flames as positive and harmless to you, as you slowly but steadily walk through them. Aldram smiles as you sign his book once more. You insert the brass key and the Gate swings open.

When you pass through the Gate, you find yourself standing in the exact center of the Five Inner Rings. The circular boundary wall hides everything from view that is not inside the Center. The ground beneath your feet is thick, lush grass.

There are four dragons standing by four gates in the boundary wall. You know that no one can enter these four gates without permission of the dragon before each Gate. Each portal leads to a different, higher Mystery School in another level of this same area. The School behind each Gate specializes in one ancient type of magick and spirituality. One by one, the dragons introduce themselves by telepathy and give you information about their Mystery School.

Durka, the dragon at the Northern Gate, has the heavy, broad, four-legged body of a European dragon. The triangular head sits at the end of a long sinuous neck. The snakelike tail ends in a barbed tip. His two leathery wings are long and strong. Ridges of thick, sharp-edged scales frame the eyes, which are golden with rims of greenish-yellow. The claws on all four feet are steel gray. This dragon is covered with scales colored in swirls of green shades, from pale green to almost black.

The Northern Higher Mysteries teach deep secrets of the Scandinavians, Celts, and dwellers of those areas before recorded history, particularly those who built Stonehenge in Britain.

Hun-Ton, the dragon in the East, is a kaleidoscope of yellow-gold and orange. Although she has the body of a very thick, long snake, she has two small front feet with black claws. Her scales change colors and patterns with movement. The two small wings on her back by her legs have diamond patterns. Her head is long and narrow and merges with her body with no neck. Her eyes are a piercing, glittery black. Three red stripes run parallel to each other from the tip of her nose to the end of her pointed tail.

The Higher Mystery School of the East teaches ancient wisdom from Atlantis, Egypt, and Crete. There are also special studies connected with Africa, the Polynesian Islands, Australia, New Zealand, and the Americas.

Im-Miris, in the South, reminds one of the dragons of Babylon and Chaldea. He has a thick body and a head with the blunt muzzle of a huge canine. Each of his four paws has four dark red claws. His front two feet are shaped like lion paws while his two back feet are reminiscent of huge bird feet. He has two wings with featherlike scales. His coloring is a mixture of rich desert hues mixed with brick-red and deep, sparkling brown. His neck is short, and his glittering eyes are bright red.

The Higher Mysteries of this School teach forgotten knowledge of the Chaldeans, Babylonians, Mesopotamians, and other Mediterranean and ancient Arab cultures.

Gark-Yin, of the West, is an azure blue dragon with gold edging on her scales. Red thread-thin whiskers wave from over the top of her eyes and around her nose. Her long, slender body has four legs with four dark gold claws on each foot. These legs are small in proportion to her body. There is no discernible division to show where her neck would be. Her head is wide and blunt. Long, feathery antennae rise from the top of her head like those of a moth. The antennae are colored in a beautiful pattern of gold, azure blue, and pure red, twisting and turning as she senses the air for changes in vibrations, especially in emotions and mental thoughts.

The Higher Mystery School of the Western Gate concentrates on the ancient, hidden secrets of all the areas of the East, plus those of Lemuria, the Indonesian Islands, and the Philippines. It teaches wisdom from Russia, the Balkans, the Tartars and Huns, and Alaska.

The key given to you at your initiation keeps wavering in shape. As you stand thinking, your co-magician dragon appears at your side.

"You must decide what a 'key' means to you, what 'key' you need for your future life or future studies," your friend says. "Tradition says that keys are a symbol of the deeper Mysteries and magick. In the Osirian Mysteries of ancient Egypt, the key represented a secret word of occult power (hekau) that was concealed from everyone except initiates. The key had the same meaning in the Greek Eleusinian Mysteries. In magick spells, a real key symbolizes locking or releasing of any kind."

"If I don't use this key," you say, "then I'm locked here. If I use it on the Gate to a Higher Mystery School, I unlock a door to more knowledge." You look at your dragon friend, who smiles and nods.

"You may make a choice now of being satisfied with your exploration of the Five Inner Rings, knowing you haven't seen all there is to see," your co-magician says. "You may rest for a time before deciding. Or you can apply at once to one of the Mystery Schools, knowing it will be much more difficult than any studies you have undertaken. Aldram, these inner Gate guardians, and the Dragon Elders will give you a certain period of time to consider the choice, if you ask."

You make whatever decision is right for you. The column of light catches you and takes you to your physical body.

Use the ritual ceremony ending on page 54.

SIX

Continuing the Great Journey

The concepts, knowledge, and magickal practices in this book are not all that you can learn. They are a mere drop of water in the ocean. If one had the tenacity, courage, financial independence, and pure spiritual commitment, the amount of dragon magick to be discovered is endless. However, higher dragon magick demands total dedication of all your time.

If you have broader interests in different ways of approaching and doing magick, you can work with the Fae (human-sized faeries) for all of nature; the Phoenix (both Middle Eastern and Eastern) for strong, completely committed spiritual growth and enlightenment; the entire wild cat clan for bringing criminals to justice and revealing life errors to others to help them grow; or perhaps you can work with the elements to aid in keeping the Multiverse balanced and safe. And then there are the four Hidden Dragons who offer passage to the four ancient Mystery Schools of advanced dragon magick. There are areas and systems of magick without number that are interesting and rewarding to curious magicians.

The Great Journey, of which all dragons speak, is the journey of life after life until we stand in the Center of All and ask to be reabsorbed by the Power that made us. That choice, however, will not be given to us until we, like the dragons and other fantastical creatures, teach the truth about magick and the Multiverse to all those worthy who come to us to learn. By that time, we will easily know how to determine the worthy ones by their actions, their auras, and their hearts.

Think back to your own reservations on magick as an Apprentice of the Five Inner Rings. You will be amazed at how much you changed and grew in knowledge by the time you reached the status of Mystic. During the Apprentice Ritual, you may even have thought you could never reach the center of the Rings.

There are two laws of the Multiverse that apply to all creation, laws with which we all must work every day. There are only two ways to go: forward or backward. And nature (creative power) will not tolerate a void in anything. The void will be filled with whatever is closest at hand, so do your best to fill voids with positive energy. The magician must keep learning and moving forward. Once your feet are on the path, though, you will not want to stop your magickal adventures. Your moving forward, your never-ending learning, and your constant curiosity about the Multiverse will ensure there are never any voids in your life that need to be filled.

I wish for you only the best and most exciting adventures on your Great Journey. May the dragons always be there whenever you need a guide and a teacher.

BOOKS OF INTEREST

Addison, Charles G. *The History of the Knights Templar*. Kempton, IL: Adventures Unlimited Press, 1997. First published in London in 1842.

Andrews, Ted. *The Magickal Name*. St. Paul, MN: Llewellyn, 1991.

————. *Sacred Sounds*. St. Paul, MN: Llewellyn, 1992.

Ash, Heather. *The Four Elements of Change*. San Francisco: Council Oak Books, 2004.

Bailey, Alice. *Esoteric Astrology*. 3 volumes. New York: Lucis, 1976.

Bryant, Page. *The Magick of Minerals*. Santa Fe, NM: Sun Publishing, 1987.

Churchward, James. *The Sacred Symbols of Mu*. Las Vegas, NV: Brotherhood of Life, 2001.

Cirlot, J. E. *A Dictionary of Symbols*. 2nd ed. New York: Philosophical Library, 1978.

Clow, Barbara Hand. *Chiron: Rainbow Bridge Between the Inner and Outer Planets*. St. Paul, MN: Llewellyn, 1999.

Conway, D. J. *Advanced Celtic Shamanism*. Freedom, CA: The Crossing Press, 2000.

————. *Animal Magick*. St. Paul, MN: Llewellyn, 1997.

————. *By Oak, Ash & Thorn*. St. Paul, MN: Llewellyn, 1995.

————. *Crystal Enchantments*. Freedom, CA: The Crossing Press, 1999.

————. *Dancing with Dragons*. St. Paul, MN: Llewellyn, 2001.

————. *Elemental Magick*. Franklin Lakes, NJ: New Page Books, 2006.

————. *A Little Book of Healing Magick*. Freedom, CA: The Crossing Press, 2002.

Cunningham, Scott. *Cunningham's Encyclopedia of Magickal Herbs*. St. Paul, MN: Llewellyn, 1985.

_____. *Earth Power*. St. Paul, MN: Llewellyn, 1983.

_____. *Magickal Herbalism*. St. Paul, MN: Llewellyn, 1983.

Dale, Cyndi. *New Chakra Healing*. St. Paul, MN: Llewellyn, 1996.

Daniels, Estelle. *Astrological Magick*. York Beach, ME: Samuel Weiser, 1995.

Doore, Gary. *Shaman's Path: Healing Personal Growth & Empowerment*. Boston: Shambhala, 1988.

Eason, Cassandra. *The Illustrated Directory of Healing Crystals*. London: Collins & Brown, 2003.

Elliott, Paul. *Warrior Cults*. London: Blandford, 1995.

Emoto, Masaru. *The Hidden Messages in Water*. Hillsboro, OR: Beyond Words, 2004.

_____. *The Secret Life of Water*. New York: Atria Books, 2003.

Farmer, Steven D. *Power Animals*. Carlsbad, CA: Hay House, 2004.

Fontana, David. *The Secret Language of Symbols*. San Francisco: Chronicle Books, 1994.

Gawain, Shakti. *Creative Visualization*. New York: Bantam Books, 1982.

Gaynor, Mitchell L. *Sounds of Healing*. New York: Broadway Books, 1999.

Gonzalez-Wippler, Migene. *The Complete Book of Amulets & Talismans*. St. Paul, MN: Llewellyn, 1991.

Hall, Jamie. *Half Human Half Animal*. Bloomington, IN: unpublished, 2003.

Hall, Judy. *The Crystal Bible*. Cincinnati: Walking Stick Press, 2004.

Hamilton-Parker, Craig with Jane Hamilton-Parker. *The Psychic Workbook*. London: Vermilion, 1995.

Harris, Bill. *The Good Luck Book*. New York: Gramercy Books, 1998.

Hauck, Dennis William. *The Emerald Tablet: Alchemy for Personal Transformation*. New York: Penguin Compass, 1999.

Hersh, L. S. *The Buyer's Guide*. Bearsville, New York: no publisher, 2001. (Photographed and written by the owner of Montgomery Crystal Company, retrieved from www.montgomerycrystalco.com).

Hoult, Janet. *Dragons: Their History & Symbolism*. Glastonbury, UK: Gothic Image, 1990.

Huxley, Francis. *The Dragon: Nature of Spirit, Spirit of Nature.* London: Thames & Hudson, 1979.

Ingerman, Sandra. *Soul Retrieval: Mending the Fragmented Self.* San Francisco: Harper & Row, 1991.

Janse, Eva Rudy. *Singing Bowls.* Havelte, Netherlands: Binkey Kok, 1992.

Johnson, Cait. *Earth, Water, Fire & Air.* Woodstock, VT: Skylight Paths, 2003.

Kalweit, Holger. *Dreamtime and Inner Space.* Boston: Shambhala, 1988.

Lady Passion and Diuvei, *The Goodly Spellbook.* New York: Sterling Publishing, 2004.

Lady Rhea with Eve Le Fey. *The Enchanted Candle.* New York: Citadel Press, 2004

Lambert, Mary. *Crystal Energy.* New York: Sterling Publishing, 2005.

MacGregor, Trish. *The Everything Spells & Charms Book.* Avon, MA: Adams Media Corporation, 2001.

McArthur, Margie. *Wisdom of Elements.* Freedom, CA: The Crossing Press, 1998.

McColman, Carl. *The Complete Idiot's Guide to Paganism.* Indianapolis: Alpha Books, 2002.

McFarland, Phoenix. *The Complete Book of Magickal Names.* St. Paul, MN: Llewellyn, 1996.

Meadows, Kenneth. *Earth Medicine.* Rockport, ME: Element Books, 1996.

Melody. *Love is in the Earth.* Wheat Ridge, CO: Earth-Love Publishing House, 1998.

Mickaharic, Draja. *Magickal Practice.* Tinicum, PA: Xlibris, 2004.

Murphy-Hiscock, Arin. *Power of Spellcraft for Life.* Avon, MA: Provenance Press, 2005.

Musashi, Miyamoto. *A Book of Five Rings.* New York: One Overlook Drive, 1974.

Newark, Tim. *The Barbarians.* New York: Sterling Publishing, 1985.

Page, James Lynn. *Applied Visualization.* St. Paul, MN: Llewellyn, 1991.

Penczak, Christopher. *The Witch's Shield.* St. Paul, MN: Llewellyn, 2005.

Pennick, Nigel. *Magickal Alphabets.* York Beach, ME: Samuel Weiser, 1992.

Perkins, John. *Shape Shifting.* Rochester, VT: Destiny Press, 1997.

Richardson, Wally and Lenora Huett. *Spiritual Value of Gem Stones.* Marina del Rey, CA: De Vorss & Co., 1983.

Roeder, Dorothy. *Crystal Co-Creators.* Flagstaff, AZ: Light Technology Publishing, 1994.

Silbey, Uma. *The Complete Crystal Guidebook.* New York: Bantam, 1996.

_____. *Crystal Ball Gazing*. New York: Simon & Schuster, 1998.

Simmons, Robert and Naisha Ahsian. *The Book of Stones*. Montpelier, VT: Heaven & Earth Publishing, 2005.

Stearn, Jess. *The Power of Alpha-Thinking*. New York: New American Library, 1976.

Sun Tzu. *The Art of Strategy*. Translated by R. L. Wing. New York: Broadway Books, 2000.

_____. *The Art of War*. El Paso, TX: El Paso Norte Press, 2005.

Trayer, Patricia. *Crystal Personalities: A Quick Reference to Special Forms of Crystal*. Peoria, AZ: Stone People Publishing, 1995.

Tresidder, Jack. *Dictionary of Symbols*. San Francisco: Chronicle Books, 1998.

Uyldert, Mellie. *Metal Magick*. Wellingborough, UK: Turnstone Press, 1980.

Walker, Barbara G. *A Woman's Dictionary of Symbols and Sacred Objects*. San Francisco: Harper & Row, 1988.

Warlick, M. E. *The Philosopher's Stones*. Boston: Journey Editions, 1997.

Wilson, Colin. *From Atlantis to the Sphinx*. York Beach, ME: Red Wheel/Weiser, 1996.

Wolfe, Amber. *In the Shadow of the Shaman*. St. Paul, MN: Llewellyn, 1990.

Zerner, Amy and Monte Farber. *The Alchemist: The Formula for Turning Your Life into Gold*. New York: St. Martin's, 1991.

A native of the Pacific Northwest, author D. J. Conway has made the occult fields a life-long quest and study. Her search for knowledge has covered every aspect of Paganism, Wicca, New Age, and Eastern philosophies, and their histories, customs, mythologies, and folklore. In 1998, she was voted Best Wiccan and New Age Author by *Silver Chalice*, a Pagan magazine. She was awarded the Prolific Pagans Award for Excellence and the EarthSongs Readers' Choice Award. D. J. also tied for second place in the 2006 COVR Visionary Awards. She lives a rather quiet life with her husband and fur people, with most of her time spent researching and writing.

She can be contacted through her website: www.djconway.com.

Dancing With Dragons
Invoke Their Ageless Wisdom & Power

D. J. Conway

Access one of the most potent life forces in the astral universe: the wise and magickal dragon. Dragons do exist! They inhabit the astral plane that interpenetrates our physical world. Now, *Dancing with Dragons* makes the vast and wonderful hoard of dragon power available to you. Learn to call, befriend, and utilize the wisdom of these mythical creatures for increased spiritual fulfillment, knowledge, health, and happiness.

Dancing with dragons is a joyful experience. Whether you are a practicing magician, a devotee of role-playing games, or a seeker looking to tap the dragon's vast astral power, this book will help you forge a magickal partnership with these magnificent astral creatures.

ISBN: 978-1-56718-165-4
320 pp.
56 illus. $18.95

Magickal Mystical Creatures
Invite Their Powers into Your Life

D. J. CONWAY

(**Formerly titled** *Magickal, Mythical, Mystical Beasts*)
Unicorns . . . centaurs . . . gorgons and gargoyles. Long ago, strange and fabulous beasts filled the tales of storytellers and the myths of many cultures. In those times, humans not only believed these creatures truly existed, but they also credited them with great knowledge and called upon them for aid.

These mythical beasts do exist, and they're alive and well on the astral plane. This one-of-a-kind guide describes how you can enlist the special energies and talents of over 200 of these fabulous creatures to empower your magickal workings, rituals, and potential for success. Call upon a Magical Serpent for that financial windfall. Let the Phoenix help you resurrect your hope and energy. Invoke the Centaur for artistic inspiration. The mystical beings in this book are waiting to enhance your life with their legendary wisdom and power.

ISBN: 978-1-56718-149-4
272 pp. $14.95

The Comlete Magician's Tables
STEPHEN SKINNER

Anyone practicing magic won't want to miss this comprehensive book of magician's correspondences. Featuring four times more tables than Aleister Crowley's *Liber 777*, this is the most complete collection of magician's tables available. This monumental work documents thousands of mystical links—spanning pagan pantheons, Kabbalah, astrology, tarot, I Ching, angels, demons, herbs, perfumes, and more!

The sources of this remarkable compilation range from classic grimoires such as the Sworn Book to modern theories of prime numbers and atomic weights. Data from Peter de Abano, Abbott Trithemium, Albertus Magnus, Cornelius Agrippa, and other prominent scholars is referenced here, in addition to hidden gems found in unpublished medieval grimoires and Kabbalistic works.

Well-organized and easy-to-use, *The Complete Magician's Tables* can help you understand the vast connections making up our strange and mysterious universe.

ISBN: 978-0-7387-1164-5

432 pp. $44.95

White Spells for Protection
ILEANA ABREV

Nasty gossip, raging bosses, a nit-picky mother-in-law . . . we've all experienced our share of negative energy. Why not try a little magic to protect yourself, your home, and your loved ones?

This beginner's spellbook introduces defense magic and offers three levels of spells depending on your needs. There are simple "quick fix" spells—such as protecting your children with tiger-eye crystals and guarding your finances with fresh basil. And there are also powerful rituals for shielding yourself from strong negative forces, curses, and hexes. Each spell is safe and ethical, and the magical tools you'll need—candles, essential oils, herbs, and the like—are easy to find.

This adorable yet dynamic spellbook also includes spells to break self-inflicted curses responsible for depression, overeating, guilt, envy, fear, and more.

ISBN: 978-0-7387-1085-3
192 pp. $8.95

Goddess Alive!
Inviting Celtic & Norse Goddesses into Your Life

MICHELLE SKYE

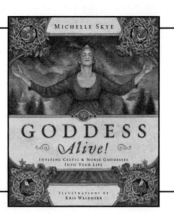

The seasons, moon phases, and even our personal experiences can be linked to the Divine Feminine. They have a face . . . they have a name . . . they have a goddess!

Meet thirteen vibrant Celtic and Norse goddesses very much alive in today's world. Explore each deity's unique mythology and see how she relates to Sabbats and moon rites. Lyrical meditations will guide you to otherworldly realms where you'll meet Danu, the Irish mother goddess of wisdom, and Freya, the Norse goddess of love and war. As you progress spiritually, you'll begin to see Aine in the greening of the trees and recognize Brigid in a seed's life-giving potential.

Goddess Alive! also includes crafts, invocation rituals, and other magical activities to help you connect with each goddess.

ISBN: 978-0-7387-1080-8
312 pp. $18.95

Natural Witchery

Intuitive, Personal & Practical Magick

ELLEN DUGAN

Natural Witchery offers dozens of ways to hone your intuition, enchance your magickal powers, and enliven your everyday practice.

Ellen Dugan goes to the heart of what it means to be a natural Witch. Forget about lineage, degrees, and politically correct titles. Her thoughtful observations and wise words will guide you back to what's important: forging your own unique spiritual path. These engaging exercises will help you look within yourself and stretch your psychic talents, discover your elemental strengths, and charge up your personal power.

Dugan's personal anecdotes and humor liven up the lessons and keep you grounded throughout the daily joys and trials of life as a natural Witch.

ISBN: 978-0-7387-0922-2
288 pp. $16.95

ORDER LLEWELLYN BOOKS TODAY!

Llewellyn publishes hundreds of books on your favorite subjects!
To get these exciting books, including the ones on the following pages,
check your local bookstore or order them directly from Llewellyn.

Order Online:

Visit our website at www.llewellyn.com, select your books, and order them on our secure server.

Order by Phone:

- Call toll-free within the U.S. at 1-877-NEW-WRLD (1-877-639-9753). Call toll-free within Canada at 1-866-NEW-WRLD (1-866-639-9753)
- We accept VISA, MasterCard, and American Express

Order by Mail:

Send the full price of your order (MN residents add 7% sales tax) in U.S. funds, plus postage and handling to:

Llewellyn Worldwide
2143 Wooddale Drive
Woodbury, MN 55125-2989, U.S.A.

Postage and Handling:

Standard (U.S., Mexico, and Canada). If your order is:
Up to $25.00, add $3.50
$25.01 - $48.99, add $4.00
$49.00 and over, FREE STANDARD SHIPPING
(Continental U.S. orders ship UPS. AK, HI, PR, and P.O. Boxes ship USPS 1st class. Mex. and Can. ship PMB.)

International Orders:
Surface Mail: For orders of $20.00 or less, add $5 plus $1 per item ordered. For orders of $20.01 and over, add $6 plus $1 per item ordered.

Air Mail:
Books: Postage and handling is equal to the total retail price of all books in the order.
Non-book items: Add $5 for each item.

Orders are processed within 2 business days.
Please allow for normal shipping time. Postage and handling rates subject to change.